PERSONAL FINANCIAL PLANNER

Debbie Harrison

London · Hong Kong · Johannesburg · Melbourne · Singapore · Washington DC

PITMAN PUBLISHING
128 Long Acre, London WC2E 9AN
Tel: +44 (0)171 447 2000
Fax: +44 (0)171 240 5771

A Division of Pearson Professional Limited

First published in Great Britain in 1997

© Pearson Professional Limited 1997

ISBN 0 273 62517 9

British Library Cataloguing in Publication Data
A CIP catalogue record for this book can be obtained from the British Library

10 9 8 7 6 5 4 3 2 1

Typeset by Northern Phototypesetting Co. Ltd, Bolton
Printed and bound in Great Britain by Redwood Books, Trowbridge, Wiltshire

The Publishers' policy is to use paper manufactured from sustainable forests.

ABOUT THE AUTHOR

Debbie Harrison is a freelance financial author and journalist who specialises in personal and institutional investment. She writes regularly for the *Financial Times* and is the author of four FT reports on pension provision and investment in Europe. She is the main editorial contributor to the 1997 FT *Unit Trust Year Book*. Her consumer books include *The Investors Chronicle Good Peps Guide*, published by Pitman, and *Pension Power*, published by John Wiley. Debbie has won a number of press awards including the 1994 British Insurance and Investment Brokers Association 'Journalist of the Year' and the Alexander Clay & Partners 'Pensions and Investment Journalist of the Year'. She was highly commended for her work for the *Financial Times* in the Bradford & Bingley 1996 Freelance Journalist of the Year awards.

CONTENTS

Section III
TAXATION

Section V

SAVING FOR LONG-TERM PROJECTS:
SCHOOL FEES AND MORTGAGE REPAYMENTS

Section VI
PENSIONS

SERIES FOREWORD

Today, more than ever, we need to make our savings and investments work hard for us. Changes to the welfare state – and the likelihood of further changes to come – mean that managing our capital properly is a key factor in financing the purchase of our home, our healthcare, our children's education and – perhaps most important – our retirement planning.

De-regulation of the financial services industry, which began in the 1980s, has led to a sometimes bewildering proliferation of financial products. The quantity and complexity of products mean investors need guidance. True, there is a world of information out there – some of it free, a lot of it cheap – but is it any good?

The *Investors Chronicle* series of investment books – like the weekly magazine – has been produced to help answer that question, with objective and authoritative advice, written from the investor's point of view.

The aim is to provide readers with a practical, jargon-free guide to all areas of personal finance and investment. Thus, whether you are a sophisticated investor, keen to learn more about the DIY approach to investing, or are new to investment, the books will arm you with the facts and understanding that you need. As such, they should be the natural complement to the high-quality, independent assessment that the magazine aims to provide every week.

MARK VAN DE WEYER, Publisher, *Investors Chronicle*,
FT Magazines

FOREWORD
by Julie Lord,
Chairman of the Institute of Financial Planning

What is financial planning?

The definition of financial planning used by the Institute of Financial Planning is as follows:

'Financial planning is a professional service for clients who need objective assistance in organising their personal or corporate financial affairs to more readily achieve their goals.'

You will notice that this definition makes no reference to financial products, or to the sale of such products. The financial planner is there to help you identify the objectives you wish to achieve, and then to show you how these objectives might be best fulfilled. In practice, financial planners will strive to help you define, review and attain your financial objectives with less risk and cost than if you tried to do it yourself.

We can, therefore, clearly distinguish the provider of financial services from the financial planner as follows:

The provider of financial services is concerned with choosing the best or most appropriate products for your needs. The financial planner's concern is to identify and advise on the best solution to the overall management of your affairs.

The provider of a financial service is 'product-orientated' and sells products. The financial planner is 'client-orientated' and sells advice. In the UK at present, there are many providers of financial services, but relatively few financial planners.

The financial planner will take a comprehensive and strategic approach to your circumstances and will start by identifying your objectives and reviewing the strengths and weaknesses of your current arrangements. This will not be confined to a single area of personal finance, but will cover all areas including risk management, cash and credit management, investments, personal taxation, retirement planning and estate planning. The financial planner recognises the inter-dependencies that connect all areas of personal finance, and will view the separate strands of your financial affairs as a total picture.

The financial planner, therefore, provides an identifiable professional service, and is happy to call upon other expert professionals where their advice might be helpful or necessary. The planner is not in competition with other professions and therefore will be pleased to work with your existing professional advisers or to suggest appropriate firms if you require professional help.

The profession of financial planning has already attracted people from the related disciplines of accountancy, banking, insurance, taxation, stockbroking, education and the legal profession. Professional and well-qualified financial planners will have a broad depth of knowledge across all of these disciplines in order to provide his/her client with an holistic solution.

The process of financial planning

These are the six main stages of personal financial planning:

- **Stage one:**   gathering data
- **Stage two:**   establishing your objectives and/or problems
- **Stage three:**   processing and analysing information
- **Stage four:**   recommending a comprehensive plan
- **Stage five:**   implementation of the plan
- **Stage six:**   monitoring the plan.

The description of financial planning as a six-stage process is a helpful model, but like all models, an over-simplification of the actual process. The stages in practice do not necessarily follow in clear-cut sequence. For example, processing and analysing of information frequently will require the planner to reconsider your objectives with your help.

It is important to appreciate that financial planning is a continuous process. The plan has to be updated and modified to allow for changes in the financial environment or in your personal circumstances.

A typical financial plan will contain reference to some or all of the following areas and will provide professional recommendations where appropriate:

- Life goal planning
- Cashflow planning
- Investment planning
- Personal insurance planning
- Personal protection assurance planning
- Tax planning and mitigation
- Retirement planning
- Estate planning
- Education planning

A professional financial planner will address your overall needs, and those of any other people directly affected by your plan. Planners deliberately divorce their planning and advice services from recommendations relating to financial products. Indeed, many planners offer their clients the option of purchasing essential financial products as a completely separate step, perhaps even with an unconnected third party.

For this reason, most financial planners prefer to offer their advice on a fee basis. In this way you can be confident that you are paying for a service which is not linked or dependent on the sale of a product.

In conclusion, financial planners are the general practitioners of the financial world. They give professional advice on a broad range of subjects, bringing in specialist expertise where necessary. Your planner will play a central role in the successful achievement of your goals.

JULIE LORD FIFP CFP ASFA FLIA (dip), Certified Financial Planner, Chairman of the Institute of Financial Planning

PREFACE

Labour's plans for personal finance

Labour's first months in power indicated the party would make some substantial changes to the world of finance – both at the institutional and individual level. However, many proposals will be implemented only after a period of consultation between the government, financial institutions and consumer organisations. This is particularly true of proposed changes to the welfare state where the government hopes to encourage the introduction of private plans and insurances to help shift the burden of provision from the over-stretched National Insurance Fund to the individual.

This book explains the law and regulatory regime as they currently stand but the following comments highlight some of the chief areas where we can expect to see significant developments over the coming years.

Regulation

The system of self-regulation which was introduced by the Financial Services Act (1996) was a great improvement on what had gone before but increasingly critics have voiced concern about the inefficiencies inherent in a system where those responsible for the policing of the regime can be the very perpetrators of the crimes. The failure of the system to prevent or deal effectively with the Maxwell scandal, where millions went missing from pensioners' funds, won the regulators no fans. Nor did the mass mis-selling of personal pensions in the late 1980s and early 1990s.

The departing chairman of the Securities and Investments Board (SIB), Sir Andrew Large, made public his views on the flaws in the system, saying that it lacked efficiency and credibility. He supported a merger of the main regulators and was also keen to place responsibility on top managers in financial institutions to put the right controls in place and to be held to account if they failed in this duty.

Labour proposes to unite the regulators under a single statutory body, which would take the form of a strengthened SIB. It also intends to transfer the role of banking supervision from the Bank of England to the new super-regulator.

However, it will be some time before the impact of the regulatory overhaul on the individual investor can be assessed. Clearly, any move to improve the efficiency of the system must be welcomed, provided it is not undermined by increased complexity. In the meantime caveat emptor (buyer beware), as always, should be your guide.

Pensions

Labour's plans for pensions are surprisingly similar to those of the Conservatives. Political dogma aside, this has to be good news for investors who need long-term stability in the pensions arena. Labour accepts that the present unfunded system of state pensions, where the National Insurance contributions of today's workers pay the pensions and related benefits of the retired, is inappropriate given the dwindling number of employed and the growing elderly population.

For this reason the government plans to consult with all the relevant consumer and financial organisations to determine the best way forward.

Unfortunately, changes to the taxation of equity dividends for pension funds, announced in Labour's first Budget, put even more pressure on funds to perform well and on younger investors to increase their contributions.

Long-term care

The cost of care for the growing number of frail elderly is an increasing problem for most western governments. So far Labour has indicated that it will consult on this issue but it is unlikely to make any dramatic moves until it has sorted out the problems of funding mainstream retirement through the right balance of state and private provision. Meanwhile no doubt the financial institutions will continue to launch new investment and insurance products to encourage people to fund their own liabilities.

Education

Parents who want to send their children to private schools and to further education are likely to face bigger bills. Labour's focus will be on reducing class size in state schools and increasing the quality of education. One source of extra funds is expected to be the abolition of assisted places schemes which provide subsidies for parents on lower incomes to send their children to private schools. At the same time the burden of funding university and other higher education costs is likely to fall increasingly on parents.

Taxation

Labour's election manifesto pledged to leave intact for five years the current rates of income tax. This means that significant changes are likely to focus on capital gains tax and inheritance tax. Under threat is the annual CGT exemption (£6,500 for the 1997/98 tax year) – the amount of capital gains (adjusted for inflation) individuals can make before paying CGT at their top rate of income tax. CGT currently can also be avoided on gifts between spouses.

IHT has long since been viewed by the wealthy and their accountants as a voluntary tax because there are so many ways to avoid or mitigate its impact. This entire area is under review and many a loophole is expected to be closed, particularly the use of trusts which are set up purely for tax mitigation purposes.

New regime for tax-efficient investments

A new generation of Individual Savings Accounts will be launched in 1999, which will probably incorporate tax-exempt special savings accounts (Tessas) and personal equity plans (Peps). Labour's aim is to encourage more people to save for the long term on a regular basis.

Conclusion

In future sensible financial planning will take into account the decline of the welfare state and will automatically include suitable investments for retirement and adequate protection insurances. At the same time government changes will make it less attractive for investors to use artificial arrangements to mitigate CGT and IHT. This will be no great loss to the sensible investor. After all, good financial planning has always insisted that investments should be appropriate for an individual's circumstances and should never be undertaken solely for tax purposes.

INTRODUCTION

The era of the welfare state has passed. As we head towards the Millennium and the 21st century, it is increasingly clear that the key to financial security lies in the hands of the individual, not the government. For some, this will be a welcome challenge. For others, it will be a daunting responsibility.

Whether you view the subject of finance with enthusiasm or trepidation, this book is for you. Financial planning is about setting the right goals for your circumstances, and building up a well-integrated package of insurances, investments and taxation arrangements to meet those goals.

Step 1: Find the right adviser

Clearly, the success of your financial plan will depend largely on the competence of your chosen adviser. But finding the right firm will not prove easy. There are literally thousands of so-called financial advisers out there, ranging from the fully qualified, fee-based professionals to the archetypal insurance salesman whose only hope of earning a crust is to persuade you to buy a policy you probably don't need, or an investment plan which combines the twin evils of lousy performance and high charges.

To save you a lot of time and money, this book explains how to find a good firm of advisers. Here you will learn how the advice channels in the UK operate, what questions to ask, what qualifications to look for, and what research and information technology a good adviser should have. Moreover, since the financial services regulators do not provide a list of 'jolly good' advisers, we show you how to draw up your own from a tried and tested shortlist of organisations dedicated to good-quality, independent financial advice.

Admittedly, no system is 100 per cent foolproof. If you do feel you have been hoodwinked into buying the wrong insurance policy or investing in an inappropriate fund, we also explain how to make a successful complaint and who to turn to for help.

Step 2: Protect your family

The best-laid plans to generate a good income for your family from earnings and investments will come to nothing if you do not protect your chief sources of revenue in the event of your death or serious illness. For this reason, before we look at investments, Section II of this book deals with the essential protection insurances.

Many of these products are complicated and riddled with small print. Most are not regulated by the Financial Services Act. When disaster strikes you could find out too late that the small-print exclusions render the policy worthless. Section II, therefore, will help you assess the levels of cover you need and determine which type of policy suits your circumstances. We explain how to get the best from:

- life assurance
- income protection plans (lump-sum and regular-income)
- mortgage payment protection plans
- private medical insurance
- long-term care for the elderly.

Throughout we highlight the pitfalls and the most important policy terms, so you can avoid the products and providers whose only guarantee is that you will be let down in an emergency.

Step 3: Taxation

Before you embark on your tax-efficient investment planning we draw your attention to the most important tax matters. Tax planning is not an isolated exercise, but an integral element in your overall financial plan. For this reason, taxation is dealt with at various stages throughout this book as it affects your insurance and investment decisions. In addition you need to understand how to get the best value from your annual allowances and exemptions, how income and capital gains tax work, and how you can avoid inheritance tax.

Don't forget the old adage – 'Where there's a will there's a relative'. Two in three people do not have a will, and as a result impose unnecessary administration and costs on their families and have no control over the beneficiaries. This section explains the importance of making a will and highlights the main points this document must cover.

Step 4: Successful investing

Once you have dealt with protection insurance and taxation you can turn to savings and investment. This section will help you understand risk, return, the most important asset classes, and how to use them to achieve your short-, medium- and long-term investment goals. It will also help you decide whether to invest directly in equities and bonds or via collective funds which spread risk and offer economies of scale. Armed with this vital information you can sift through the chapters which follow, make your choice and find out how to buy, monitor and sell your investments. We include:

- deposits and comparatively 'safe' investments such as Tessas, National Savings, gilts (held to maturity), guaranteed income and guaranteed growth bonds
- unit trusts, investment trusts and open-ended investment companies
- personal equity plans
- life assurance investments
- and, for the risk-takers, enterprise zone trusts, enterprise investment schemes, venture capital trusts and timber …

Step 5: Long-term investment goals – mortgages and school fees planning

Although part of your overall investment strategy, your mortgage and, where applicable, your school fees plan, are likely to be your largest liabilities throughout your working life. Section V explains how to define your mortgage requirements and set sensible debt limits. We also explain how the different types of mortgage work, including:

- repayment mortgages
- endowment mortgages
- Pep mortgage
- pension mortgages
- the bells and whistles: fixed-rate, discounts, low-start, foreign-currency
- the sting in the tail: the penalties you may face if you want to switch to a different type of mortgage or want to pay off your debt early
- home income plans.

For some parents, private schooling is an essential requirement. It can start from as early as age 2 or 3 when the children attend private nurseries, and can continue to age 22 or 23 if the children go to university. (Remember, even if you manage to send your children to a good State school, the chances are you will qualify for very little, if any, help towards further education.) The cost is phenomenal and few parents can afford to fund the entire bill direct from income. Part of the cost must be derived from a sensible investment portfolio. Section V provides all the information you need to get started on your education fees plan, including:

- the choice of school
- State assistance, scholarships and grants
- special fee schemes
- educational trusts
- investment plans
- insurance
- organisations worth contacting.

Step 6: Your pension

Over 10 million employees and their dependants rely on private pension funds for their financial security in retirement, and for important family protection insurances during their working lives. A further 8 million are covered by individual plans, while thousands of small businesses and partnerships operate pension schemes which in some cases are unique to the UK.

But all pensions are not equal and for the same level of contributions, different schemes and plans will produce very different results. This section tells you how to spot the difference. We examine:

■ state pensions

■ company pension schemes

■ topping up your company scheme

■ special schemes for higher earners

■ personal pensions

■ annuities.

Guide to the organisations and the jargon

Finally in Appendices I, II and III we provide a glossary of financial jargon, contact details for the most important organisations and a guide to making complaints.

Author's note

Throughout this book, unless stated otherwise, the male gender is used to denote both male and female.

The professional firms of financial planners can also be described as financial advisers, but there are many 'advisers' who certainly could not be described as professional financial planners. The important difference between planners and advisers is explained in the Foreword and in Section 1, but elsewhere, for the sake of simplicity, the book uses 'adviser' as a generic descriptive term.

ACKNOWLEDGEMENTS

Many people helped with this book but there are several experts I would like to thank for their inspired ideas and equally inspired technical support. In particular, Simon Philip, Director of Financial Planning at chartered accountants Arthur Andersen, gave up much of his precious time in order to help plan the synopsis and to read the final manuscript. Simon is a fellow and council member of the Institute of Financial Planning and is author of *Kelly's Financial Planning for the Individual*.

I would like to thank Kate Gill, chief executive of the Institute of Financial Planning and Julie Lord, IFP chairman and also managing director of the Cardiff firm of financial planners, Cavendish Financial Management. Kate and Julie courageously battled with my cynicism and ignorance, and finally convinced me that financial planning is not the preserve of wealthy investors but rather, provides an eminently practical approach to all aspects of finance and is available to everyone. Provided, that is, they know what to look for and where to find it. I hope this book will help with that quest.

Robert Hall, principal in the insurance practice of consultants Watson Wyatt, provided considerable technical support for the chapters on pensions and personal equity plans. Chris Wicks, financial planning manager with Manchester independent advisers Kidsons Impey Scott Lang, helped with the chapters on risk insurance and offered excellent all-round support. Martin Jones, partner of the London firm of chartered accountants Blick Rothenberg, provided technical support for the chapters on taxation and on the tax issues which affect every saving and investment scheme mentioned in this book.

Finally, I would like to thank the *Financial Times* for granting permission to use in this book some of my work originally published in the *Weekend Money* and the *Surveys* sections of the *FT*. The publisher John Wiley & Sons gave me permission to use some of the factual material contained in my consumer guide to pensions, *Pension Power*. Much of the detail on Peps was derived from my other Pitman Publishing title, *The Investors Chronicle Good Peps Guide*.

DEBBIE HARRISON

June 1997

CALL ON THE EXPERTS

HOW TO FIND A GOOD FINANCIAL PLANNER

The UK has over 22,000 'independent financial advisers', several thousand more professional advisers and a further 60,000 company representatives. Trying to find a good firm may resemble an exercise involving a large haystack and a very small needle. In practice, however, it is possible to eliminate most of this army of advisers by considering carefully what *you want*, not what *they sell*.

Some of the best advisers in the UK are more correctly described as 'financial planners'. Don't worry too much about the labels, but do focus on the range of advice, the qualifications and experience of your adviser.

■ WHAT IS FINANCIAL PLANNING?

Financial planners take what they call an 'holistic' or integrated approach to your financial affairs. The reasons for this integrated approach are obvious when you consider the following 'shopping list', typical of most families' financial requirements:

- protection insurances (life assurance, income protection, mortgage protection)
- general investments and savings
- retirement provision (State, company and private pensions)
- funding for major liabilities (investing for specific items like school fees and mortgages)
- income and capital gains tax planning
- estate planning (passing on your wealth, inheritance tax planning, making a will)

■ **FINANCIAL SNAPSHOT**

The term 'financial adviser' is a bit like 'consultant' and 'engineer'. It can mean a one-man band which sells everything from motor insurance to mortgages, to well-resourced, qualified professional firms of stockbrokers, chartered accountants, actuaries and solicitors.

Each item has an impact on one or more of the other categories, so rather than deal with your mortgage or your pension in isolation, financial planners would tackle them in the light of all your investments, tax and insurance needs.

■ WHO ARE THE FINANCIAL PLANNERS?

Although financial planners have been around for a long time, it is only fairly recently that they have adopted a higher profile and recognisable identity which distinguishes them from other advisers. This is partly due to the greater involvement in financial services of the professional firms – in particular the accountants and solicitors, who represent about 50 per cent of the financial planners.

A good firm of financial planners will have access to a wide range of technical expertise, covering everything from protection insurance and taxation to general savings and specific investments for pensions, mortgages and school fees. If the firm is too small to cater for all these requirements, it should have a close working relationship with other professional firms which can supply the missing elements. In order to provide the best financial plan, firms must be able to draw on every available good-quality insurance product, savings scheme and taxation arrangement. Above all, they should not be influenced by the amount of sales commission offered by the product providers.

But before looking at who can give you advice, it is helpful to understand the system of regulation in the UK and how it protects you.

■ AUTHORISATION AND REGULATION

The 1986 Financial Services Act set up a system of self-regulation for financial services in the UK. Under this system each firm or company is regulated by a self-regulatory organisation (SRO) or, in the case of the professional bodies, by a recognised professional body (RPB). The Labour government plans to unite all these organisations under one super-regulator.

The FSA covers every firm or company providing investment advice or an investment service. If someone gives you advice on products covered by the Act and is not himself authorised, he is breaking the law. Check authorisation by calling the Securities and Investments Board, which runs a comprehensive database. See Appendix III.

Bear in mind that not everything sold as an 'investment' has to be authorised. For example, tangible assets directly purchased – gold coins, rare stamps, antiques, vintage cars and wines, for example – are not classed as investments under the Act.

As a rule of thumb you can regard an 'investment' as a non-tangible asset. The Act's definition of 'investments' includes shares, debentures and other securities (government securities or 'gilts' for example), certain options and warrants, unit trusts and other forms of collective investments, futures contracts and some long-term life assurance contracts. 'Investment business' includes dealing, arranging deals in, managing and advising on investments, as well as setting up and operating collective investments. Investment business is distinguished from deposit-taking business, which is covered by the Banking Act and Building Societies Act.

This may all seem rather academic but the point is this: *If you buy something which is not covered by the Act, the FSA regulators cannot investigate your case and you are not entitled to compensation if things go wrong.*

Who gives the advice?

Under the FSA, advisers are split into two broad categories, namely, 'representatives' of a company and 'independent financial advisers'.

Representatives

Company representatives (also known as 'direct salesmen' and 'tied agents'), are employed by – and work solely for – just one company. Their income consists of a basic salary and a commission element. Some representatives are remunerated purely by sales commission which means if they don't sell you a policy, they don't eat. Fortunately, an increasing number of representatives receive quite decent basic salaries, so there is less need for them to verbally beat you into submission. Where commission is paid, the total bill will depend on the level of premium or contribution, whether this is a one-off or a regular investment contract, and the investment period.

> Many advisers are not independent. This does not mean that they will necessarily give inferior advice but it does mean that the range of products on which their recommendations are based is very limited.

Buying direct from a company is not necessarily a bad thing. Some of the best insurance and investment products – as well as some of the worst – are sold in this way. The important point to remember is that this type of adviser is permitted by law only to sell the products of the company he represents and through which he is authorised. You might be lucky and pick a winner, but unless you are prepared to thoroughly research the market for the best combination of charges, potential investment returns and flexibility, frankly, buying direct is a gamble.

> If you buy direct, you might be lucky and pick a winner, but unless you are prepared to thoroughly research the market yourself, frankly it's a gamble.

Appointed representatives are companies which have a contract with a financial institution to sell one or more of their products in return for commission. The appointed representative is not necessarily employed or owned by the institution and, confusingly, may act independently in other lines of business.

A typical example is a building society which conducts a full range of its own mortgage facilities, but sells the endowment, personal equity plan or personal pension products of one life company only (often its own). So, if you want a Pep mortgage, you will borrow XYZ Building Society's money, but there will be no choice of Pep products – you will have to take the ABC Company's Pep – or go elsewhere.

The appointed representative, like the company representative, is not obliged to tell you how competitive the products he sells are in terms of charges and performance.

Independent financial advisers

Independent financial advisers (IFAs) are not tied to one company. Their job is to examine your needs and to search the market for the product that offers the best value in terms of performance, charges, and contract flexibility, among other factors.

In theory at least, you stand a better chance of coming away with the right insurances and investments than if you go to a company or appointed representative. However, the term 'independent' is not synonymous with 'expert'. IFAs vary considerably in their level of competence.

How to make your choice

Your choice of adviser will be dictated partly by your pocket and partly by your requirements. However, there are certain features worth checking.

Qualifications

Qualifications are becoming increasingly important in the financial services sector and are a good indication of a firm's commitment to high standards. If you are interested in direct equity investment as well as collective funds, you probably need the services of an investment manager or stockbroker. Stockbrokers are regulated by the Securities and Futures Authority and in order to give you advice they must first pass the SFA's 'Registered Persons Examinations'.

A committed investment adviser is also likely to be a member of The Securities Institute. To become a full member the adviser needs to pass the Institute's Diploma, which is a professional level qualification for practitioners who have already gained experience in such areas as securities, derivatives, corporate finance and investment management.

For more general investment advice, you can go to a firm of independent financial advisers or financial planners. This category includes an increasing number of chartered accountants and solicitors who specialise in this area.

By the end of June 1997, all advisers must have a 'benchmark' or basic qualification. There are several of these, but you are most likely to come across the Financial Planning Certificate (FPC). This is examined by the Chartered Insurance Institute (CII). The Securities Institute also runs a benchmark exam for independent advisers – the Investment Advice Certificate. Accountants and bankers have their own benchmark regulatory qualifications.

The next stage up from the FPC is the Advanced Financial Planning Certificate (AFPC), which includes a personal investment planning syllabus. Of the 82,000 advisers and representatives operating in Britain, at the time of writing only 2,500 had this qualification. The AFPC allows advisers to become full members of the Society of Financial Advisers (SOFA) – the financial services arm of the CII. SOFA has also launched associate and fellowship qualifications.

The AFPC also allows advisers to become associate members of the Institute of Financial Planning. Through the Institute, members can acquire Certified Financial Planner status, which is recognised in six countries – the UK, US, Canada, Japan, Australia and New Zealand. According to the Institute, the UK's top qualification for planners/advisers currently is its fellowship exam. However, these are rare birds – at the time of writing there were fewer than 100 in the UK. All of the fellows are fee-based and independent.

Research and technology

Technology is no substitute for experience and expertise but there are some first-class systems designed to help an adviser eliminate the companies which are financially weak, have a poor performance track record, high charges, and inflexible contract conditions – for example, exit penalties if you stop the plan early.

For mortgages, a firm might subscribe to the Moneyfacts *Mortgage Screen*, for example, an on-line database which is updated daily. For protection insurance, pension plans and life assurance investments many firms of advisers use the *Aequos* system from The Research Department. Pension specialists may also subscribe to the best annual surveys. The Bacon & Woodrow annual survey of unit-linked personal pensions identifies the top providers in terms of company strength, past performance, investment strategy, volatility, risk and charges. Also popular with professional advisers is the *Life and Pensions Review*, an on-line and paper-based service from actuaries and employee benefits consultants, Buck Consultants.

If you are interested in unit and investment trusts, either for general savings or for a specific purpose such as school fees and mortgages, probably the best source of information an adviser can buy is Standard & Poor's *Fund Research*. This provides performance ratings, explains how the performance was achieved and keeps track of fund managers. If a leading light defects to a rival investment company, Standard & Poor's *Fund Research* swiftly checks the credentials of the new manager and if necessary re-rates all the relevant funds. The screening process analyses the quality of the investment group as a whole as well as the individual manager and the team. If your adviser does not subscribe, he can still check if the unit or investment trust he wants to recommend has an 'A', 'AA' or 'AAA' rating. This in itself tells you a lot – for example only the top 20 per cent out of the 1,600 unit trusts available achieve even an 'A' rating.

Fund Research also analyses discrete results, and any firm of investment advisers worth its salt should do the same. Discrete results show year on year rather than cumulative performance. This is important because a good cumulative result over five years might hide an outstanding (possibly lucky) short-term performance followed by several years of mediocrity. Most published statistics are cumulative, and discrete results are difficult to analyse without access to a major statistics database such as *Micropal* or *HSW Hindsight*.

Apart from professional qualifications, stockbrokers and other firms advising on direct equity investments should be able to demonstrate quality of research and analysis. Larger firms will have several UK companies analysts – the primary market for private clients. To supplement this research, the firm probably will use Reuters for company news and the monthly *Estimate Directory*, which provides aggregate earnings and company forecasts for about 1,300 UK companies covering the FTSE All-Share index and the Alternative Investment Market.

The second source of company research is the market makers through which the stockbroker buys and sells shares. The main sources of information here are BZW, Kleinwort Benson, NatWest Securities, Merrill Lynch, S G Warburg and Winterflood Securities (which specialises in smaller companies). Daily research from the institutional heavyweights is good news – an on-line link is ideal.

Paying for advice

Stockbroker/investment manager charges fall into two categories. First, there are the commissions which are charged on purchase or sale of securities – usually a percentage of the money invested. Alternatively, the firm may charge a fee once or twice a year for a continuing investment management service. Some firms use a combination of both fee and dealing commissions.

Other professional advisers – accountants and solicitors for example – are fee-based and any sales commission would be offset against fees or re-invested in your plan. The broader band of independent financial advisers (IFAs) may operate on a fee basis or accept commission. Some do both.

Fee-based advisers charge anything from around £50–£300 per hour depending on whether you go to a local high street adviser or a leading firm of consulting actuaries or chartered accountants. As a rough guide, however, for good advice you can expect to pay at least £80–£130 per hour.

One of the particularly daft aspects of the tax system is that you pay fees out of your taxed income, on top of which you have to pay VAT. If you pay through the commission route, not only do you avoid VAT, but in the case of pension plans, effectively you get tax relief at your highest rate on the payment. This is because the commission is deducted from your pension contributions, which themselves benefit from full tax relief.

Commission and flexibility

Since January 1995, life assurance companies have been required by the financial services regulators to disclose all their charges in full, including sales commission, in a pre-sale 'key features' document. Similar rules came into force in May 1997 for unit and investment trust managers.

Commission rates vary depending on the size of premium and the term of the contract. As a rough guide you can assume that on a 'single premium' or one-off payment to a pension or life assurance investment plan, the sales commission will be 4–6 per cent of your investment. For a 25-year 'regular premium' plan, where you agree to pay a certain amount each month or each year, the commission is likely to be worth about 70 per cent of the value of your first year's contributions.

Now, over the long term there is very little difference between the total commission cost for a regular premium plan and a plan where you pay in the same amount, but your contributions are classed as a series of single premiums. However, regular premium plans can be inflexible. This is because many life and pension companies, particularly the direct sales operations, pay advisers upfront all of the commission that would otherwise have been paid over the entire investment period. This means that if you pull out in the early years you will have very little to show for your money.

If you do buy commission-based products, your best bet is to ask for single premium or 'recurring' single premium terms. Under this system, each contribution is treated as a one-off, and only the commission related to that amount is paid to the adviser. However, to encourage regular savers, some companies have low charges on regular premium contracts, so do ask before signing up.

Impact of charges on your fund

Your adviser will give you a pre-sale 'key features' document which shows what your fund would be worth at different stages during the investment period, assuming a certain growth rate. The purpose of this is to show you the impact of the companies' charges on your returns. This can be used to compare different companies' charges to check if you are getting good value for money. As a quick guide, refer to the 'reduction in growth' figure which shows by how much the charges would reduce the annual yield of 9 per cent.

A low reduction in growth figure for one level of contribution does not indicate that charges are low across the board. Different charges apply to different premium levels and the effect of a flat-rate monthly fee, for example, will be proportionately greater on lower premiums.

Charges are very important, but should not be the sole selection criterion. If your investment company turns out to be one of the worst performers in its category, it is little comfort to know that the charges are modest.

The client agreement

If you plan to use your adviser on a regular basis, you should have a written agreement which sets out the firm's terms and what services it will provide. A clearly worded client agreement gives you a bench-mark against which you can judge the adviser's performance, particularly where the firm has direct responsibility for investing your money.

The following checklist includes the main points in a client agreement. You should add any further points that apply to your particular circumstances.

- The regulation of the adviser under the Financial Services Act 1986.

- Which services this entitles the adviser to carry out and the services it is not authorised to undertake. For example, is the adviser authorised to hold client money?

- Permission (required by the Consumer Credit Act 1974) for the adviser to act on your behalf to negotiate mortgages, loans and overdrafts.

- The period of agreement and period of notice on both sides (usually a minimum of 30 days).

- Your responsibility to provide the information the adviser needs.

1

(For example, to give appropriate advice, your adviser needs a clear idea of your existing investments and your attitude to risk).

- Details of access to your other advisers, for example your bank manager, accountant and pension provider.
- Your right to veto any recommendations.
- A confidentiality clause.
- Details of how your documents will be stored.
- Fee rates per hour for different level of advisers within the firm and details of any due dates for regular fees.
- Details of VAT likely to be charged.
- Treatment of commissions if the adviser acts on a fee basis – for example, does the firm re-invest this money or offset it against fees.
- Treatment of complaints and disputes.

■ SUMMARY

- **Unless you are sure of your ability to research the market thoroughly, seek *independent* advice.**
- **Check in particular the level of qualifications held by the staff and the firm's research resources.**
- **Ideally pay for your advice by fees rather than commission, as this removes any potential bias in the firm's recommendations.**

■ GLOSSARY OF TERMS

Company and appointed representatives advise on the products of just one company.

Independent financial advisers should consider all the products and investments available and select the best for your circumstances.

Further information

For a list of regulators, professional bodies and adviser organisations, see Appendix II. For a guide to making a complaint, see Appendix III.

PROTECTION COMES FIRST

PROTECT YOUR FAMILY IF YOU DIE

If you die, your family gets very little from the State. Therefore if you have any dependants who would suffer financially as a result of your death, you need life assurance. Fortunately this is relatively cheap and easy to buy.

The 'sum assured' – that is the amount of cover you take out – should do two things:

- ■ It should repay any outstanding loans including the mortgage, and
- ■ It should allow your family to maintain its standard of living by replacing your income in full or by topping up any other benefits you may receive.

■ HOW MUCH DO YOU NEED?

The amount of cover you buy must be geared to your liabilities. As a rough guide, you could multiply your salary by 10 to provide a lump sum for your dependants which, when invested, will generate a reasonable replacement annual income. A more precise method is to calculate the income you actually need to meet expenditure, including the cost of outstanding loans.

Consider carefully the period you need to insure. One way of looking at this is to cover the period during which any borrowing remains outstanding, and until the children have ceased to be dependent – up to age 23 if you expect them to go to university. However, more wealthy individuals who plan to retire early should provide cover until earnings stop and pensions start. Don't forget that where there are young children, the partner responsible for childcare must also be insured. The cost of a full-time nanny could easily run to £8,000 a year.

> **■ FINANCIAL SNAPSHOT**
>
> Women tend to live longer than men, and so generally can expect to pay less for their life assurance policies than a man of the same age, because there is less chance the insurance company will have to pay up.

The basic calculation, then is 'income requirement plus debt minus any existing cover'. Existing cover may be provided by your company pension scheme or other private insurances. Pension schemes can provide up to four times the level of your annual salary as a tax-free cash lump sum if you die. They should also provide a spouse's pension and possibly a pension for your children if they are under 18.

Personal pension plans also provide life cover. However, in this case, the value will not be linked to your salary, but instead will depend on how much is in your fund. If you have only recently started a pension plan, this could be very little, so you will need to pay for extra life assurance while your fund is building up. You can also use up to 5 per cent of your personal pension contribution, allowance to pay for life assurance. However, you may need to pay maximum contributions to your pension, so think carefully before you use this option.

The main drawback with life assurance linked to your company pension scheme is that it applies only while you are working and contributing. If you are in this position, make the most of it while it lasts, but be prepared to top up with private insurance if your employment circumstances change.

In particular, make sure the cover provided by your old and new jobs overlaps. A common mistake is to go off for a holiday between jobs and to forget to arrange stopgap insurance.

■ WHICH TYPE OF POLICY?

Once you identify the shortfall in your provision, you can use one of the methods listed below to fill the gap.

The two simplest products are **level term assurance** and **family income benefit**. The term assurance lump sum can be invested to provide an annual income and/or used to pay off debt, while family income benefit can directly replace the shortfall in annual income.

Most life assurance policies work on the 'you drop dead, we pay up' principle. However, some companies offer **whole of life** plans which combine insurance and investment by deducting the cost of life cover from your savings plan.

The two simplest products are *level term assurance* and *family income benefit*. The term assurance lump sum can be invested to provide an annual income and/or used to pay off debt, while family income benefit can directly replace the shortfall in annual income.

The following descriptions explain your basic options.

Level term assurance

Level term assurance provides a tax-free cash lump sum if you die within the period insured. However, if you die the day after the term expires, you get nothing. Unless the policy is assigned to cover a specific liability – for example your mortgage debt – it is sensible to write it under trust, so that the lump sum does not form part of your estate if you die. In this way, the policy proceeds could be passed on to your children, for example, without having to wait for probate to be granted to your executors (see Chapter 7).

Life assurance can be written on a single or joint life basis. A joint life policy covers more than one person – typically a husband and wife. It may be written to pay out if just one of the spouses dies ('joint life first death') or only when both have died ('joint life second death'). Experts reckon it is usually better – and only slightly more expensive – to arrange individual policies.

Remember, wherever you share ownership, you have an insurable interest, so it is important to take appropriate cover. Young people often buy houses together to share the cost, while older couples may purchase a holiday home with friends.

Term assurance comes in other forms.

- **Convertible renewable** term assurance gives you the right to extend the insurance period without further medical underwriting or, in some cases, to convert to an investment-linked plan. The former can be useful if you need to increase your life cover when you are older. Generally you would be asked to undergo a medical, and could pay much higher premiums if you are not in good health.

■ *Decreasing* term assurance reduces at regular intervals and can be used to protect a debt which reduces in a similar way – for example, where the outstanding debt decreases over the loan period at regular intervals. However, repayment mortgage protection insurance is structured in a slightly different way to accommodate the specific pattern of the capital debt reduction (see page 28).

Decreasing term assurance can also be used as a means of covering an inheritance tax (IHT) liability where you have transferred assets to someone other than your spouse (known as a 'potentially exempt transfer') and there would be a reducing IHT liability if you died during the seven years following the transfer. Remember, the insurance need only cover the potential tax liability – that is, a maximum of 40 per cent of the asset value in excess of £215,000 – not the whole of the gift.

■ *Increasing* term assurance automatically increases the level of cover – usually in line with retail price inflation or a fixed amount – say, 5 per cent – without further medical underwriting. If you opt for this type of insurance, your annual premiums will also increase.

■ *Personal pension* term assurance is available to the self-employed and employees not in company schemes. Premiums attract full tax relief, provided they fall within your overall annual contribution limits. However, if you stop earning, you must also stop the plan. As mentioned above, although you can use up to 5 per cent of your annual pension contribution allowance to pay for life assurance, you may not want to do so if you need to pay the maximum amount to your pension plan.

Family income benefit

Family income benefit (FIB) provides a regular income from the date of death until the end of the insurance period. Tax treatment is favourable, because although the proceeds are paid in the form of a regular monthly income, technically they are classed as capital, so there is no income tax to pay. You can arrange for the income to remain the same ('level') or to increase each year. FIB is particularly useful where you have a young family and you want to insure the life of the spouse who stays at home to look after the children, so if he or she dies you can afford to employ a nanny and/or continue the school fees payments.

Whole of life plans

Whole of life plans, as the name suggests, pay a benefit whenever you die: there is no specific term. Given the certainty that the policy must pay out at some point, naturally the premiums tend to be higher than for term assurance. Whole of life policies combine insurance and investment. Your monthly premiums are invested and from this fund the insurance company deducts the amounts necessary to provide the life cover. When you die you get the fund value or the sum assured, whichever is greater. One common use for this type of policy is to provide a lump sum to cover your inheritance tax liability when you die.

■ TIPS ON BUYING YOUR INSURANCE

As a general rule, it is better to avoid products that combine insurance and investment. If what you need is a sensible amount of life cover, then simple term assurance is likely to offer best value. If you want to build up some capital for your dependants, you could, for example, invest in tax-efficient personal equity plans and take out a decreasing term assurance plan to provide a lump sum if you die early before your fund has had the chance to build up.

The premium you pay for your insurance will depend on your age, sex and your state of health, among other factors. You have duty to complete the proposal form honestly and accurately. If you are considerably overweight or you smoke, your premiums may be 'loaded' – in other words, you pay more because there is a greater chance of an early death. Certain dangerous sports will also raise eyebrows in the underwriting department, and in turn may raise your premiums. In some cases your policy may not cover you while you indulge in these activities.

You have a duty to complete the proposal form honestly and accurately. If you are considerably overweight or you smoke, your premiums may be 'loaded' – in other words you pay more because there is a greater chance of an early death.

The proposal form will also ask if you have ever been tested for HIV (AIDS). If you are a single man and want a substantial amount of cover, you will probably be requested to complete a 'lifestyle' questionnaire which is designed to discover whether your private life exposes you to a higher than average risk of AIDS or other sexual diseases.

■ THE MEDICAL

Both men and women who want to take out a large amount of cover should expect to be asked to undergo a medical examination. Despite the aversion most people have to this, it does actually work in your favour. Where policies are not fully medically underwritten (this is usually the case with policies sold by direct mail or through off-the-page advertising), the underwriters assume there will be a much greater incidence of claims, so the premiums may be much higher than a medically underwritten contract.

The premium will also depend on the company. Life assurance is a very competitive market, which is why independent advice is essential. These days a good adviser will have access to a comprehensive database which will enable him to select the right features and the best rates available at any given time.

Your adviser should also make sure your premium rate is guaranteed. The cheapest rates often are offered by companies which reserve the right to 'review' premiums at any time. With reviewable premiums, effectively you are writing the insurance company a blank cheque.

2

■ HOW TO PAY

You may be offered a choice of payment options – for example, you could pay annually by cheque, or monthly by direct debit. Direct debit is probably the safest method, because the payments are guaranteed. If by mistake, you overlook a reminder for your annual cheque, your cover may lapse, and if you have to re-apply, you may find that rates have increased due to your increased age or a change in your state of health.

■ LIFE ASSURANCE AS INVESTMENTS

Many companies sell investment plans which offer an element of life assurance. For details, see Chapter 16.

■ SUMMARY

- **If you have dependants who would suffer financially if you die, you need life assurance.**

- **As a rough guide to how much cover to take out, multiply your salary by 10, add in the value of any outstanding loans and deduct any existing cover, for example, from a company pension scheme.**

- **Don't forget to top up your life assurance if your company benefits package changes when you change jobs.**

- **Take out life assurance for the spouse who looks after the children. If he/she dies you will need to pay for childcare or work part time.**

- **Opt for a guaranteed premium. Some companies retain the right to 'review' (upwards) the premium whenever they want to.**

■ GLOSSARY OF TERMS

Level term assurance provides a tax-free lump sum if you die during the insured period.

Joint life covers two people, and can either pay out on the first death or only when the second person dies.

Family income benefit pays a regular income for the insured period.

Convertible renewable term assurance gives you the right to extend the insurance period without further medical underwriting, or in some cases to convert to an investment-linked plan.

Decreasing term assurance reduces at regular intervals, and can be used to protect a decreasing debt.

Increasing term assurance automatically increases the level of cover – usually in line with retail price inflation or a fixed amount – say, 5 per cent – without further medical underwriting.

Personal pension term assurance is available to the self-employed and employees not in company schemes. Provided you have an earned income, premiums attract full tax relief.

Whole of life plans pay a benefit whenever you die and combine insurance with an investment plan.

INCOME PROTECTION INSURANCE

Life assurance protects your family if you die, but it is equally, if not more important to insure against loss of income due to illness or disability. If you are not convinced, consider this. In April 1995, the government cut long-term sickness benefits and changed the definition of qualifying disability from 'can't do *own* job' to 'can't do *any* job'. This means that even though your medical condition prevents you from continuing your profession, if you can sweep the streets, you will be classed as fit for work.

The change in the eligibility rules wiped an estimated 250,000 people off the list of the 1.6m who previously claimed the old invalidity benefit. The new incapacity benefit is taxed, and if your claim started after 13 April 1995, you will not get an earnings-related top-up, previously worth up to £85 per week.

This leaves not so much a gap in welfare provision as a gaping chasm. If you are not covered by a group scheme, you need private insurance.

There are two products which protect you if you become seriously ill or disabled. 'Income protection plans' (also known as 'permanent health insurance' or PHI) provide a regular income, while 'critical illness' insurance pays out a lump sum on diagnosis of a serious condition. A third product you will come across is mortgage protection insurance which essentially is a combination of the two.

Price is the crucial factor when you buy insurance, but independent advice is essential, given the range of products and the complex medical underwriting criteria applied by the insurance companies.

■ FINANCIAL SNAPSHOT

Women typically pay 50 per cent more for income protection than men, due to the higher incidence of claims.

■ PERMANENT HEALTH INSURANCE

PHI pays a maximum of about two-thirds of your earnings (less any State and company benefits) if you are prevented from working through disability or long-term illness. The income is tax-free and is payable for the full period insured, which is usually up to the date you start to draw your pensions.

This type of insurance should itself carry a health warning, as the policies often are riddled with small print. The premium you pay will depend on age, sex, occupation and level of earnings covered. Most insurers will only cover earnings of up to about £45,000, so high earners may not be able to fully protect their income.

If you are on a tight budget, to keep premiums down, you could insure the minimum income you need to survive and increase cover later (but first check your policy will allow you to do this). You can also cut premiums if you opt for a long waiting period between the date you fall ill or become disabled, and the date you claim benefit. The minimum waiting period is four weeks, but premiums reduce if you sign up for a three-, six- or 12-month 'deferment' period. If you opt for a long deferment period, then make sure you have enough savings to manage while you are waiting for your income protection plan to kick in.

Advisers stress that it is essential to link the insured income to retail price inflation – both during the insurance period and during the payment period. This will cost extra, but without it the purchasing power of your insured income would quickly be eroded.

Misleading contract features

With PHI, there are two vitally important but potentially misleading contract features – the premium basis and the definition of disability.

The premium basis

An apparently cheaper policy may have a 'reviewable' premium. As mentioned in Chapter 2, this means that you have no control over future rate increases. Over 40 companies sell PHI, but only a handful, including Sun Alliance, Friends Provident and Swiss Life, at the time of writing offered premiums guaranteed not to rise. Several companies sell investment-linked PHI policies, which review premiums in line with claims experience and investment returns. They may

> The best definition of disability is 'unable to follow *own* occupation'. Avoid policies that say they will only pay up when you are unable to follow *any* occupation. Under the latter, you have got to be totally incapacitated in order to claim – as is now the case with the State scheme.

also pay a lump sum at the end of the insurance period. However, these complex products are not necessarily cheaper than the guaranteed premium version. As a general rule, it is wise to keep your investments separate from your protection insurance.

The definition of disability

This is the deciding factor when the insurance company judges whether you are too ill to work, and therefore are eligible to claim benefit. The best definition is 'unable to follow *own* occupation' with the possible addition of the phrase 'or an occupation suitable by training, education, experience and status'. The worst definition to avoid at all costs is 'unable to follow *any* occupation'. Under the latter, you have got to be totally incapacitated in order to claim – as is now the case with the State scheme.

■ CRITICAL ILLNESS INSURANCE

Critical illness insurance is often regarded as the poor man's PHI. This type of insurance pays the owner of the policy – which could be you, your spouse or even your business partner – a tax-free lump sum on the diagnosis of up to 36 illnesses or accidents. Most policies use six standard definitions:

- cancer
- heart attack
- stroke
- coronary artery bypass surgery
- kidney failure
- major organ transplant.

If you are self-employed, the best way to protect your family should you become too ill to work is through a PHI policy. Critical illness may be a cheaper way to insure against some of the worst possible illnesses, but unless your condition is on the list, you will not receive a penny even though you are unable to work. A good policy will include 'permanent total disability' on the payment list.

> **Beware of vaguely worded exclusions relating to pre-existing conditions, as this type of clause can be interpreted very widely.**

Critical illness insurance may create a potential inheritance tax bill. If you have a major illness before you die, your insurance lump sum will boost the value of your estate, and in the 1997/98 tax year anything above £215,000 will be subject to IHT at 40 per cent. As mentioned, with term assurance you can avoid IHT by writing the policy in trust for your beneficiaries – your children or cat for example (yes, it does happen!). However, with critical illness you cannot do this if you yourself are the beneficiary.

■ MORTGAGE PAYMENT PROTECTION PLANS

There is nothing unique about mortgage protection plans – these are usually a combination of term assurance and a restricted version of PHI or critical illness insurance.

Term assurance is the simplest way to provide mortgage protection as this pays off the loan if you die. A special type of decreasing term assurance can be used where the debt reduces with time – as is the case with a repayment mortgage. For an interest-only loan, where the debt remains constant throughout the mortgage, you need level term assurance.

Where the policy you are offered includes an element of income protection, do check your existing cover first. If you take out more term assurance than you really need, at least your family will reap the benefits. However, if you over-insure with some of the income protection plans, you are not entitled to the excess, so some of your premiums will be wasted. As a rule, advisers reckon it is usually better to buy term assurance and critical illness or PHI separately to provide the right type and level of cover.

Another option you may be offered is **accident, sickness and unemployment (ASU)** insurance. This covers your monthly mortgage payments if you become too ill to work or are unemployed. The accident and sickness element is like a short-term PHI policy. Unemployment insurance is available through a few specialist companies, but is very expensive, so ASU may be the only way to get it.

Following social security changes, if you are a new borrower and become unemployed, you now have to wait nine months before you can claim benefit to cover your mortgage – longer if you have savings of £8,000 or more. You can use ASU to insure the nine-month gap and in some cases can cover yourself for up to two years. However, experts warn that you should treat this type of insurance as a way of buying some breathing space if you need to re-assess your finances in the light of illness or unemployment. It does not provide a long-term replacement income.

■ SUMMARY

- **From April 1995 you can only claim state incapacity benefit if you are unable to do *any* job.**

- **Income protection or permanent health insurance plans can be used to replace up to two-thirds of your regular income.**

- **Specialist advice is essential – these policies are riddled with small print and vaguely worded clauses about pre-existing conditions.**

- **Make sure the premium rate is guaranteed not to rise, or is restricted to the rise in inflation. 'Reviewable' premiums can be increased at any time.**

- The definition of eligibility for benefit should be 'unable to continue *own* job'.

- A good critical illness policy will include 'permanent total disability' on the eligible conditions list.

■ GLOSSARY OF TERMS

Income protection or **permanent health insurance** (PHI) pays a regular income, usually until you reach pension age.

Critical illness policies pay a lump sum if you are diagnosed as having one of a list of illnesses.

Mortgage protection usually combines life assurance to repay the debt if you die, and PHI, to cover payments if you are too ill to work.

Accident, sickness and unemployment plans can be used to cover the nine-month period between loss of income and eligibility to claim the State benefit.

LONG-TERM CARE

The problem of supporting a growing elderly population is not confined to the UK, although Germany is the only European country so far to introduce a tax specifically for nursing care. To date, the UK government has limited its consultation on long-term care to voluntary insurance and savings plans. About 20,000 people have this type of insurance and most of these are in the 65–75 age range.

Under the NHS and Community Care Act 1993, the responsibility for assessing need and the payment of nursing home fees shifted from the Department of Social Security to the already financially overstretched local authorities. The rules are simple. If you have assets and investments worth over £16,000, you must pay your own bills. Since your house is an asset, this is likely to be the first item to fall under the auctioneer's hammer unless you have a spouse or other dependent relative still living at home.

> At present, an estimated 40,000 homes are sold each year to pay for nursing home costs.

At present an estimated 40,000 homes are sold each year to pay for nursing home costs. Once your house is sold, with typical nursing home fees of £15,000 to £20,000 per annum, depending on area, it will not take long to spend your children's entire inheritance.

■ PROPOSALS IN THE PIPELINE

Following a year of discussions with government agencies, charities and insurance companies, in May 1996 the Conservative government published a consultation paper in which it proposed several options, mostly aimed at asset protection. These include a US-style 'partnership' scheme where you are encouraged to insure a certain amount –

■ FINANCIAL SNAPSHOT

Seven per cent of the over-75s live in care. The figure for the over-85s is nearer 30 per cent and growing. The number of people aged 75 and over will rise from 3.9 million now to 6.3 million by the year 2030.

---

say £30,000 – and after this is exhausted, the State steps in. Your assets up to a prescribed limit are not used to pay for care.

Other proposals build on existing products such as equity release schemes or home income plans (see Chapter 21), and 'impaired life annuities' (see page 35). No date has been set for the implementation of such proposals.

In the meantime an estimated 200,000 people a year enter care. For these people and their relatives, any future partnership schemes will come too late. Besides, critics argue that the partnership concept will only help those with an asset base of less than £100,000, including the family home.

■ CHECK YOUR OPTIONS CAREFULLY

If you are interested in LTC, do seek the help of a specialist independent adviser. Most of these plans are complicated, expensive and they are not governed by the strict financial services regulatory system. One organisation well worth contacting is IFACare, which is a voluntary association for independent advisers who agree to adhere to a high standard of ethics and a strict code of practice to ensure best advice is given on LTC. You should also seek legal advice. If you want to act on behalf of an elderly parent, for example, you must have enduring power of attorney in order to appoint a professional adviser to help manage your relative's affairs.

> Given that the average age of long-term care policyholders is 70, and that they are investing substantial sums, they should consider carefully whether an offshore fund which is not covered by the UK Policyholder Protection Act is a good idea.

Before considering a dedicated LTC policy, check if you are covered under other protection insurance plans. Some critical illness policies pay a cash lump sum if you suffer 'loss of independence'. Companies selling this type of plan include PPP Lifetime, Axa Equity & Law, Norwich Union and Sun Life. BUPA's permanent health insurance product pays out in cases of 'lifelong' disability.

Finally, if you are tempted to give away all your worldly goods in order to qualify for full financial support under the social services means test, think twice. If you make a substantial gift within six months of entering care, your local authority may be able to claw back the assets. Where the gap is longer, the authority could take you to court.

■ What the State provides

■ If you have over £16,000 in assets you will get no help towards nursing home fees. There is a sliding scale of benefits if you have between £10,000 and £16,000 and where your assets fall below £10,000 you qualify for the full assistance available, although this will vary from area to area.

■ Local authorities which follow government guidelines paid a maximum of £346 a week towards a London private nursing home and £303 outside London in 1996. You would also get £13.75 a week 'spending money'.

Source: Department of Health and PPP Lifetime

■ HOW TO INSURE THE COST OF LONG-TERM CARE

There are two ways to insure the cost of long-term care. With a 'prefunded' plan you pay regular premiums or a lump sum ahead of the time when you may need to claim. If you are elderly and not insured, an 'immediate care' plan would guarantee a regular income to pay the nursing home fees, but for this you would need to invest a substantial sum.

Pre-funding plans

At the time of writing, only half a dozen insurance companies offered pre-funding plans. These included PPP Lifetime, BUPA, Commercial Union, Prime Health, Hambro Assured and Allied Dunbar (a branded version of PPP Lifetime's plan). The policies pay the benefit to your nursing home or, in some cases, to your carer. You may also qualify for help towards the cost of home alterations where this would enable you to stay put. Annual benefit, which is tax-free, usually is limited to about £25,000. However, most people can insure for much less than this if they have other sources of income from pensions and investments.

To qualify for benefit, you must fail two or three 'activities of daily living' (ADLs). ADL tests – also used by social services for those who qualify for State help – include washing, dressing, feeding, continence and mobility. Cognitive impairment should also be on the list, given the rapid increase in the number of sufferers of Alzheimer's Disease and similar conditions.

As with income protection, you can reduce premiums if you opt for a long 'deferment period' before receiving the first payment. This can be anything from four weeks to two years. You can also reduce premiums if you restrict cover to a limited payment period – for example two to three years. However, whether you would enjoy peace of mind with this type of policy is questionable. Certainly, conditions that involve cognitive impairment can result in a lengthy stay in care.

The cost of insurance varies, but as a rough guide, a man aged 65 who wants to insure an annual benefit of £12,000 would pay monthly premiums of about £70 or a single premium of £9,500.

Immediate care annuities

If a relative needs to go into a home you might consider an immediate care annuity, although to fund this, you may need to sell their house. Where the elderly person could stay at home, provided certain care was available and alterations were carried out, a home income plan might be more appropriate (see Chapter 21).

An annuity provides a regular income for life in return for your lump sum investment. One option for this age group is an 'impaired life annuity', as this offers a higher income if you have an illness which is likely to reduce your life expectancy.

The impairment must adversely affect life expectation and not just impact on the quality of life. Qualifying impairments include AIDS, Alzheimer's, cancer, cirrhosis, coronary disease, diabetes and stroke. Depending on your impairment, you could secure an income up to 30 per cent higher than that offered by a standard plan.

The few companies which specialise in this type of annuity include Pension Annuity Friendly Society, Scottish Widows, Stalwart, Commercial Union, Eagle Star, Equitable Life, General and Sun Life. If you are interested, do go to an annuity specialist who will select the best terms for your particular circumstances.

Unlike pre-funding plans, the annuity payments are not tax-free. Part of the income is treated as a return of capital so this is not taxed. The interest element is taxed but this reduces with age.

LTC investment alternatives

Long-term care is an insurance product, not an investment. Insurance relies on the pooling of risk, so the benefits of those who need to claim are paid for by the premiums of those who do not. This may be a price worth paying for peace of mind, but some investors regard it as money down the drain

There is an alternative which combines investment and insurance, but it is relatively new and untested. Only a handful of companies offer this type of product. Under an LTC investment plan, you pay a lump sum into a fund from which the insurance company deducts monthly premiums to cover the LTC risk. The products currently available use funds which, for one reason or another, are able to offer gross roll-up (that is, the fund does not pay income and capital gains tax). This means that if your fund does well and the investment growth covers the cost of the monthly insurance, your LTC premiums effectively are tax-free.

If you need to claim, initially, you draw your agreed annual benefit from your fund and when this is exhausted, the insurer picks up the tab for as long as you remain in care. In some cases, for an extra cost, you may be able to protect part or all of your fund so that the insurance covers the benefit payments from the outset. However, if you remain healthy to the end and do not make a claim, you can pass your investment on to your dependants.

■ SUMMARY

■ **200,000 people a year enter care.**

■ **Currently about 30 per cent of the over-85s live in nursing homes.**

■ **Typically a resident can expect to pay between £15,000 and £20,000 a year in fees.**

■ **If you have over £16,000 in assets, including the value of your house, you will get no help from the State.**

■ **If you buy a long-term care policy make sure it covers cognitive impairment.**

■ **Only consider an investment-linked LTC product if you are happy with the level and cost of insurance and the risk level *and* performance of the fund.**

■ GLOSSARY OF TERMS

Pre-funded long-term care policies require you to pay regular premiums or a lump sum ahead of the time when you might need to claim.

Immediate care plans (annuities) guarantee a regular income for life in return for a lump sum investment.

Impaired life annuities offer a higher regular income because the insurance company assumes your life expectancy is less than a healthy person of your age.

Activities of daily living (ADLs) include washing, dressing, feeding, continence and mobility. To qualify for benefit you must fail two or three of these tests.

Further information

A list of independent firms of advisers who abide by the IFACare code of conduct is available from: Andrea Beech, IFACare Administration, Bridge House, Severn Bridge, Bewdley, Worcs DY12 1AB.

4

Source material

Meeting the costs of continuing care, The Joseph Rowntree Foundation, The Homestead, 40 Water End, York YO3 6LP. Price £5.00.

Inheritance in Britain: The boom that never happened, an independent survey commissioned by PPP Lifetime Care, PPP Lifetime House, Elm Court, Stratford-upon-Avon, Warwickshire CV37 6PA.

PRIVATE MEDICAL INSURANCE

The waiting list for many operations under the National Health Service is still well over a year, and that does not include the often lengthy period between GP referral and seeing a specialist. Regional variations in the provision of care can also make a huge difference to how quickly your particular condition will be treated.

If you want to jump the queue you have to pay. While the more wealthy may decide to draw on cash reserves, for most people the only realistic option is to take out private medical insurance (PMI). About 11 per cent of the population has some form of private cover at a cost of over £1.5 billion in annual premiums.

■ HOW IT WORKS

PMI is a complex product and contract conditions can be lengthy. With over 25 companies each offering a range of options, it is wise to seek independent financial advice. An adviser should identify the best plan for your needs and price range and will know which insurers offer good service and are prompt with payments. Some advisers are able to offer better terms than are available if you buy direct from the PMI company.

> Watch out for clauses that promise a 'full' refund and then qualify this statement in the small print by restricting payment to 'what is fair, reasonable and customary'. This can mean just about anything.

It is important to understand what conditions private medical insurance does and, in particular, does *not* cover. PMI pays for private treatment for *acute curable conditions* – that is, cases where an operation or a short-term course of treatment can put right things

■ FINANCIAL SNAPSHOT

The provident associations, which dominate the PMI market, are being challenged by the heavyweight composite insurers. Norwich Union launched in 1990, and now has an impressive 10 per cent market share. Legal & General is likely to make similar inroads following the 1996 launch of its budget plan.

right permanently. It does not pay for emergency treatment. Nor does it pay for treatments for chronic illness.

This can lead to confusion. For example, under your policy you may qualify for private treatment to have a condition investigated and diagnosed, but if it is a long-term illness rather than an acute curable condition, you could find yourself back on the NHS.

The premiums you pay for your PMI will depend on the level of cover you require, your age and medical history. It will also depend on the type of hospital you choose to attend. Most

> Under your policy you may qualify for private treatment to have a condition investigated and diagnosed, but if it is a long-term illness rather than a curable condition, you could find yourself back on the NHS.

insurers group hospitals into three bands – London teaching (the most expensive), national and provincial. Your adviser can help you choose the appropriate band for your area.

■ DIFFERENT TYPES OF PMI

It is very hard to compare PMI policies because they all seem to offer something slightly different. However, most fall into three broad categories:

- standard
- budget
- over-60s.

Standard cover

Standard cover should pay for virtually everything but if you want private alternative medicine, GP and dental treatment, among other features, you will probably have to pay for a deluxe version.

Budget plans

Budget plans limit the insurer's risk in several ways. Each carries a risk, so do consider your priorities carefully. For example a plan might restrict the treatment to a 'menu' of the most common operations. If your condition qualifies then you receive prompt treatment. If it doesn't, tough. A second method of reducing the insurers' costs is to set a monetary limit either per annum or per treatment. PMI companies claim these limits are usually generous enough to cover most major operations but there is always the concern that you might run out of money half way through a course of treatment, particularly if complications set in.

An alternative budget concept is the 'six-week' plan which provides standard levels of cover, but only if you cannot be treated under the NHS within six weeks of the consultant's diagnosis. A six-week wait may not sound too onerous but do bear in mind that you may have a long delay between your GP's referral and actually seeing your consultant – unless of course you pay for a private consultation, which is unlikely to be covered by this type of policy.

Finally, some insurers contain costs by asking you to agree to pay an excess – that is, the first £100 or so of every claim. This is probably the most acceptable method of cutting premiums although the reductions achieved are not so dramatic as under the other budget plans.

Over-60s plans

Over-60s plans cover the 60 to 75 age range and until the Labour budget of July 1997 offered basic rate tax relief on premiums. However, this was abolished immediately for new policies and at the time of the annual renewal for existing policies.

■ MANAGED CARE

One of the latest trends in PMI is the use of managed care to contain costs. With managed care the insurer monitors the claim from the outset, before treatment has started and before the first penny has been spent. This means you have to check the insurer will pay up before you actually start treatment (this is known as 'pre-authorisation'). You may also be asked to use certain groups of hospitals where the insurer has negotiated special rates.

■ MEDICAL HISTORY

Unless you are in a top of the range group scheme run by your employer, the PMI insurer will exclude most pre-existing conditions. This will be done in one of two ways. Where the contract is *fully underwritten*, you must disclose your complete medical history and the insurer may impose exclusions as a result. If there is a *moratorium clause*, you would not need to disclose your medical history but all pre-existing conditions would be excluded for a period of time – typically two years – after which they would also be covered. Some pre-existing conditions – heart disease and psychiatric illness for example – may be permanently excluded.

■ PREMIUM INCREASES

When selecting your plan, your adviser should consider the PMI company's track record on premium increases. As with any form of general insurance, when your policy comes up for renewal each year, insurers can increase premiums without warning. Medical inflation tends to outstrip retail price inflation and typical rate increases in 1995 and 1996 were over 7 per cent. Much higher increases have been experienced in previous years.

If you are unhappy with the new premium, your only option is to vote with your feet and leave. However, if you already have a claim under way it may be impossible to switch insurers. It will also be awkward if you have made claims in the past five years since a new insurer would class any recent health problems as pre-existing conditions and exclude them. If your health has been particularly poor, you might even find yourself uninsurable.

■ CHECK YOUR EXISTING COVER

As with any form of protection insurance, it is important to check existing cover before buying. There are two likely sources – the State and an employer's scheme.

What the State provides

The National Health Service aims to provide a full range of medical services for all residents regardless of their income. These services are financed mainly out of general taxation. Most forms of treatment, including hospital care, are provided free of charge 'at the point of delivery', to use the jargon. However, some treatment – eye tests for example – must be paid for directly by the individual.

The length of time you have to wait for an operation will depend on where you live. According to Department of Health figures for March 1995, the number of patients waiting more than a year was over 14,700 in the North Thames region but was less than 100 in the West Midlands and in the South and West of the country. The North-west region claimed it had no patients waiting for more than 12 months.

What your employer provides

Many employers offer group PMI as part of an employee benefits package but the level of cover varies considerably and there is a general trend to reduce costs. Some group schemes have increased the number of exclusions – for example stress-related conditions are likely to be excluded since these can be very complicated and expensive. Your employer may also ask you to pay an excess, or he may agree to pay your premiums but will not cover the rest of your family. Premiums paid by your employer are treated as a benefit in kind and are therefore taxable.

If you are in a group scheme find out what happens when you leave the company if you want to continue the insurance on an individual basis. This is particularly important if you are coming up to retirement, where your age and past medical treatment could result in very high individual premiums. Some insurers offer a discount if you move from a group scheme to a private plan.

If your employer does not provide a scheme, check with your trade union or professional association to see if they offer discount terms. Other organisations such as the AA and RAC also offer affinity group discounts.

5

■ SUMMARY

■ **PMI covers private treatment for *acute curable conditions* – that is cases where an operation or short-term treatment can put things right permanently.**

■ **If you want to arrange private treatment always check first with your insurer that your policy covers the treatment you need and at the hospital of your choice. Ask for written confirmation.**

■ **Try to keep costs down and check your bill. Even though the insurance company is paying, if the hospital and consultant charges are excessive, eventually the cost will be passed on to policyholders through higher premiums.**

■ **If you are in your employer's scheme, check if you can continue on an individual basis if you leave or retire.**

■ GLOSSARY OF TERMS

Standard PMI covers all mainstream treatment, but may not cover alternative medicine, and dental treatment. Some insurers offer deluxe plans which would include these extras.

Budget plans limit treatment by restricting cover to certain operations or by setting a monetary limit. Some budget plans offer private treatment only if you cannot be treated under the NHS within six weeks of diagnosis.

Over-60s plans currently offer tax relief on premiums.

Managed care means that the insurer monitors costs throughout and pre-authorises treatment.

Moratorium clauses exclude all pre-existing conditions typically for the first two years of the contract.

Source material

Risk, Insurance and Welfare, published by the Association of British Insurers. Tel: 0171-600 3333.

Laing's Review of Private Healthcare 1996, Laing & Buisson, Lymehouse Studios, Block B, 38 Georgiana Street, London NW1 0EB. Tel: 0171-284 1268.

TAXATION

6

TAXATION AND YOUR INVESTMENTS

This book does not attempt to explain tax law and practice in great detail – its main concern is with saving and investing wisely, and where applicable, making use of tax breaks to improve your returns. For this reason, most of the details on taxation are dealt with as they arise in the relevant chapters – on investments and protection insurances, for example.

Before you consider investing your spare capital, it is worth checking you are making the most of your tax-free allowances and exemptions. This costs you nothing and can save you thousands of pounds. However, do not use your quota just for the sake of it. First look at how much tax you will save, and find out if

> Do not use your tax allowances and exemptions just for the sake of it. First look at how much tax you will save and find out if this is negated by complicated and expensive administration.

this is negated by complicated and expensive administration, as might be the case where you have to set up a trust.

Also, do bear in mind that security and peace of mind are important. Gifts made to avoid tax must be outright, otherwise the Revenue will see through the arrangement and continue to assess you on their value. Tax-efficiency aside, you may rue the day you gave your favourite shares to your spouse or children.

■ INVESTMENT SNAPSHOT

Since April 1990 married couples have been taxed separately. This means that a husband and wife each has a personal allowance for income tax and inheritance tax, as well as the annual exemption from capital gains tax.

Table 6.1 Main tax allowances and rates 1997/98

Allowances/exemptions	
Personal allowance	
under 65	£4,045
Married couples	
under 65[1]	£1,830
Annual CGT	
exemption	£6,500
Income tax	
Lower rate 20%	£1–4,100
Basic rate 23%[2]	£4,101–26,100
Higher rate 40%	over £26,101
Inheritance tax	
40%	over £215,000

[1] Relief restricted to 15%. [2] 20% on interest and dividends

Source: Inland Revenue

Table 6.1 shows the main tax rates, allowances and exemptions. For more specific details consult your accountant or the Inland Revenue. This chapter summarises the most important allowances and exemptions which do not require expensive and complicated arrangements.

The personal allowances and exemptions for the 1997/98 tax year, which apply to both spouses and children, are:

■ Income tax annual personal allowance – £4,045

■ Capital gains tax annual exemption – £6,500

■ Inheritance tax annual exemption for gifts – £3,000

■ INCOME TAX PERSONAL ALLOWANCE

Your personal allowance is the amount you can earn before paying income tax. The source is irrelevant – it can be earned income or investment income. One of the best ways to save on income tax is to share income between spouses to make full use of the non-working or lower earning spouse's allowance.

For example, transferring income from a higher-rate tax-paying spouse to a non-earning spouse can save up to £1,500 in tax for the current year. If you also make use of the spouse's lower and basic rate allowance you can save up to £6,000. You can achieve these savings either by giving your spouse income-producing assets or, if you run your own business, by paying your spouse a salary. If you opt for the latter method, do make sure you can justify the income to the Inland Revenue, and that you actually do pay it.

Don't forget that the allowance also applies to children. You could give your children income-producing assets, but you may need to set up a trust so that the income is not classed as your own. As a rule, if the annual income from your gift is over £100 you, as parents, will be taxed on the lot. There are special trusts which avoid this, known as 'bare trusts', but do check that the cost of setting up and running a trust is worth the tax saving. Remember, where the gift is from someone else – doting grandparents for example – any income generated is classed as the children's and can be offset against the personal allowance.

> If you transfer income from a higher rate tax paying spouse to a non-earning spouse can save up to £1,500 in tax for the current year. If you also make use of the spouse's lower and basic rate allowance you can save up to £6,000.

■ CAPITAL GAINS TAX EXEMPTION

The exemption is the amount of post-inflation capital gains you can make in the current tax year before you pay CGT. Gifts between spouses are exempt, so it makes sense to share assets in order to make use of both of your CGT exemptions.

For example, the partner with a potentially high CGT bill could give shares to his or her spouse who can then bed and breakfast the shares – that is, sell them, realise the capital gains using the annual exemption and buy them back – usually the following day.

B&B is a valuable exercise (although again, keep an eye on the balance between the transaction costs and the potential tax savings). This is how it works. You incur a CGT liability when you make a 'chargeable gain' – that is, when you sell an asset and its value has increased since the time of purchase. The gain is the difference between the original purchase price and the sale price, allowing for an adjustment for inflation, known as the 'indexation allowance'.

If you don't B&B, the potential gain on your shares will grow each year (assuming you invested wisely), and at some point will exceed the annual exemption. When this happens, if you sell, you will have to pay CGT at your highest rate of income tax. For this reason, it makes sense to pocket the increase in value on a regular basis by selling and re-purchasing. This allows you to use the CGT exemption annually to absorb gains and cancel the tax bill. In years when you do exceed the exemption, you can also use B&B to realise a capital loss, which can be offset against the gain.

■ INHERITANCE TAX EXEMPTION

If you die, your estate will be liable to inheritance tax (IHT) on anything over £215,000 (for the 1997/98 tax year). Gifts between husbands and wives are exempt, but there are several other ways of making a cash gift without building up an IHT liability. Probably the most useful is the £3,000 annual gift which can be made by both spouses. You can increase this by a further £3,000 if you did not use last year's exemption.

In fact, there is nothing to stop you giving away any amount in excess of the exemption, but if you die within seven years, the tax assessment is based on when you made the gift and the date of death. A sliding scale operates, so the longer the period between the two dates, the lower the liability. This transaction, where you give assets to someone other than your spouse, is known as a 'potentially exempt transfer'.

If you and your spouse are likely to create a substantial IHT liability, then discuss with your solicitor or accountant whether it is worth taking out a life assurance policy to cover the bill (see page 21). 'Joint life, second death, whole of life' policies written in trust are often used for this purpose. These combine insurance and investment. Your monthly premiums are invested, and from this fund, the insurance company deducts the amounts necessary to provide the life cover. When you both die, the beneficiaries get the fund value or the sum assured, whichever is greater, free of tax. For potentially exempt transfers, where the potential liability decreases over the seven-year period after making the gift, you could use a decreasing term assurance policy to cover the bill. Remember, you only need to cover the potential tax liability – not the value of the entire gift.

There are several other useful IHT exemptions. For example, if your children get married you can give them each £5,000, while other relatives can give up to £2,500 free of any IHT liability. You can also make unlimited gifts to charities and political parties.

One further, under-used exemption is modest gifts from income. These are gifts that are normal or habitual and leave sufficient income for the donor to maintain his normal standard of living.

■ SUMMARY

- **Do not invest or set up complicated tax arrangements just for the tax benefits.**

- **The main tax allowances and exemptions you can take advantage of are income tax, capital gains tax and inheritance tax.**

■ GLOSSARY OF TERMS

Bed and breakfasting is where you sell shares and re-purchase, usually the following day, to pocket the gain by making use of the CGT annual exemption

Potentially exempt transfers are where you give assets to someone other than your spouse. If you survive for seven years there is no IHT to pay.

MAKING A WILL*

For most people, making a will is a simple and cheap exercise, and represents a small price to pay for your own peace of mind and for the ease and comfort of your family. Yet only one in three adults bothers.

If you die without a valid will you die 'intestate'. If you have not yet made your will, remember the old saying, 'Where there's a will, there's a relative'. If you don't choose your beneficiaries, the government will do it for you.

> Remember the old saying, 'Where there's a will, there's a relative'. If you want to choose the beneficiaries of your estate, you must make a will – otherwise the government will effectively choose for you.

This means the laws of intestacy will decide which of your dependants receive your money, while your friends and favourite charities will receive nothing. In particular, if you have young children, you will not have had the chance to make careful arrangements for their inheritance of capital (this would happen automatically at age 18 under the intestacy rules), and you will not have appointed the executors, the trustees and the children's guardians who will oversee their upbringing.

Remember also that there are certain events that render it essential to re-write your will – in particular if you marry, divorce or re-marry. As a general guide, even if there are no major changes relating to marriage or children, it is worth checking your will is up-to-date every five years.

---

* This chapter is based on Section 14 of *Kelly's Financial Planning for the Individual* by Simon Philip, published by Gee Publishing Ltd. Sections reproduced are by kind permission of the author.

7

Making a will does not involve a huge amount of work, unless your finances are very complicated. Most solicitors do the legwork for you, and simply ask you to complete a short form which provides the information they need to draw up a draft.

■ WHAT HAPPENS IF YOU DON'T MAKE A WILL

The main disadvantages of dying intestate are as follows:

- Your estate may not be distributed in accordance with your wishes.

- The appointed administrators may not be people whom you personally would have chosen – or even liked.

- It may take longer for the estate to be distributed, whereas when a will has been made an executor can take up his duties immediately after death occurs.

- The costs may be greater, leaving less to pass on to your beneficiaries.

- Children will receive capital automatically at age 18, whereas you may have preferred this to take place later at a less 'giddy' age. What's more, the family home where your widow or widower lives may have to be sold in order to raise the capital.

- A testamentary guardian is not appointed for young children.

- Trusts may arise under an intestacy which produce complications, including statutory restrictions on the trustees' power to invest and advance capital.

■ POINTS TO CONSIDER

When making a will, there are several common mistakes which can be easily avoided. For example, you should make sure you dispose of all of your estate, because if you do not, then this could result in partial intestacy. You should also make provision for the fact that one of your main beneficiaries may die before you. Above all else, consider the legal rights of your dependants. If you do not make suitable provision, then they may be able to claim their right to a sensible provision under the law. Remember in this context that 'children' refers to legitimate, illegitimate and adopted children, although it does not usually include stepchildren.

You should also include any gifts to charities or specific gifts of assets to specific beneficiaries (for example your jewellery to your daughter/granddaughter). The trust powers of the trustees should also be set out here.

Don't forget – you can use your will to make some important arrangements about your own wishes. For example, if you have a strong preference for burial or cremation, and know where you wish to be buried/your ashes to be scattered, this is the place to make your wishes known.

You should also discuss any specific role with an appointed executor or trustee before you put it in writing. These responsibilities can be onerous, or may conflict with some other role the individual already performs. Where you have young children, the appointment of willing and responsible guardians is essential, particularly where only one parent is alive.

Finally, if you own any property overseas, you should draw up a will under the terms of that country, with care to ensure consistency with your UK will.

■ EXECUTORS AND TRUSTEES

The executor is responsible for collecting your estate, and distributing it in accordance with the law. This can include paying any outstanding taxes and dealing with other financial affairs. The executor takes over from the date of your death, but is not officially appointed until the will is 'proved', and the appointment is confirmed by a grant of probate.

Most people appoint as an executor a spouse or close relative, plus a professional – for example, your solicitor or accountant. Where the will includes a trust, it is helpful if the executor and the trustees are the same people.

■ DISTRIBUTION OF AN ESTATE UNDER THE LAWS OF INTESTACY

The following details refer to the law in England and Wales. The laws that apply in Northern Ireland and in Scotland differ. 'Issue' refers to children (including illegitimate and adopted), grandchildren and so on. It does not include stepchildren.

If the deceased dies leaving:

- *A spouse but no issue, parent, brother, sister, nephew or niece:* The spouse takes everything.

- *A spouse and issue:* The spouse takes £125,000, personal 'chattels' (car, furniture, pictures, clothing, jewellery etc) plus a life interest – that is the income only – in half of the residue. The children take half the residue on reaching age 18 or marrying before that age. In addition, on the death of the deceased's spouse, the children take the half residue in which the spouse had a lifetime interest.

- *A spouse, no issue, but parent(s), brother(s), sister(s), nephew(s) or niece(s):* The spouse takes £200,000, plus personal chattels, plus half the residue. The other half goes to whoever is living in order of preference: parents, but if none, brothers and sisters (nephews and nieces step into their parents' shoes if the parents are dead).

- *No spouse:* Everything goes to, in order (depending on who is still alive): issue, but if none, parents, but if none, brothers and sisters (nephews and nieces step into their parents' shoes). The pecking order then moves on to half-brothers and -sisters or failing them, their children, but if none, grandparents, but if none, uncles and aunts (cousins step into their parents' shoes), but if none, half-uncles and -aunts (failing that, their children). If all of these relatives have died, then the estate goes to the Crown.

Where part of the residuary estate includes a dwelling-house in which the surviving spouse lived at the date of death, the spouse has the right to have the house as part of the absolute interest or towards the capital value of the life interest, where relevant.

■ SUMMARY

■ **Only one in three adults has made a will in the UK.**

■ **If you fail to make a will you will cause delays in the distribution of your estate and you have no control over the choice of beneficiaries.**

■ **Do use expert help when you draw up your will. A DIY will, unless very carefully worded, may prove invalid, in which case the laws of intestacy apply.**

■ **Make sure all of the important details about your professional advisers and your financial affairs are set out for your executors.**

■ GLOSSARY OF TERMS

Executors are the people who sort out your financial affairs after your death and are appointed in your will.

Guardians are appointed to help with the upbringing of your children.

Intestacy is where you die without a valid will. The laws of inheritance under intestacy are outlined above.

Issue refers to children (including illegitimate and adopted), grandchildren and so on. It does not include stepchildren.

Trustees are appointed to run any trusts you have – for example your children's inheritance which is held for them until they are 18 or older. Normally the trustees would be the same people as the executors.

SUCCESSFUL INVESTMENT PLANNING

THE RULES OF THE GAME

Many of the investments covered in this section are tax-effi-cient for at least one, sometimes several categories of investor. In some cases, you benefit from income tax relief at your top rate, in others, you qualify for tax relief on income and dividends at the 'savings rate' of 20 per cent.

But if there is one piece of advice central to successful investing, it is this: never invest purely for the sake of obtaining tax relief. Your investments must be suited to your circumstances and must be able to stand up with or without the tax breaks. You only have to recall the hundreds of ill-advised investors who ploughed into now infamous business expansion schemes (BES) – and lost virtually everything – to see that this caveat makes sense.

So what criteria should you use in order to make the right choices? To answer this question, it is helpful first to go back to basics. In this chapter, we explain the relationship between risk and return and describe the most common asset classes. Your choice of assets – whether you hold them directly or through a collective fund – will be determined by your investment goals and your attitude to risk.

■ RISK

As an investor you will frequently come across the terms 'risk' and 'return'. Where an investment guarantees or aims to protect you from risk, you should be specific

As an investor you need to come to terms with that four-letter word 'risk'.

about the type of risk involved, and whether protection from one cat-egory exposes you to another. A good example is a building society deposit account. You can't get any safer than that. Or can you? The answer depends on which type of risk concerns you most. A deposit

■ INVESTMENT SNAPSHOT

Equities are considered more risky and volatile than bonds because they behave in an unpredictable way whereas, provided the company or government backing a bond is secure, the return on a bond held to maturity is predictable.

account with a major building society will protect you from capital loss, but in real terms, the interest rates offered rarely protect you from inflation. Your capital is 'safe', but it is exposed to inflation risk, so its real value – that is, its spending power in today's terms – will be eroded over time by inflation.

Historically, if you wanted to match or beat inflation over the long-term, you would have had to invest in equities. However, with equities, unless your fund provides a guarantee (and these inevitably lead to increased charges), your capital is at risk. Bonds – a type of IOU – offer the prospect of higher interest than a deposit account, but there is a risk that your capital may be eroded in order to provide you with a good regular income. Also, bonds generally pay a fixed rate of interest, and so do not offer any protection against increases in inflation. This is also true of deposit accounts.

> **Historically, if you wanted to match or beat inflation over the long-term, you would have had to invest in equities.**

■ RETURN

Risk and return are inextricably linked. Any change to one will automatically affect the other. Essentially risk is the trade-off for return or, to put it another way, 'return' is the increase in value of your investment, and represents your reward for taking a risk. If the risk pays off, your return could be substantial but the reverse is also true. And clearly, the greater the level of risk, the greater the potential reward or loss. So, if you invest all your money in a single company's shares, and it does well you will be in clover. If the company goes bust, you could lose everything.

You can spread risk through collective funds such as unit and investment trusts, and the new open-ended investment companies, or through insurance company investments. But even here the risk rating ranges from higher-risk small specialist funds to large international funds which offer greater immunity to the capricious behaviour of particular markets and shares. Bear in mind, however, that even the most broadly diversified funds will be hit when stockmarkets crash.

■ ASSET CLASSES

Savings and investment institutions are very adept at dressing up what are essentially quite straightforward assets which can be used to meet certain needs. For example, if you are saving for the short-term and need a steady and secure income, the assets most likely to match this requirement are fixed-interest securities, bonds and cash – all of which are low-risk investments that generate a stream of income. If, however, you are saving over 25 to 30 years for your pension or to build up a fund to repay your mortgage, then you should consider taking greater short-term risks in return for potentially higher rewards. In this case you are more likely to invest in equities.

Stocks and shares

Investment literature often is confusing and it helps to understand the jargon. Commonly used (and misused) terms include 'securities', 'stocks' and 'shares'. 'Securities' is the general name for all stocks and shares. Broadly speaking, stocks are fixed-interest securities and shares are the rest. The four main types of securities listed and traded on the UK Stock Exchange are:

■ UK ('domestic') equities – ordinary shares issued by UK companies

■ Overseas equities – ordinary shares issued by non-UK companies

■ UK gilts – bonds issued by the UK government to raise money to fund any shortfall in public expenditure

■ Bonds or fixed-interest stocks – issued by companies and local authorities, among others.

The following guide may help the uninitiated.

UK equities

UK equities are the quoted shares of companies in the UK and tend to dominate most private investors' portfolios, whether the investments are held directly or are pooled. Companies 'go public' by being quoted on the Stock Exchange or Alternative Investment Market in order to raise finance by issuing shares. A share literally entitles the owner to a specified share in the profits of the company and, if the company is wound up, to a specified share of its assets.

The owner of shares is entitled to the dividends – the annual or six-monthly distribution to shareholders of part of the company's profits. The 'dividend yield' on equities is the dividend paid by a company divided by that company's share price. This is an important feature for income seekers.

There is no set redemption date for an equity: if the holder wishes to realise its value he must sell it through a broker. The price will vary from day to day, so the timing of the purchase and selling of shares is critical.

There are different classes of shares. 'Ordinary' shares give the holder a right to vote on the constitution of the board of directors. 'Preference' shares carry no voting rights but have a fixed-dividend payment and have preference over ordinary shareholders if the company is wound up.

The return achieved by UK equities, when measured over the long-term, has exceeded both price and earnings inflation (see page 67).

There are several sub-classes of equities or equity-related investments.

Convertibles and warrants

Convertibles (also known as a convertible loan stocks or convertible bonds) confer a right to convert to an ordinary share or preference share at a future date. You might also come across warrants, which confer a right but not an obligation on the holder to convert to a specific share at a pre-determined price and date. The value of the warrant, which itself is traded on the stock market, is determined by the difference or premium of the share price over the conversion price of the warrant.

Derivatives

Derivatives, as the name suggests, derive their value from the price of an underlying security. This is the generic term given to futures contracts and options, both of which can be used to hedge risk in a fund or even in a large private portfolio.

A futures contract binds two parties in a sale or purchase at a specified future date at a price that is fixed at the time the contract is taken out. These can be used by institutional funds to control risk by quickly increasing or reducing exposure to an existing asset class. Futures have also proved popular as a cost-cutting mechanism, particularly in index-tracking funds and other funds where there are rapid changes of large asset allocations.

Options are more speculative financial instruments, whereby the payment of a sum of money confers the right but not the obligation to buy or sell something at an agreed price on or before a specified date.

Derivatives can be extremely risky, and great care should be taken to check that an investment manager is following prescribed guidelines. In general, it is considered less risky if derivatives are used for hedging and similar risk management techniques rather than speculation, but in some cases this may be a difficult line to draw. Also, guarantees do not come free, and if derivatives are used for this purpose, you will pay more for the investment management as a result.

Overseas equities

These are similar in principle to UK equities, but there are differences in shareholder rights. Investment overseas offers the opportunity to gain exposure to foreign currency and younger, fast-growing economies, but there can be tax penalties on the investments, because some or all of the withholding tax on dividends deducted by the foreign country may not be recoverable. Moreover, in the case of developing markets, there may be a risk of sequestration.

Bonds

Bonds behave like a sophisticated IOU. UK bonds are issued by borrowers, for example the government (these bonds are known as 'gilt-edged securities' or just 'gilts') and companies (corporate bonds).

Bonds are also issued by local authorities, overseas governments and overseas companies.

In return for the loan of your money, the borrower agrees to pay a fixed rate of interest for the agreed period, and to repay your original capital sum on a specified date, known as the maturity date.

UK domestic bonds are either secured on the company's underlying assets – for example the company's property – or they are unsecured, in which case there is no physical asset backing the bond's guarantee to pay interest, and to repay the capital at maturity. Secured bonds are known as debentures, and unsecured bonds are known as loan stocks. Since the security offered by debentures is greater than for loan stocks, the former tend to pay a lower rate of interest.

The point to remember about fixed-interest securities is that the investment return is determined more by the level of interest rate than the issuing company's profitability. Provided the issuer remains sufficiently secure to honour the future coupon payments (the regular interest) and redemption payment (the return of the original capital), you know exactly what your return will be if you hold the bond to maturity. Gilts offer the highest degree of security because they are issued by the UK government.

If the fund manager sells a bond before its maturity date, then the value of the future coupon and redemption payments will depend on the prevailing interest rates at the time of sale. If interest rates are high, then the value of the fixed-interest security will be lower because you could get a similar return for less money elsewhere. Conversely, if interest rates are low, then the value of the fixed-interest security will be higher, because it provides a greater stream of income than you could get from alternative sources. This volatile pattern of behaviour is more apparent with fixed-interest securities which have a long period to run to maturity, since they are more likely to be traded before redemption date.

Index-linked gilts
Index-linked gilts are issued by the UK government and are guaranteed to provide interest payments and redemption proceeds which increase in line with inflation. For this reason they are one of the lowest risk asset for income seekers. The return on index-linked gilts

in excess of the retail price index varies, but usually it is possible to buy these securities in the marketplace at a price which guarantees a real rate of return to the holder, assuming that the stock is held to maturity.

Cash

Cash does not refer to stacks of £10 notes stuffed under the mattress. Institutional investment in cash is very similar to an individual's investment in a building society or bank deposit account. Deposits have the advantage that the value in monetary terms is known and is certain at all times. What is unknown is the interest that will be received.

Property

In investment terms, 'property' usually refers to the ownership of land and buildings that are used by a business or other organisation. The owner receives income from rent charged to the tenant and, over time, this rent is expected broadly to keep pace with inflation. The dominant factor in the value of a property is the desirability or other-wise of its position.

There are several problems with property. First, it is often sold in large blocks which cannot be easily split for investment purposes. As a result, only the larger institutional funds can afford (or are wise enough) to own property directly. Second, property is a very illiquid asset and it can take several years for the right selling conditions to arise. Also, unless you invest via a collective fund, you cannot dispose of your investment piecemeal to make best use of your annual capital gains tax exemption, but instead could be landed with a whopping CGT bill on your profits.

Comparing equities, bonds and cash (deposits)

It is common practice to compare returns on equities and bonds with cash (deposits). These returns are illustrated in the box, and this demonstrates that when inflation is taken into account deposits do not keep pace with inflation. If you put your money in a deposit account, it will increase with the interest earned, but over the long-term the value of its real spending power will fall.

Barclays de Zoete Wedd Securities' annual *Equity-Gilt Study*, (see Source material), first published in 1956, provides data and analysis of yearly returns from investments in UK equities, gilts and cash since 1918 (see Box).

The one overriding message from the study is that over the long-term, an equity investor is rewarded for taking risk. Historically, the degree of that payoff – in the form of an enhanced return – has been substantial relative to both gilts and cash. Although gilt returns have performed relatively well in recent years compared with equities, the total returns to an equity investor have been higher.

BZW's *Equity-Gilt Study* reveals the following key facts:

■ £100 invested in equities in December 1918 with all income re-invested gross was worth £710,556 in December 1996. The equivalent figures for gilts was £8,917 and for cash £6,101. When inflation is taken into account, the returns were £36,528 (equities), £458 (gilts) and £314 (cash).

■ The average real return (that is, the return in excess of inflation) for equities for the entire period 1918-96 was 7.86 per cent a year. For gilts the real return was 1.97 per cent and cash produced an annual real return of 1.48 per cent. The average dividend yield for the period was 5.1 per cent and the average bond yield was 6.7 per cent.

Note: See the graphs in Figures 8.1 and 8.2.

It is important to remember that these index figures do not make any allowance for the charges that would be deducted on your savings and investments. For example, if you invest directly in equities, you would pay dealing costs, including stamp duty and the stockbroker's charges, while for unit or investment trust Peps you would have to take account of the plan manager's initial and, in particular, annual charges.

Figure 8.1   The BZW Indices

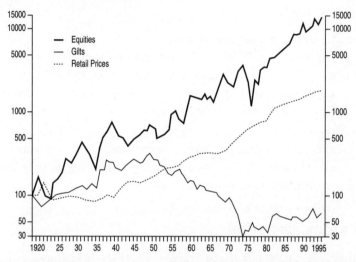

The nominal capital value of gilts and equities beginning December 1918 (=100). Historically the return on equities has outstripped both gilts and the retail price index.

Figure 8.2   The BZW Investment Funds, Net Income Re-invested in Real Terms

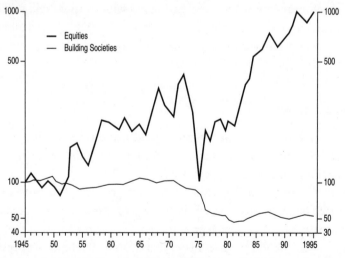

Real returns from equities and building societies since 1945. Historically the return on equities has outstripped building society deposit rates of interest.

Period of investment

Clearly, long-term returns on equities, gilts and cash should be viewed with some caution and certainly should not be treated as a guide to the future. While it does seem likely that equities will provide a better return than bonds over the medium- to long-term, there is an important caveat. 'Medium- to long-term' means a minimum of five years, preferably longer. If you go into the stockmarkets for shorter periods, you are in danger of getting your fingers burned either because the markets take a tumble just before you want to get out, or because the fixed costs associated with setting up your investment undermine the return in the short-term.

■ STOCK SELECTION

Stock selection refers to the process where the investment manager chooses individual securities. The following paragraphs over-simplify the process but nevertheless may help explain the jargon that investment managers love to use to confuse.

One important point to remember is that large institutional funds can make money on minor price changes because of the sheer volume of their transactions. Moreover, compared with a private client, many institutional funds – the big pension and charity funds, for example – also benefit from very low dealing costs and automatic exemption from income and capital gains tax.

Active managers

Active investment managers aim to add value by deviating from a specific benchmark – for example a stockmarket index. There are two basic techniques used in active stock selection.

The starting point for active managers who adopt a **bottom-up** approach is the company in which the manager is considering making an investment. The manager will look at in-house and external research on the company's history and potential future prospects. This will include an examination of the strength of the balance sheet, the company's trading history, the management's business strategy and the price/earnings ratio (the market price of a share divided by the company's earnings/profits per share in its latest 12-month trading period). From the company analysis, the manager will proceed to look at the general performance and prospects for that sector (oil, transport and so on) and then take into consideration national and international economic factors.

The **top-down** manager works in reverse, looking first at the international and national economic factors that might affect economic growth in a country or area such as emerging markets, and gradually working down to the individual companies.

Passive managers

Passive managers aim to track or replicate a benchmark. This style is also known as index tracking. It may sound simple, but in practice this is a complex process based on emulating the performance of a particular stockmarket index by buying all or a wide sample of the constituent shares, using a computer model to achieve this. The passive manager does not consider the merits of each stock, of different sectors and economic cycles. If it is in the index then it must be represented in the fund. Where the process tries to outstrip the index returns by deviating in a specific way it is known as quantitative management.

Comparing different investments

Before you consider the various investment options outlined in the following chapters, get acquainted with the benchmarks set out below. It doesn't matter if you are looking at plain vanilla deposit accounts or high-risk arrangements such as enterprise investment schemes, which invest in the shares of unquoted trading companies – the benchmarks will help you judge them all. They will also help you to focus on the important fundamentals as opposed to the bells and whistles that are used in marketing literature to make products look clever.

■ **Aims:** What are the stated aims, benefits and possible uses of the investment?

- **Returns:** Compare the potential net returns with after-tax returns on very low-risk investments such as 120-day notice building society deposit accounts, short-term conventional gilts and National Savings. Is the potential outperformance of your chosen investment really worth the additional risk?

- **Alternatives:** Which other investments share similar characteristics? Are they simpler/cheaper?

- **Direct investment or collective funds?** Everyone's financial circumstances and requirements are different, but as a rough guide experts suggest that for those with £100,000 or more to invest (some put the figure as high as £200,000) it may be cost-effective to build a direct equity and bond portfolio, using collective funds to gain access to specialist sectors and overseas markets. For investors with less than £100,000 it makes sense to use collective funds for the main core holdings where economies of scale reduce dealing and administration costs, and the spread of investments within the fund reduces risk and provides better access to overseas markets.

- **Investment period:** Never mind the flannel, for how long is your money really tied up? Check how the charges undermine returns in the early years and make sure you know about any exit penalties.

- **Risk:** What is the most you can lose if you stay the course or pull out early? Check how risk affects your capital and income and look at the likely effect of inflation. Find out how the investment is regulated and what happens if the firm/investment manager goes bust.

- **Cost:** Look at the establishment costs and ongoing charges. Watch out for high annual management charges, particularly for long-term investments as these will seriously undermine your return.

- **Tax:** The way the fund and you, the investor, are taxed is important because it will reduce your ultimate return. Check for income and capital gains tax implications.

■ SUMMARY

- Building society deposit accounts have their place as a home for an emergency fund and short-term cash, but interest rates are unlikely to match inflation over the long-term, especially for tax-payers.

- Your choice of investment will be determined by how much risk you can afford to take to boost your chances of an enhanced return.

- Historical data show that over the long-term, equities have sub-stantially outperformed bonds and deposit accounts.

- You can spread risk through collective funds but you must still consider your exposure to risk and examine how well a fund or your portfolio is diversified.

- Use the benchmarks provided to compare the most important features of different types of investment.

■ GLOSSARY OF TERMS

Active managers aim to beat a stockmarket index through research into companies and markets.

Bonds are IOUs issued by governments and companies, amongst others. In return for your loan of money, the borrower pays you a fixed rate of interest while the loan is outstanding and, at a specific date in the future repays the capital. Bonds can be **secured** – for example on the company's property – or **unsecured**.

Convertibles confer a right to convert to an ordinary share or preference share at a future date.

Collective funds spread risk because they invest in many different equities and/or bonds and/or other securities. Your money buys you units (in the case of unit trusts) or shares (in the case of investment trusts) in the fund.

Derivatives literally 'derive' their value from the price of an underlying equity. This is the generic term used to describe futures contracts and options, both of which can be used to hedge risk.

Equities are the ordinary share capital of a company. In return for your investment, you receive a share in the company's profits.

Gilts are bonds issued by the UK government.

Passive managers aim to keep returns in line with an index performance by replicating some or all of the index companies.

Securities is the general name for stocks (fixed interest) and shares (equities).

Stock picking: *Bottom-up stock picking* means your investment manager will analyse company details first, and then consider the results in the context of the prospects for that sector, and in the context of national and international economic forecasts. *Top-down stock picking* is the reverse where the manager will start with international factors, proceed to country forecasts, economic forecasts, and then focus on the prospects for a particular sector. Individual stock picking is the final stage in the top-down process.

Warrants confer a right but not an obligation on the holder to convert to a specific share at a pre-determined price and date.

Source material

The BZW Equity-Gilt Study, price £100, is available from Barclays de Zoete Wedd Securities, Ebbgate House, 2 Swan Lane, London EC4R 3TS. Tel 0171-956 3511.

The author would like to thank consultants Bacon & Woodrow for their help with the definitions of asset classes and investment management style.

BUYING, SELLING AND MONITORING YOUR INVESTMENTS

This chapter explains how to buy, sell and monitor some of the most popular types of investments. Savings which offer a fixed or variable rate of interest – deposit accounts, National Savings, gilts and bonds, among others – are examined in Chapter 10.

Most investment managers would argue, quite rightly, that good performance more than outweighs a high initial or annual management charge. However, since it is impossible to predict future performance, it makes sense to ensure that returns are not undermined by excessive costs.

Be particularly careful when you are looking at the so-called 'tax-efficient' investments. Your best approach is to ignore the

> Since it is impossible to predict future performance, it makes sense to ensure that returns are not undermined by excessive costs.

hype and consider instead a simple question: Do the charges outweigh the tax advantages? This is particularly important for those investing smaller sums and for basic and lower-rate taxpayers where the charges may be disproportionately high compared to the tax benefits.

Peps are a good example. If the annual management charge is 1 per cent, then the income tax savings for a basic rate taxpayer investing in shares yielding less than 4 per cent is also about 1 per cent so the saving is illusory.

From January 1995, for life offices, and from May 1997 for unit and investment trust companies, it is a regulatory requirement to provide investors with a pre-sale 'key features' document which sets out the charges and how they build up over different investment periods. This will help you make comparisons between different managers

■ **INVESTMENT SNAPSHOT**

If you use a nominee account, you are unlikely to qualify for any shareholder perks, so do check on this point – you might be missing out on free samples (booze and chocolates!) or a discount on purchases.

who offer essentially the same product, and also between entirely different investments.

■ THE CHARGES

The following section looks at the charges for one of the most popular investments – unit trust Peps.

The initial charge

The initial charge is deducted immediately from the original capital invested. It is calculated as a percentage of the lump sum – typically 5 per cent on a UK unit trust. The charge may include your adviser's sales commission, if applicable, which is likely to account for about 3 per cent. An increasing number of the low-cost index-tracking funds keep their charges to a minimum by eliminating the middle man and selling direct to the public. In this case there may not be an initial charge at all (but see *Initial vs annual charge* below).

The bid/offer spread

The initial charge does not reveal the full upfront costs, which instead are shown in the bid/offer spread (the difference between the buying and selling price). This is likely to be 0.5 per cent to 1 per cent higher than the initial charge, and in some cases the increase may be as much as 3 per cent.

The bid price is the price the manager will buy back the units – and therefore the price at which the investor sells. The offer price is the price at which the manager sells units – and therefore the price at which the investor buys. The 'spread' includes stamp duty, among other items, and as such represents the true purchase cost of the investment.

The annual management charge

This represents the cost of the investment management and adminis-tration and is deducted as an annual percentage of the fund – so its value grows along with your fund. The annual charge also includes the cost of any 'renewal' commission paid to financial advisers – that is the annual commission that is paid from Year 2 onwards – typically 0.5 per cent of your fund value. Although included in the annual charge, your key features docu-ment will separate out the cost of the advice – that is, the commis-sion paid – if applicable.

> Although the initial charge often appears the most significant deduction, advisers warn that it is the compound effect of high annual charges that most damage your prospects of a good return over the long-term.

Most managers deduct the annual charge from income, but some deduct from capital. The latter practice has the effect of artificially inflating the yield and has proved contentious in the con-text of corporate bond Peps, where it would almost certainly lead to capital erosion.

Typical annual management charges, currently shown as about 1.25 per cent, could rise to 1.4 per cent – higher for some funds – when all the costs are taken into account. The costs which were unlikely to be disclosed before the key features document became compulsory include trustee, auditor, registrar, custodial and regula-tory fees.

Initial vs annual charge

Although the initial charge often appears the most significant deduc-tion, advisers warn that it is the compound effect of high annual charges that most damage your prospects of a good return over the long-term.

For this reason, you should watch out for unit trust Pep companies which have lowered or abolished altogether their initial charges (often compensated by equally high 'exit' charges if you pull out early), and raised their annual charge. A typical exit penalty might be 4.5 per cent of your fund in Year 1, 4 per cent in Year 2, 3 per cent in Year 3, 2 per cent in Year 4 and 1 per cent in Year 5.

Pep charges

Unit trust managers may add an extra layer of cost on top of the charges for the underlying unit trust to cover Pep administration. In practice, however, most managers charge the same whether or not the client invests through a Pep wrapper, and several companies reduce the initial unit trust charge to encourage Pep investment. The effect of any additional costs or discounts for the Pep wrapper must be shown in the key features document.

■ HOW TO GET THE BEST DEAL

Unless you are an experienced investor, you probably should seek help from an independent financial adviser, and accept that you will have to pay for the advice. However there are opportunities for investors who know what they want, and are looking for the cheapest way to buy.

Several companies offer a discount by cutting the initial charge when they sell direct, or if the adviser has given up some or all of the commission. Do remember though, that unit trust managers have a degree of discretion over their initial charge, and if you plan to make a substantial investment, it is worth haggling. You should also adopt these tactics when you switch units within the same management group. In some cases you will automatically purchase units at or near bid price, but it is always worth asking.

■ BUYING AND SELLING

Shares

How you buy your shares – this includes investment trust shares – will depend on the nature of the agreement you have with your stockbroker or investment manager. If you have a discretionary or advi-

sory manager, the firm will act on your behalf once you have completed a terms of business agreement and paid a cash and/or stock
deposit. The firm automatically will provide a tariff of charges.

Rolling settlement and nominee accounts

In the past all deals completed over a two-week period had to be settled on just one day. With the current system, known as rolling settlement, a transaction must be settled a set number of days after
dealing. This means that settlement takes place every day. Under
five-day rolling settlement your stockbroker or other professional
adviser must pay for the shares you buy, or deliver the shares you sell
five business days after the transaction was made. As an investor, you
must make sure that you supply your adviser with money or share
certificates and signed transfers in good time to meet the deadline.

To help meet the deadlines you may be asked to use a nominee
account. Under a nominee account, you are still the beneficial owner
of the shares, but the share certificates are kept by the nominee company which is the registered shareholder. This means that the nominee company's name appears on the share register for the companies
in which you invest. The nominee company, which is legally separate
from your stockbroker, can offer a range of services including administration and banking.

Nominee companies do not have to be authorised by one of the
financial services regulators, so if you use a nominee account, do check
that your investment adviser accepts responsibility for any losses.

Buying your shares

Buying is quite straightforward. You contact your broker and ask for
a price (which will depend on the size of the deal). The stockbroker
then executes the 'bargain', and sends you a contract note which will
record the price, the number of shares, the cost (including the stockbroker's dealing charges plus stamp duty), and the settlement date.
Shortly afterwards, the registrar will send you a share certificate,
except where you are using a nominee service.

Most major investment trust houses have their own share-dealing
service, set up by the management company to help its own shareholders buy and sell. Effectively, this is just an intermediary service

between shareholders and the market makers. Nominee companies may also be used.

If you have some shares already, you might consider a share exchange scheme, whereby you swap your direct holdings in return for the same or different shares or a collective fund held within a Pep. This can be attractive if you have a few small holdings of shares – for example, in the company where you work or from privatisation issues. It could be cheaper to swap these rather than for you to sell at private investor rates.

In the case of single-company Peps, if your shares have recently come from an Inland Revenue-approved all-employee savings-related share option or profit-sharing scheme, a privatisation issue or from a preferential offer, you do not even have to sell them if you wish to retain the same holdings within your plan.

Execution-only

With an execution-only service, your stockbroker will carry out your requests and provide you with all the necessary documents. If you are investing direct for the first time, the company should also explain clearly which documents require your signature and must be returned.

With some execution-only services, you can either ask the company to obtain the best price available at the time of your deal or you can set a limit – a ceiling on the price you are prepared to pay, rather like an auction bid. When the market is closed, you can still place orders ready for execution as soon as trading re-opens. Again, you may have the choice of dealing at the best price or setting a limit.

Following a sale, you should receive a cheque on the due settlement day, or you can ask the dealer to pay funds directly into your account. Alternatively, the dealer can send the proceeds to your bank by direct credit – again on settlement day.

Collective funds

Buying units in a unit trust, an open-ended investment company or unit linked insurance company funds is also simple. All you have to do is contact the company direct, or through an adviser and ask for an application form. You complete this, and send it back with your cheque. Alternatively you may be able to place your order by phone and the company will send you a contract note.

Pricing may vary slightly. For example, with unit trusts, the price at which you buy will depend on which pricing basis the company uses (see the box on page 82 for an explanation of forward and historic pricing). The number of units you purchase will depend on the buying or offer price. You may also be offered two types of units.

- *Income units:* if you hold these units any income generated by the trust's investments will be paid to you on set dates.

- *Accumulation units:* with these units the income generated remains within the fund.

Within a few days of sending off your application or placing your order, you will receive a contract note which will confirm your investment, giving details such as the price, type and number of units.

Assuming you are satisfied that the timing is appropriate, it is easy and quick to sell unit trusts. You can sell either your total holding or just some of your units, provided you leave in sufficient to meet the manager's minimum investment requirements.

The documents you receive when you make your investment and the regular manager's reports should include an explanation of how to sell units. This may involve completing a special withdrawal form on the back of your unit trust certificate, or it may be enough to send a written instruction. Alternatively you could ask your adviser to arrange a withdrawal for you.

Once the manager receives your instruction you should get your cheque, accompanied by a 'sell' contract note within a week.

Income payments

If you elect to receive income, you will do so on fixed dates each year, half-year or at whatever frequency you have agreed. Income is usually paid directly into your bank account unless you ask for it to be re-invested.

Investments held within a Pep

Buying and selling investments held within a Pep is quite different from the usual practice for shares and collective funds held outside of the plan. You can buy direct from the plan manager or through your financial adviser. The adviser will handle all the paperwork for you, and help you with any questions you may have. Some advisers are authorised to handle client money, but many are not. If he is not authorised to handle client money you must make all cheques out to the investment manager, not the adviser's firm.

An increasing number of Peps and other collective funds are sold through advertisements in the Press. Here the regulators insist the company provides a considerable amount of detail so that you can make an informed decision. If you decide to go ahead, you will deal directly with the investment manager. The whole idea is to eliminate the middle man and so to cut costs.

With a Pep, although the investor is the 'beneficial' owner, generally it is the Pep manager who is the title owner and who deals with all the paperwork. As a Pep investor, you would not usually receive a copy of the reports and accounts of the companies in which you invest. You may not even receive the Pep manager's report unless you specifically request it.

■ MONITORING PERFORMANCE

The weekly *Investors Chronicle* provides first class coverage of company news. For daily share prices the best source of information is the *Financial Times* share guide – or, if you have access, even more frequent updates are provided by Ceefax and Teletext. The *IC* and *FT* also cover collective funds but there are several additional sources of reference, for example the useful articles, surveys and statistics which appear in financial publications such as *Money Management*, *Investors Chronicle*, *Planned Savings* and *Moneywise* – all of which are available from newsagents.

Chase de Vere publishes an annual guide to Peps and updates its performance supplement every six months (see page 286).

Another excellent source of informed commentary on Peps is BESt Investment's *Personal Equity Plan* publication. In addition to its recommendations, the company also runs a 'Spot the dog' column which lists all the funds you should avoid, or from which you should consider making a rapid exit.

For investment trusts, probably the most useful source of performance data is the monthly information sheet (MIS) from the Association of Investment Trust Companies, which shows the results of £100 invested in each investment trust share and the performance of the underlying net assets. The latter is considered a far better measure of the company's investment expertise because it disregards the impact of market forces on the company's share price.

If you have the time, you could build up a more detailed record of performance fluctuations by monitoring your fund's price changes, although this would not show the impact of dividend re-investment. With unit trusts, for example, your unit trust manager should send you a quarterly or six-monthly valuation which will show the unit price. For more frequent updates, you can check the price in the authorised unit trusts pages in the *Financial Times*. On Saturdays, the information appears in 'Weekend Money', while on weekdays you will find these figures in the 'Companies and Markets' section. Compare percentage price changes with changes in an appropriate benchmark. The FTSE A All-Share is probably the best general index for UK equity-based unit trusts since it covers the full 900-plus companies capitalised at over £40m.

If you find reading the pink pages rather daunting, a basic description of the column headings is provided in the *FT* itself, but a more detailed source is the *Financial Times Guide to Using the Financial Pages* (see Further information below).

Personal pension plan performance is covered by surveys in *Money Management*, among others. Your adviser will probably also subscribe to *Aequos*, an on-line database which includes comprehensive product details and performance statistics. However, ideally the firm will also subscribe to one of the top consultants' annual surveys which provide detailed analysis of performance, how that performance was achieved and whether the team responsible is still in place. The surveys also consider the strength of the company and the flexibility of the contract. The best known surveys are from Bacon & Woodrow and Buck Consultants.

■ Keep track of your unit price using the FT Authorised Unit Trust service

Name of the investment group, its pricing system and trust names: This is shown as, for example, 'Fleming Private Fund Mngt Ltd (1200)F' followed by the company's address and telephone number for dealing or enquiries. Use this number if you want to get a free copy of the management group's most recent report and scheme particulars. Under each company are listed its authorised unit trusts.

The figure in brackets in the heading is the basis of the company's pricing system. This refers to the time at which the price was measured (using a 24-hour clock) and the basis of calculation. 'F' means forward pricing, where orders are taken from investors and the price of units is determined by the next valuation. All larger groups have a valuation point each day, often at noon. So, if you phone your order at 10am, the price will be struck at noon that same day. An investor who phones at 1pm will have to wait for a price until the following midday valuation.

Some groups still deal on an historic price basis, indicated by 'H'. This means they buy and sell using the price agreed at the last valuation point.

Initial charge (Init chrge): The second column shows the percentage charge deducted from your investment to cover certain costs – for example administration and the sales commission paid to advisers, if applicable. If the charge is 5 per cent, then £95 out of every £100 will actually be invested in your chosen fund.

Notes: The third column lists symbols and letters which represent particular features. For example, 'E' indicates there is an exit charge when you sell your units, 'C' indicates that the manager's annual charge is deducted from capital, not income. A full list of notes can be found at the end of the 'FT Managed Funds' section.

Selling price: This is also known as the 'bid price' – the price at which investors sell units back to the manager.

Buying price: This is also known as the 'offer price' – the price at which investors buy units.

Price change (+ or -): The sixth column compares the mid-point between the bid and offer prices with the previous day's quotation.

Gross yield (Yield Gr's): This column shows the gross income paid by the unit trust as a percentage of the offer price. The quoted yield reflects income earned by the fund during the previous 12 months and therefore relates only to past performance.

Figure 9.1 Authorised unit trusts

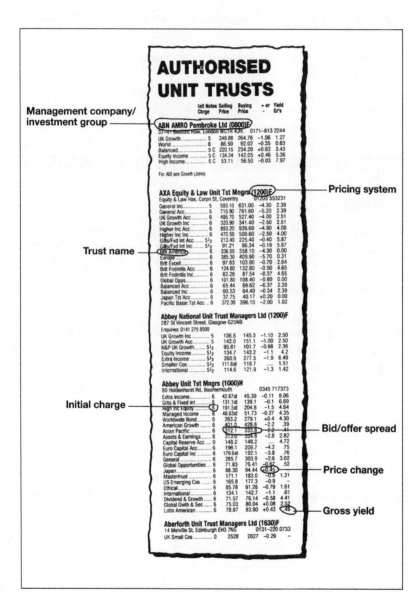

Periods of measurement

The costs of buying shares, whether direct or through a unit or investment trust, combined with the short-term volatility of markets, has meant that performance tends to be measured over the medium- to long-term – typically over a minimum period of five years. While this is a sensible approach for private investors it should be backed up by more regular monitoring which will pick up on changes in fund management style or personnel.

SUMMARY

■ **The annual charge is the one to watch on medium- to long-term investments.**

■ **Under new rules, which come into force in 1997, your adviser or plan manager must disclose the full cost of your investment in a pre-sale 'key features' document.**

■ **If you plan to make a substantial investment, try haggling over the charges.**

■ **For Pep investments, find out exactly what information you will receive – for example if you want to see the company or trust's annual report and accounts, do you have to pay extra?**

■ **Be prompt when your adviser asks for the money/shares and other paperwork necessary to settle a deal.**

■ **Nominee accounts can help speed up settlement, but do check that your adviser accepts responsibility for any losses made by the nominee company.**

GLOSSARY OF TERMS

Accumulation units If you buy this type of unit in a unit trust, the income generated remains within the fund.

Advisory management is where you and your manager discuss investment decisions and the manager cannot act without your prior approval.

Annual management charge This is the percentage of your fund which is deducted by the financial institution to cover investment management and administration.

Bid/offer spread The difference between the price at which you buy (offer price) and sell (bid price) your units. This includes additional items such as stamp duty, which are not included in the initial charge so the 'spread' shows the full cost of your plan.

Discretionary management is where your plan manager makes all the investment decisions for you.

Execution only is where you make all the investment decisions and your stockbroker simply buys and sells on your instructions. No advice is provided.

Exit charges Additional charges imposed as a penalty if you pull out early.

Income units If you hold these units in a unit trust, any income generated by the trust's investments will be paid to you on set dates.

Initial charge The cost of buying your Pep, including sales commission to your adviser, if applicable.

Nominee account Your adviser may suggest you have a nominee account to speed settlement. You are still the beneficial owner of your shares but the nominee company, which is legally separate from your adviser, is the registered owner.

Pound/cost averaging theory indicates that saving on a regular basis provides some protection from market volatility.

Rolling settlement Each deal has to be settled or completed five days after it has taken place.

Further information

The Stock Exchange publishes useful leaflets on buying and selling shares and on rolling settlement and nominee accounts. For copies, telephone 0171-797 1000 or write to the Stock Exchange, London EC2N 1HP.

Money Management is published by FT Magazines, price £4.50. Subscriptions/back issues enquiries: PO Box 461, Bromley, Kent BR2 9WP. Tel: 0181-402 8485.

Chase de Vere Pep Guide, price 12.95 (refunded if you buy a Pep through the company). Contact Chase de Vere Investments plc, 63 Lincoln's Inn Fields, London WC2A 3BR. Tel: 0800 526 092.

BESt Investments *Personal Equity Plan Recommendations*. For a complimentary copy and details of the free review of your portfolio, contact BESt Investment, 20 Masons Yard, Duke Street St. James's, London SW1Y 6BU. Tel: 0171-321 0100.

The Financial Times Guide to Using the Financial Pages, by Romesh Vaitilingam, published by the Financial Times and Pitman Publishing, price £15.99. Contact the Professional Marketing Department, Pitman Publishing, 128 Long Acre, London WC2E 9AN. Tel: 0171-379 7383.

The London Stock Exchange *How to Buy and Sell Shares*. Contact the Stock Exchange, London EC2N 1HP.

For a free sample copy of the AITC *Monthly Information Service*, write to the Association of Investment Trust Companies, Durrant House, 8–13 Chiswell Street, London EC1Y 4YY. If you want to receive the *MIS* each month, the subscription price is £35 a year. For a quarterly service, the price is £20 a year.

'SAFE' SAVINGS AND INVESTMENTS

'Safe', like 'risk' means different things to different people. It might be 'safe' to shift your pension fund into long-dated gilts and deposits in the run-up to retirement, but it would be far from prudent to adopt the same investment strategy for a personal pension in your early thirties. The phrase 'reckless conservatism' aptly sums up the hidden risks in going for investments which appear to be safe, but in fact are wholly inappropriate, and therefore expose you to the risk that inflation will seriously damage your long-term returns.

This chapter, which is aimed primarily at those with short-term savings needs and investors looking for income, takes you through the various savings and investment opportunities where important guarantees are offered – but at a price. The trick is to recognise the guarantees for what they are, use them wisely, but avoid the trap of investing too much in products which are not designed to provide capital growth.

> The phrase 'reckless conservatism' sums up the hidden risks in going for investments which appear to be safe but fail to protect you from the ravages of inflation.

Before you invest any money, it is important to be sure it really is surplus. Check first that you have the essential protection insurance for you and your family (see Section II).

■ EASY ACCESS DEPOSITS FOR RAINY DAYS

All investors need an immediate access emergency fund to pay for unforeseen events, such as sudden repairs on the house and car. How-

---

■ INVESTMENT SNAPSHOT

Since the Second World War, inflation has averaged over 6 per cent. At this rate, in retirement, if your investment income from gilts, bond funds and deposits is a level £10,000 a year, its purchasing power after seven years will shrink to £6,450.

---

ever, this is not a role for mainstream investments such as unit trusts or Peps. If you have to pull out of a Pep in a hurry, you could lose money, particularly in the early years when your investment is 'working off' the effect of initial charges or when the investment manager may impose an exit charge.

The traditional home for cash is the building society. Stick with it, but avoid the common mistake of keeping too large a reserve when part of your money could be earning a potentially better return elsewhere.

The size of your emergency fund should be determined by your monthly expenditure, your liabilities and the level of 'padding' you feel is appropriate for your lifestyle and peace of mind. As a very rough guide, it is worth keeping three times your monthly outgoings in an account which has one week's notice. Accounts offering a higher rate of interest with, say, three months' notice, can be used for known future capital expenditure – for example a new car, a holiday or school fees. If you manage your cashflow carefully then you can feed money from your other investments to your high-interest-rate account well in advance of the dates these more substantial bills fall due. Do keep a regular check on your longer-term deposits as rates change frequently.

There are several good sources of information on savings products, including the *Investors Chronicle*, the weekend family finance pages of the national newspapers, and, in particular, the specialist finance magazines such as *Moneywise* and *Money Observer*. Also useful is *Moneyfacts*, which covers savings accounts, children's accounts, cheque accounts, credit cards, store cards, bonds, gilts, mortgages, National Savings, and loans. *Moneyfacts* also publishes a separate monthly guide to life assurance and pension products.

You can also find useful information on the best rates for a variety of savings accounts in the personal finance pages of the weekend newspapers. Most papers publish useful summaries of best buys for different types of products and accounts (many of which are provided by *Moneyfacts*).

Safety at a price

When you consider fixed-income products, remember that if interest rates rise you will have committed yourself to a low rate of return. Of course if the reverse happens, and you lock in before rates plummet, you will congratulate yourself on doing the right thing. However, if the experts consistently make errors in their predictions of interest rate trends, the chances of you getting it right are slim.

> **The hidden cost of income guarantees is a reduction in the real purchasing power of your capital.**

10

Second, for most people, some form of inflation-proofing is an essential element in their income-generating portfolio of investments. The purchasing power of £100 will be worth just £64 after 15 years of inflation at 3 per cent, and £48 if the inflation rate is 5 per cent.

The hidden cost of income guarantees is a reduction in the real purchasing power of your capital. As a rule, guaranteed income products limit, or exclude altogether any prospect of capital growth. With some products, part of your capital could be used to bolster income if returns are lower than expected. Exposure to this type of investment should be limited.

If investing for income *growth* is a better way of describing your requirements, then you should include at least some equity investments within your portfolio. Clearly this introduces risk, but provided you aim for diversity and avoid the exotic, your main concern will be fluctuations in income rather than the fear of losing everything.

Tax status

This is a crucial factor in your choice of savings products. For example, the income from National Savings Pensioners' Bonds is paid gross, but the income from insurance company guaranteed bonds in effect is paid net of basic rate tax and you cannot reclaim this. In theory this should make the NS bonds a clear winner for non-taxpayers, but the slightly higher income available on the insurance bonds can offset this tax advantage. Depending on rates at the time, non-taxpayers should consider both products.

■ INCOME EARNERS

In the following pages we outline some of the most popular savings and investment options for income seekers.

National Savings

National Savings offers a wide range of accounts and bonds designed for every age and tax status. **Income bonds**, for example, have a three-month notice period for withdrawals, and the bonds must be held for a minimum period of one year. If you don't give the required notice you lose 90 days' interest. For savers looking for capital growth there is also a **Capital bond** which offers a fixed return.

NS Savings certificates can be either fixed-rate or index-linked, and both run for five years. All returns are tax-free even with early repayment, although if you don't go the full five years, the interest rate drops. **NS Pensioner bonds** can be bought by anyone over age 60 and offer a monthly tax-free income guaranteed for five years. Finally, NS also offers two accounts with a pass book – the investment account, which requires one month's notice – and the ordinary account which offers instant access at post office counters.

One of the attractions of NS products is that you can buy them through the Post Office and there are no charges. Bear in mind though that NS changes its interest rates less frequently than building societies, so you should always compare rates before committing yourself.

For details of the complete range of NS products, ask at your local post office or use the contact details provided at the end of this chapter (see Further information). Remember, NS does not pay commission to advisers – which may explain why many commission-based advisers fail to recommend them.

Tax-exempt special savings accounts

Taxpayers prepared to lose access to capital for five years should also consider investing the maximum (£9,000) in tax-exempt special savings accounts. Tessas are not specifically designed to generate income but it is possible to make partial withdrawals of the interest and retain the tax-exempt status. Most Tessas pay a variable interest rate, although a few societies offer a fixed rate for either one year at a time or for the full five years. Unfortunately, switching between Tessas is rarely worthwhile, due to the transfer charges or the loss of interest penalties imposed by providers.

If your first account has matured, provided you act within six months of the maturity date, you can transfer the capital (up to a maximum of £9,000) to a new account and enjoy a further five years' tax-free growth. If the transfer is for less than £9,000, you can make additional contributions to your new Tessa to bring it up to the £9,000 maximum.

Tessa maximum contribution limits

The total maximum over five years is £9,000, divided as follows: up to £3,000 in Year 1, and £1,800 in Years 2 to 5 (but only up to £600 in Year 5 if you paid maximum contributions in Years 1 to 4). If you prefer, you can make regular savings of up to £150 per month.

The rules are different if you transfer capital from an earlier account. For example, suppose you transfer £6,000 from your first, mature Tessa to a new account. You could then contribute £1,800 in Year 2 and the balance of £1,200 in year 3, taking you up to the maximum investment of £9,000.

Gilts and bonds

As explained in Chapter 8 (see page 63), gilts effectively represent an IOU – you lend the money and in return the borrower promises to repay the loan in full at a fixed date in the future. With conventional gilts and bonds the borrower pays interest, known as the coupon, twice a year at a fixed rate. As a general rule, the longer the term, the higher the rate – but also the greater the drop in the real value of your capital.

Gilts pay interest gross. Previously this was only possible where you bought through the National Savings Stock Register (NSSR). The NSSR remains convenient for non-taxpayers and also the cheapest way to purchase. However, NSSR applications must be made by post, so you will not know the buying price in advance.

Both gilts and qualifying bonds (not convertibles and preference shares) are free of capital gains tax on any profits because the 'return' is classed as income. This is paid net of lower-rate tax, which can be reclaimed by non-taxpayers.

■ How to assess bond income

To assess the income from gilts and bonds you need to look at three figures.

- ■ The *nominal* value represents the original purchase price (which is not necessarily the price at which you buy). This is the amount you receive at redemption.

- ■ The *coupon* tells you the interest rate that applies to the nominal value throughout the loan period.

- ■ The *market price* is the present value if you buy or sell.

The coupon and nominal figures determine the level of interest but the actual return or yield will depend on the buying price. If the buying or market price of a gilt or bond goes up, the yield goes down because you have paid more than the nominal value, and therefore the interest rate will be smaller in comparison. So, if the nominal price is 200p and the interest rate is 10 per cent, but you buy at 240p, then the interest is still only 10 per cent of 200 – that is 20p, so the yield is 8.33 per cent (20p as a percentage of 240p).

If the situation was reversed, so the nominal is 240p, the interest rate 10 per cent and you buy at 200, you will still get 10 per cent of 240p, which is 24p – a yield of 12 per cent.

Guaranteed income bonds

These are offered by many insurance companies – usually for a period of one to five years. Naturally, the income is higher the longer you are prepared to commit your money. Do note the point mentioned above on taxation: interest on GIBs is paid net of basic rate tax and this is not reclaimable even by non-taxpayers. However, since these bonds generally pay slightly higher rates of income than the tax-free NS products, it pays to consider both options.

The minimum investment in GIBs is usually about £5,000, but some companies offer higher rates if you invest £20,000 or even £50,000. Income is paid monthly, but if you can manage with annual payments you can secure a slightly higher rate.

For more information on insurance company investments, see Chapter 16.

■ CAPITAL OPPORTUNITIES

10

Two other options that guarantee to return your original capital are **National Savings premium bonds** and **guaranteed equity bonds**. However, both are unsuitable for income seekers. In the case of premium bonds, no income is paid, and you have to rely on the probabilities of winning to earn the equivalent of interest on your investment.

Guaranteed equity bonds use derivatives to guarantee a percentage of stockmarket growth or to guarantee the unit value of fully invested funds. A few of these funds offer to pay an income but only when the relevant index has achieved a specific return.

■ HALFWAY HOUSES

Many investors, particularly pensioners, need to squeeze as much income as possible from their savings, and are reluctant to take any risks with the capital. The trouble with this approach is that inflation eats into the real value of both capital and income. This is why most advisers recommend that income seekers should have at least a portion of equity-based investments in their portfolios.

But if you genuinely believe you cannot afford the risk of ordinary shares it is worth considering a halfway house – that is, investments which offer some capital protection plus a rising income. This category of investments includes **index-linked gilts**, **corporate index-linked debentures**, **escalator bonds** and the **stepped preference**

shares of split-capital investment trusts. A recent and welcome addition to the group is the corporate bond personal equity plan. This type of Pep is examined in Chapter 13 on page 122.

Index-linked gilts

These bonds are issued by the government and guarantee to increase both the six-monthly interest payments and the 'nominal' or original capital investment which is returned to you on the redemption date. The capital increases in line with the retail prices index (RPI).

Since the starting RPI figure used is eight months before the date of issue, the final value of the investment can be calculated precisely seven months before redemption (RPI figures are published a month in arrears). But, as we discussed on page 64, guarantees offered by government or corporate bonds apply only if you hold the bonds to maturity. Like conventional gilts (see page 63), the index-linked variety are traded actively, so the price and real value can fluctuate significantly between the issue and redemption dates.

Investors seeking absolute guarantees from their income-yielding portfolios may be tempted to put all their money in gilts. In this case, you might be better off with a balance between conventional gilts, which offer a comparatively high fixed income but no index-linking of the capital value, and index-linked gilts, which offer a low initial income, but protect both the income and capital from rising inflation.

From 28 February 1996, the 'accrued income scheme' applies to all UK residents except for those with securities valued at less than £5,000. Under the scheme, interest on gilts is paid in arrears, and is treated as though it is paid on a day-to-day basis between the actual payment dates, and separate from the capital value of the investment. When you sell, the accrued income is taxable as income, and cannot be treated as a capital gain. When you buy, the accrued income you purchase is offset against future interest you receive.

Corporate index-linked debentures

These bonds work in a similar way to index-linked gilts, paying interest twice a year which, along with the original capital investment, is linked to RPI. The main benefit of the corporate version is that the coupon or interest rate is higher because you are taking more of a risk since the bonds are backed by companies rather than the government.

However, advisers recommend that most investors should stick to gilts, due to the poor liquidity of the corporate market. There are very few corporate issues around and most are expensive to trade compared with gilts, so they would only be suitable for the long-term investor.

Escalator bonds

These bonds, available from certain building societies, share some of the characteristics of gilts in that the account pays a pre-determined rate of interest for the first year, and then increases the rate by a fixed amount for subsequent years. This type of investment could play a small part in your portfolio, but the interest rates are unlikely to be sufficiently attractive to make it significantly better than gilts.

Stepped preference shares of split-capital trusts

These are discussed on page 124, but briefly 'stepped prefs', (to use the jargon) offer an income which is guaranteed to rise each year at a fixed rate, and a fixed redemption price for the shares when the trust is wound up. Each trust offers a different yield and annual increase, depending on the nature of the underlying assets.

The factors to consider are the risk profile, the current dividend yield, and the gross redemption yield – that is, the total return expressed as an annual percentage, assuming the share is bought at the present price and held to maturity.

The best source of information on all types of investment trust is the Association of Investment Trust Companies (AITC), which publishes useful fact sheets and a *Monthly Information Service*, which provides a breakdown of all the member trusts and performance statistics. (For contact details, see, Appendix II).

■ PURCHASED LIFE ANNUITIES

Annuities, sold by insurance companies, guarantee to pay a regular income for life in return for your lump sum investment. The annuity 'rate' – or the level of regular income you secure in return for your lump sum – will depend on several important factors, including your life expectancy and interest rates. Women tend to live longer than men, so usually receive a lower income in return for the same level of investment. If you are in ill health, you may be able to get a better rate if the insurance company thinks your life expectancy is less than the average for your age. This is known as an 'ill health' or 'impaired life' annuity. The main point to remember with annuities is that, unless you pay extra for a capital guarantee, once you hand over your money, it is gone for good, even if you die the following day. Annuity rates are interest-rate sensitive and fluctuate considerably, so do seek expert advice over the timing of the purchase and the annuity company.

■ SUMMARY

■ **Remember that many 'safe' investments do not protect your capital from inflation.**

■ **Keep at least three times your monthly outgoings in an account which has one week's notice.**

■ **Most income seekers are actually looking for income growth, and therefore need an element of equity investment in their portfolio.**

■ **Make sure the taxation of the product is suitable for your tax status.**

■ **National Savings does not pay advisers sales commission.**

■ GLOSSARY OF TERMS

Bonds and gilts are IOUs which offer a regular income and a return of your original capital at the maturity date. Gilts are issued by the government. A rising income is available through index-linked gilts. Guaranteed income bonds are sold by insurance companies.

Corporate index-linked debentures are similar to gilts but are issued by companies.

Escalator bonds are issued by building societies and pay an increasing income.

National Savings certificates and bonds are backed by the government

Purchased life annuities offer a guaranteed income for life in return for a lump sum investment.

Stepped preference shares of split-capital investment trusts offer an income guaranteed to rise each year at a fixed rate

Tax-exempt special savings accounts (Tessas) are deposit accounts which offer tax-free returns if you hold the investment for five years.

Further information

Which? is published by the Consumers Association and is available in public libraries or by subscription. Telephone: Freephone 0800 252100.

Moneyfacts is published monthly by Moneyfacts Publications. Annual subscription £48.50. Telephone: 01692 500765. For a complimentary copy, telephone 01692 500677 or write to Moneyfacts Publications, North Walsham, Norfolk NR28 0BD.

National Savings products are available from post offices, but NS also has a sales information helpline: 0645 645000. Current interest rates are given in a recorded message on the following numbers: South: London 0171-605 9483/9484; North: Blackpool 01253 723714; Scotland: Glasgow 0141-632 2766.

11

UNIT TRUSTS, INVESTMENT TRUSTS AND OPEN-ENDED INVESTMENT COMPANIES

This chapter describes two of the most popular types of collective funds in the UK – unit and investment trusts – plus a newcomer in 1997 – the open-ended investment company. All three have many features in common, and offer a similar broad investment scope. Your choice will depend on the finer details.

■ UNIT TRUSTS

A unit trust is a collective fund with a specific investment aim. The trust can invest in a range of assets which are suitable for the relevant investment criteria, for example, it can aim to produce an income through investment in high-yielding UK equities, or to generate capital growth through investment in new or expanding industries or, more riskily, in emerging markets.

Unit trusts sold to the public are authorised by the chief financial services regulator, the Securities and Investments Board. (You may hear about another type. 'Unauthorised' unit trusts are used as internal funds by financial institutions and are not marketed to the public.) Unit trusts are 'open-ended', which means they may create or cancel units on a daily basis depending on demand.

Investors purchase units in the fund, the value of which fluctuate in line with the value of the underlying assets. In this respect, a unit trust functions in a similar way to other collective funds – insurance company bonds for example – although the tax treatment for these two types of fund is quite different.

■ INVESTMENT SNAPSHOT

The investment aims of a unit trust must be listed in the trust deed, and are also the basis for classification by the trade body, AUTIF – the Association of Unit Trusts and Investment Funds.

Why have a trust?

Trust law is based on the principle that there can be two legal owners of a fund – the actual owners or 'beneficiaries', and the trustees, whose job it is to act in the best interests of the beneficiaries – in this case the unit holders. This effectively separates the owners' assets from those of the fund management company so if the fund manager goes bust, the investors' money should be safe.

One role of the trust deed is to ensure that the fund is sufficiently diversified. For example, a unit trust may have four holdings which represent a maximum of 10 per cent of the fund. All other holdings must be limited to 5 per cent of the fund or less. This means that the minimum number of different holdings is 16.

Unit trust pricing

Currently unit trusts can be priced for dealing on a 'forward' or 'historic' basis. Where the fund deals on a forward basis, orders are taken from investors and the price of units is determined by the next valuation. All larger trusts have a valuation point each day, often at noon. Many groups still deal on an historic price basis. This means they buy and sell using the price agreed at the last valuation point.

Investment scope of unit trusts

Unit trusts can invest in 'transferable securities' (securities which can be bought and sold on the open market) listed on any market that meets the criteria set out in the European Union's Undertakings for Collective Investment in Transferable Securities (UCITS) directive. Basically, managers are free to decide which markets are suitable for their funds, but they must ensure the markets operate regularly, are

11

open to the public and that they offer the appropriate levels of liquidity.

Most funds invest mainly or wholly in equities, although the number of corporate bond funds, which invest in corporate bonds, preference shares and convertibles, among other assets, is growing rapidly. Securities funds may also hold up to 35 per cent of their assets in gilts, although there are also gilt funds which can hold 100 per cent of their assets in government stocks, but these cannot be held in a Pep.

Some Peps based on unit trusts offer capital guarantees, or guarantee to provide part of the rise in a stockmarket index and protect you from the falls. The guarantee is 'insured' through the use of derivatives – financial instruments which are used to protect a fund's exposure to market fluctuations.

For the more cautious investor, guaranteed unit trusts held within a Pep could represent a tax-efficient method of gaining a high exposure to equities without the usual risks. However, it is important to remember that guarantees carry a cost – in this case the price of the derivatives – which will be passed on to the investor through increased management charges. Some advisers argue that you might be better off gaining full exposure to an index through one of the low-cost index-tracking Peps now available, and hedging your exposure to risk by investing part of your capital in gilts or National Savings, for example.

To date, the guaranteed fund market has been dominated by insurance companies with their popular guaranteed bonds. Insurance bonds are pooled funds similar in concept to unit trusts, but there are important differences which are discussed in Chapter 16.

In all about 500 unit trusts qualify for Peps.

■ INVESTMENT TRUSTS

An investment trust is not a trust as such, but is a British company, listed on the UK Stock Exchange, which invests in the shares of other quoted and unquoted companies in the UK and overseas. As public companies, investment trusts are subject to company law and Stock Exchange regulation. The prices of most investment trusts are published daily in the *Financial Times*.

Investment trusts are controlled by boards of directors who are appointed by and answerable to their shareholders. The board presents annual accounts to its shareholders.

Difference between investment and unit trusts

Investment trusts are different from unit trusts in several important ways and offer the active investor additional opportunities. However, these opportunities also make investment trusts potentially more volatile than unit trusts.

Investment trust companies have a fixed number of shares, so unlike unit trusts, 'units' cannot be created and cancelled to meet increased and reduced demand, but instead, as with any quoted company, the shares are available only when other investors are trying to sell.

This means there are two factors that affect investment trust share prices. The first is the performance of the underlying assets in which the company invests. This factor also affects the price of units in a unit trust.

However, where unit trust prices directly reflect the net asset value of the fund, investment trust share prices may not. This leads to the second factor, which is that the market forces (supply and demand) to which investment trust shares are subject may make the shares worth more or less than the underlying value of the company's assets. If the share price is lower than the value of the underlying assets the difference is known as the discount. If it is higher, the difference is known as the premium.

> Investment trust share prices are affected by supply and demand. This may make the shares worth more or less than the underlying value of the company's assets.

Investment trusts can borrow money to invest, an activity known as gearing. This adds extra flexibility and if the shares purchased with the borrowed money do well, the company and its shareholders will benefit. A poor return on the shares will reduce the profitability of the company.

'Split-capital' investment trusts can have two types of shares – one that has a right to all the income and one that has a right to the capital growth. There are several other types of share, each offering different features, for example stepped preference shares (see page 124), which offer dividends which rise at a pre-determined rate and a fixed redemption value which is paid when the trust is wound up.

Taxation and charges

In terms of taxation, the unit and investment trust route is very similar. Where these investments are held outside of a Pep, in both cases the capital gains tax liability falls on the investor who can offset any tax liability against the annual CGT exemption (£6,500). Dividends are paid net of lower-rate tax. This can be reclaimed by non-taxpayers, but there would be a potential additional 20 per cent liability for higher-rate payers. Where funds are qualifying, both types of trust may be held in a Pep in which case income and gains are tax-free.

Charges on investment trusts are generally lower than on unit trusts, with the exception of index-tracker unit trust Peps. However, tracker funds available as Peps are confined to the UK stockmarket, and therefore do not offer such broad diversification as the larger and older international investment trusts.

In conclusion, unit trusts, with the exception of the index trackers, are generally considered slightly more expensive than investment trusts, but less sensitive to market movements.

Unit trusts vs insurance company bonds

This topic is covered in more detail in Chapter 16 on life assurance investments. Briefly, like unit trusts, a lump sum premium in an insurance company bond buys units which directly reflect the net asset value of the fund's underlying investments. The charges for the two types of collective funds are broadly similar, although insurance company bonds may have slightly lower annual charges, but tend to pay advisers higher rates of commission than unit trusts.

However, the tax treatment is quite different. Insurance company bonds pay tax broadly equivalent to the lower rate on income and capital gains. The income tax cannot be reclaimed so, generally, these bonds are not considered suitable for non-taxpayers. Moreover, the capital gains tax paid by the fund cannot be offset against an individual's exemption. Experts tend to regard this feature as a serious drawback.

However, there are circumstances in which the unique features of bonds can be attractive to higher-rate tax payers who may be able to defer or avoid altogether a proportion of the tax generated by the fund. (See page 143).

Unit and investment trusts vs offshore funds

In certain cases for more wealthy, risk-tolerant investors it may be appropriate to consider offshore funds (but not before you have used up your annual Pep allowance). Whether an offshore fund would be suitable will depend on the tax jurisdiction of the fund, the way the fund itself is taxed and your own tax position as an investor.

Points to consider with offshore funds include the charges – which often can be very high compared with UK funds, and the regulation – for example if it is outside of the UK, what protection do you have if the company collapses or the fund manager runs off with your money?

As a general rule for a UK investor investing in UK securities, once you have used up your Pep allowance, unit and investment trusts are likely to prove more cost-effective and simpler than offshore funds. There are two main types of offshore insurance bond – distribution bonds, which pay a regular 'income' and non-distribution bonds, which roll-up gross (tax-free).

Investors who may gain by going offshore include UK and foreign expatriates who are non-resident for UK tax purposes and who can benefit from gross roll-up non-distribution bonds if they do not pay tax in the country where they live. Higher-rate taxpayers may also benefit from the gross roll-up, but you do have to pay tax when you bring the money back into the UK, although of course you may have switched to the lower tax bracket if you have retired by the time the non-distribution bond matures.

■ OPEN-ENDED INVESTMENT COMPANIES

Unit trusts are a UK product and have several features – in particular the bid/offer spread pricing system – which on the Continent is

Unit trusts have several features – in particular the bid/offer spread pricing system – which on the Continent is regarded as rather quaint: hence the introduction of OEICs.

regarded as rather quaint and certainly not very user-friendly.

Open-ended investment companies (OEICs, pronounced 'oiks') can be regarded as the Euro-version of unit trusts and are similar to 'SICAVS', the French equivalent of OEICs and the most common retail investment on the Continent. Due to their popularity – and the fact that UK investors can and do buy European SICAVS through offshore centres – investment managers and regulators decided to introduce them in the UK in 1997.

OEICs, as the name implies, will have a corporate structure rather than be based on trust law. Like unit trusts, they will be able to invest in 'transferable securities' – that is securities which can be bought and sold on the open market. The fund's profits and income will be pooled. Also like unit trusts, OEICs will be 'open-ended' which means the management company can increase or reduce share capital on a daily basis – in the same way that a unit trust manager can create or reduce the number of units in line with supply and demand.

This means that investors in OEICs will buy and sell at net asset value – so there will not be the added complexity of a differential between the net asset value and the share price, as is the case with investment trusts.

One of the main differences between OEICs and unit trusts is that the former can have different classes of share, with different aims. In this respect, OEICs will offer some of the flexibility of split-capital investment trusts, which allow investors seeking income to take maximum income at the expense of capital growth, and those seeking growth to take maximum growth at the expense of income.

OEICS do not have a different selling and buying price (known as the bid/offer spread). Instead they have just one mid-market price – literally the mid-point between the bid/offer spread – at which investors both buy and sell. As with qualifying unit trusts, qualifying OEICS will be 'peppable'.

■ SUMMARY

- The structure of investment trusts offers greater investment opportunities but at the same time greater potential risk than unit trusts.

- For most investors – particularly lower- and basic-rate taxpayers, unit and investment trusts are more tax-efficient than insurance company bonds.

- Unless there is a very good reason, don't go offshore until you have used up your annual Pep allowance.

- Open-ended investment companies are said to combine the best features of unit and investment trusts, but are too new to have proved their mettle.

11

■ GLOSSARY OF TERMS

Unit trusts are collective funds which can invest in a wide range of assets. The unit price reflects the underlying net asset value.

Investment trusts are British companies which invest in shares of other companies in the UK and overseas. The share price does not necessarily reflect the value of the underlying assets.

Insurance company bonds are similar to unit trusts, but the taxation is quite different.

Open-ended investment companies are new funds which are similar to unit trusts but have a corporate structure.

Source material

Part of the information on unit trusts was drawn from the author's work for the *Unit Trust Yearbook 1997*, Financial Times Business Information, Maple House, 149 Tottenham Court Road, W1P 9LL. Tel: 0171-896 2222.

PERSONAL EQUITY PLANS – HOW THEY WORK

A personal equity plan is not an investment in its own right, but is simply a tax-efficient wrapper or basket in which you hold your portfolio to shield it from income and capital gains tax. Anyone who is over age 18 and is resident in the UK can take out a Pep. If you are a taxpayer and you want to invest in shares, corporate bonds or collective funds, then investing through a plan could improve your returns.

There are hundreds of different plans available from around 400 Pep managers, but the market is dominated by the high street banks and building societies, the major unit trust groups and some of the big retail companies – Virgin and Marks & Spencer for example. Some insurance companies and retail stockbroking groups also are significant players.

Originally, Peps were designed primarily for direct equity investment, but several rule changes since 1989 have given the plans much more flexibility. In particular, you can invest the full £6,000 general allowance in collective funds – a far more practical solution for most investors who do not have large enough portfolios to accommodate the concentration of risk incurred by direct equity holdings. The collective funds which can be held in a Pep are unit trusts, investment trusts and open-ended investment companies. These were discussed in Chapter 11.

■ QUALIFYING INVESTMENTS

The list of 'qualifying' investments that you can hold in a Pep is extensive:

Direct investment

■ The ordinary shares of companies registered in the UK or in other European Union countries.

■ The corporate bonds and convertibles (fixed-interest securities which may be converted to equities at some future date) of UK companies. The companies must not be authorised credit institutions so, for example, this would exclude banks. Corporate bonds must have a minimum lifespan of five years at the time of purchase.

■ The preference shares (shares that pay dividends at a fixed rate) of UK and other EU companies.

All the investments must be in quoted companies.

12

Collective funds (unit trusts, investment trusts and open-ended investment companies)

■ The full £6,000 allowance can be invested in 'qualifying' collective funds which hold at least half their assets in the above categories for direct investment. The investments can be in both quoted and unquoted companies.

■ Up to one-quarter of the allowance – £1,500 – can be invested in 'non-qualifying' collective funds, which are less than 50 per cent invested in the UK or EU. It is the Pep manager's responsibility – not the private investor's – to ensure compliance with these rules.

If a fund does not fall into one of these two categories, it is classed as ineligible for Pep investors.

Clearly as the years pass by, you will build up a sizeable portfolio and the rules allow you to change your direct holdings and collective funds. You can continue to invest in non-qualifying assets, provided these account for no more than the market value of one-quarter of your portfolio.

For the general plan, you can invest directly in equities and bonds or through unit trusts, investment trusts and the new open-ended investment companies, OEICs. You can only invest in one general Pep a year, but if you opt for a 'self-select' plan, you can use this to hold a range of qualifying investments, so you are not restricted to the funds of just one management group. Self-select plans are discussed in Chapter 14.

The annual Pep allowances cannot be carried forward to the next tax year, so if you do not use up your full allowance before 5 April it is lost for ever.

■ TAX-FREE INCOME

The tax benefits of Peps are considerable. If you hold bonds outside a Pep, then the interest payments are taxed at your top rate of income tax. In the case of equities, dividends paid to shareholders also are taxed at your top rate of income tax.

Within a Pep, both interest and dividends are tax-free (although the tax credit for Advance Corporation Tax will go in 1999). For a lower-rate taxpayer, Peps provide relief at the rate of 20 per cent, so your interest and dividends will be worth 20 per cent more than if you held the shares outside of a Pep. If you are a basic rate taxpayer, the relief will be at 23 per cent, while for higher-rate payers, the relief will be at 40 per cent.

Even for non-taxpayers, the tax reclaim service provided by the Pep manager is sometimes considered sufficient to justify the charges. Non-taxpayers may also welcome the protection offered by the Pep against the risk of paying tax in future.

This is good news for investors looking for a regular income, who can use the dividends from equities or the interest from bonds without eating into their original capital. Investors seeking capital growth can benefit considerably from the compound effect of re-investing dividends on their equity holdings.

The Pep manager is responsible for reclaiming the tax paid on dividends and interest. This is because UK companies cannot pay dividends and interest gross to non-taxpayers, including Pep investors. Peps do not need to be mentioned on your tax return.

UK vs foreign shares

Choice of geographical location may also be influenced by tax efficiency. The Advance Corporation Tax (ACT) deducted at source from dividends paid on shares of UK companies may be recovered within the Pep, so the investment returns on UK shares held in a Pep are genuinely free of tax. For foreign shares held within a Pep, the picture is different because some or all of the withholding tax on dividends deducted by the foreign country may not be recoverable.

In conclusion, taking into consideration the taxation of the fund and the investor, for many investors, the higher-yield UK equity plans are the most tax-efficient.

■ TAX-FREE GAINS

Normally when you sell shares, you incur a tax penalty on any 'capital gains'. The gain is simply the difference between the price at which you bought the shares, and the price at which you sell, after taking account of inflation. In other words, the Revenue only charges CGT on the gains an investment has made over and above inflation. For shares held within a Pep the capital gains are

> **For most Pep investors, it makes sense to hold higher-yielding equities in the plan to shelter these from income tax.**

tax-free. However, if you make any losses within your Pep, these cannot be offset against gains made outside the plan.

In practice, very few investors pay capital gains tax, because gains can be offset against the annual CGT exemption of £6,500 in 1997/98 tax year. Investors holding less than around £100,000 of equities usually can manage their investments in such a way that they would not expect to pay CGT.

For this reason, it makes sense to use your Pep allowance to shelter from income tax the interest on corporate bonds and the dividends on your high-yielding equities (assuming you actually like high yielders in the first place!). Shares which have a low yield, but the potential for capital growth, can be held outside the Pep where you can make use of your CGT allowance.

■ REGULATION AND CONTROL

Investment companies which manage and sell Peps must be authorised under the Financial Services Act 1986 and approved by the Inland Revenue. A Pep manager can be a bank, a fund management company, an insurance company, a stockbroker or an independent financial adviser.

■ TYPE OF MANAGER

There are two basic questions to consider here. First, do you want to invest in collective funds or direct? You can do either and with some plans you can do both. Second, do you want to make the investment decisions yourself or do you want your plan manager/adviser to make the choice for you? Again, between these two extremes there is a range of options which let you make some of the investment decisions, but also to take advice if you need it.

Managed funds

The bulk of the Pep market is in collective funds – largely in unit trusts. Here you automatically hand over responsibility for managing the fund – and your money – to the company. For obvious reasons, this type of fund is sometimes called a managed fund. Most plan managers have a range of 'peppable' funds, and usually you can make the initial choice and switch between funds if you wish. However, you are still restricted to the funds of that one manager.

Self-select

The alternative is to invest through a 'self-select' plan. In this case in effect you are buying the Pep wrapper separately from the assets. Provided you stick to the rules on investment choice you can run your own portfolio or ask a stockbroker to do this for you. The terminology varies, but essentially there are three different ways to run a self-select plan.

■ **Discretionary:** You can appoint a 'discretionary' manager (often a stockbroker) who has total control over your portfolio. Whether you opt for a combination of collective funds, directly held securities or both, the discretionary manager will make all the investment decisions for you and will report the transactions after the event.

■ **Advisory:** The advisory manager acts on your instructions, but is there to advise you and to make recommendations based on the firm's research. This arrangement provides a two-way dialogue which hopefully draws on the best ideas from you and your stockbroker. However, the important point is that advisory manager must refer to you before taking any action.

■ **Execution-only service:** Here you are totally responsible for all decisions and your stockbroker simply buys and sells on your instructions. This option is appropriate only if you have the time to manage your fund virtually on a daily basis and are confident in your expertise in fund selection and stock picking.

■ CHOICE OF MANAGER

You can invest in one general Pep and one single company plan each tax year. If you decide to subscribe to both you can use different managers. However, for the general Pep allowance, under a self-select plan you are not limited to just one manager of collective funds, but you can buy units and shares in several unit and investment trusts. The single-company Pep allowance must be used for just one company's shares at any time.

Transferring Peps between managers

The Pep rules allow you to transfer your plan from one manager to another. This is important because you may become dissatisfied with your manager's performance and wish to switch to a company which offers better prospects. It is not uncommon for a management group to lose half a dozen star managers in one major poaching exercise from a rival company. This should not automatically force you to pull out, but you certainly need to keep a close eye on future performance.

The transfer may require you to cash in all your investments and use this money to buy in to the new manager's funds. Do check the charges involved in this exercise.

Of course, with a self-select Pep it is not necessary to change the plan manager, because you are free to switch your investments within the plan as often as you like (although it is expensive to do so frequently). The overall asset allocation of your self-select portfolio must not exceed the maximum of one-quarter in non-qualifying investments.

With a single-company plan you can also change your shares at a later date if you are dissatisfied with the performance. In effect, each year's single company Pep is ring-fenced, so that if you want to sell the shares you must invest the proceeds within 42 days in the shares of just one company.

'Windfalls'

If you get any 'windfall' shares from building society or insurance company flotations, you must decide whether to sell or keep them within your portfolio. The Revenue rules allow you to transfer the shares to a Pep without incurring the cost of selling them and buying them back. However, you must do this within 42 days of issue. Windfall shares do not count against your annual general and single company allowances.

■ SHARE EXCHANGE SCHEMES

Some Pep managers offer share exchange facilities which enable you to move shares from your existing portfolio held outside a Pep into your plan. The Pep manager will sell your shares and re-invest the money through the Pep – either by re-purchasing the shares or by buying different ones. Some managers offer to do this for free, provided you have, say, a minimum of £1,000 held in a FT-SE 100 company.

■ LUMP SUM VS REGULAR SAVINGS

Most managers offer a monthly savings option with minimum investments from as little as £20 in some cases. There is an argument which suggests that regular savings plans are more efficient and less vulnerable to price changes than investing lump sums, but the theory is not watertight. In practice, the most important consideration is to adopt the savings pattern that best

> **Some Pep managers offer share exchange facilities which enable you to move shares from your existing portfolio held outside a Pep into your plan.**

suits your financial circumstances. If you are by nature a regular saver, and do not want to have to worry about timing your entry into the stockmarket, then a regular savings plan is ideal. If you are self-employed, and prefer to make a single lump sum investment towards the end of the tax year – then stick to this pattern, or opt for a lump sum plan where the manager drip-feeds your money into the stockmarkets, leaving your uninvested cash to earn interest tax-free.

One point to note when considering your savings pattern is that self-select plans are not really designed for regular savers. There are a few stockbrokers who will accept this arrangement, but only if you are investing the maximum allowance each year.

12

■ DEPOSIT FACILITY

Some Pep managers offer an interest-bearing deposit account to hold cash within the Pep. This can be useful if you decide to sell, but want time to reflect before re-investing your money.

Cash in general Peps can earn interest gross, provided the money eventually is invested in shares, bonds and/or qualifying unit or investment trusts. Clearly, however, the purpose of a Pep is to invest, not to act as a tax-free deposit account. For this reason, there is a limit of £180 on the amount of tax-free interest you can withdraw in a tax year.

■ THE COST OF YOUR PEP

With Peps, you need to ask yourself whether the plan charges outweigh the tax advantages. This is particularly important for those investing smaller sums, and for basic- and lower-rate taxpayers where the charges may be disproportionately high compared to the tax benefits. The rule of thumb we recommend is this: if the annual management charge is 1 per cent, then the income tax savings for a basic-rate taxpayer investing in shares yielding less than 4 per cent is probably slightly less than 1 per cent, particularly when you take other charges into consideration. To be fair though, this does not take into account the other useful administration facilities offered by Peps, such as the reclamation of tax credits on dividends.

■ SUMMARY

- ■ UK residents aged 18 and over can invest £6,000 in a general Pep, and £3,000 in a single-company plan.

- ■ You can choose one manager for your general Pep and one for your single-company Pep each year. You can use the same manager for both plans but this is not compulsory.

- ■ There is no income or capital gains tax on investments held within a Pep.

- ■ The allowance cannot be carried over to the following tax year.

- ■ Direct investments in a general Pep include the shares (and preference shares) of companies registered in the UK and EU, plus UK corporate bonds and convertibles.

- ■ Collective funds which qualify for investment in a general Pep include unit trusts, investment trusts and the new open-ended investment companies.

- ■ Self-select plans allow you to hold any combination of qualifying securities and funds within your plan – you are not limited to the funds of just one manager.

- ■ For most Pep investors, it makes sense to hold higher-yielding UK equities in the plan to shelter these from income tax. Growth funds and individual shares can be held outside the plan, where the annual capital gains tax exemption can be used to offset any realised gains.

- ■ You can switch your Pep investments provided you stick to the rules on the amounts invested in qualifying and non-qualifying investments.

- ■ You do not need to mention Peps on your tax return.

■ GLOSSARY OF TERMS

Advisory management is where you and your manager discuss investment decisions and the manager cannot act without your prior approval.

Convertibles are fixed-interest securities which may be converted to equities at a future date.

Corporate bonds are issued by companies that want to borrow money. The companies pay a fixed rate of interest and repay the capital on a specified future date.

Debentures are bonds secured on a company's assets.

Dividends are part of the company's profits which are distributed every six or 12 months to shareholders.

Discretionary management is where your plan manager makes all the investment decisions for you.

Equities represent an investor's 'share' in the company's ownership – including its profits. To issue shares, a company 'goes public' and is quoted on the Stock Exchange (the main exchange for UK companies) or the Alternative Investment Market (an exchange for smaller companies).

Execution only is where you make all the investment decisions and your stockbroker simply buys and sells on your instructions. No advice is provided.

Loan stocks are unsecured bonds. They generally pay a higher rate of interest than debentures but are higher-risk.

Non-qualifying collective investments can be used for one-quarter of the annual general Pep allowance. This includes a wide range of international funds.

Preference shares are shares that pay dividends at a fixed rate and have a priority over ordinary shares when a company is wound up.

Qualifying investments can be used for the full £6,000 annual general Pep allowance (the Summary above explains which investments qualify).

THE MOST POPULAR PEPS

There is a huge range of 'peppable' funds, and the experienced investor no doubt will spend many a happy hour trawling through the more exciting but potentially higher-risk options. This chapter is aimed at the less experienced investor who wants to build up a good core portfolio for growth, income or both.

In practice, for most investors this will be achieved with UK equities, held either through an index-tracking fund or an actively managed, possibly higher-yielding equity fund. Investors specifically seeking income should also consider a corporate bond Pep. This chapter focuses on these three categories.

■ UNIT TRUST INDEX TRACKERS

Unit trust index trackers are rapidly becoming one of the most popular and successful funds to 'pep' because they offer a combination of broad diversification, generally good performance and modest charges.

> Unit trust index trackers are one of the most popular and successful funds to 'pep' because they offer a combination of broad diversification, generally good performance and modest charges.

In practice, index tracking is a complex process, but the information you require as a private investor can be explained quite simply. Index tracking (also known as 'passive' investment management) is based on emulating the performance of a particular stockmarket index by buying all or a wide sample of the constituent shares, using a computer model to achieve this. The passive manager does not consider the merits of each stock, of different sectors and economic cycles. If it is in the index, then it must be represented in the fund.

■ **INVESTMENT SNAPSHOT**

With corporate bond funds, one indicator of security is the number of different bonds held. A large number of holdings spreads risk because it limits the damage if a company goes bust. The minimum number of holdings is 10, but basically, the more the merrier.

The alternative to index tracking is known as 'active' management, where the manager invests in specific shares because he or she believes they will do well. Active management relies on extensive research and considerable resources. The big investment management groups often employ several hundred fund managers and analysts worldwide to assess national and international trends, economic forecasts, the prospects for each sector (for example, mining, leisure industry, engineering and so on) and individual company analysis. The cost of this research is reflected in the annual management charge.

13

Good performance

When you compare the performance of a fund with an index, it is important to bear in mind that the index itself does not take into account the cost of dealing and stamp duty – so in a sense the index has a head start. However, this problem applies to all funds whether active or passive.

Purists are quite right, of course, when they argue that by their very nature it is impossible for a tracker to outperform the index, unless this arises inadvertently as a result of tracking error. What they are less quick to point out is that many actively managed funds also fail to outperform the index – and charge a lot more for their unsuccessful efforts.

Performance figures for tracker funds reveal that most return above average results in their sector (usually 'UK general'), and in some cases achieve top quartile positions (top 25 per cent). While it is impossible to predict whether this pattern will continue in the future, the fierce price war among tracker managers should keep charges very competitive indeed.

But there are several other reasons why for some time index trackers have outperformed the bulk of actively managed funds. Running the fund is relatively straightforward. There are no active management decisions to make because the fund simply replicates all or part of the stocks in the index tracked. When companies move in and out of the index at the quarterly index review, the fund follows suit and buys or sells the appropriate stocks.

In practice, the number of changes in the index shares is limited, so the fund's turnover of shares is low. This reduces dealing costs and helps keep tracker Peps' charges to a minimum. Most funds have no initial charge and a very low annual management charge compared with actively managed funds, so overall it can be said that with index trackers charges do not act as a drag on performance.

Fans of passive management (and this includes some of the biggest pension funds in the UK) argue that using an index as the basis for stock selection is actually very efficient because the index Review Panel removes underperforming stocks, and introduces up and coming companies.

The selection criteria for the most commonly tracked index – the FT-SE 100 – are based on market capitalisation – that is, the total share value of the company (see below). Passive managers argue that if a company's share price falls, this is usually an indication that it has some problems that affect profitability. As its share price drops, so too does its market capitalisation and as a result it may slip out of the index and hence out of the tracker fund.

Therefore, although the management is 'passive', in effect by proxy you are getting the active selection process ensured by the Review Panel – selling companies whose performance lags and buying companies whose performance is on an upward trend. Of course the main problem with relying on this system is that shares of companies on a downward spiral are held for longer than would (or should) be the case with active management. The active manager would try to spot the signs of trouble before the market capitalisation is hit.

Trackers have a particular appeal to new investors and those with limited UK equity investments looking for a good core holding. Once this is established, diversification into active management in more specialist equity markets can be considered.

The index tracked

When choosing a tracker fund, it is important to consider which stocks are held within the index itself, since this will have a strong bearing on the performance. You might also be interested in how the index is tracked – for example, does the manager fully replicate the index or only buy a representative selection of stocks? The indices and tracking methods are discussed in more detail below.

The two most popular indices used by the tracker funds are the FT-SE 100 and the FT-SE-A All-Share. A less common alternative is the FT-SE Mid 250. The main characteristics of these indices are as follows:

- **The FT-SE-A All-Share index** consists of around 915 companies and is regarded as the professional investor's yardstick for the level of the UK equity market as a whole. Its main advantages over the FT-SE 100 and Mid 250 are as follows:

  - almost complete coverage of UK shares – it represents about 95 per cent of UK stockmarket capitalisation;
  - greater diversification than other indices;
  - exposure to smaller companies which often outperform larger companies;
  - often regarded by market professionals as the 'best' index.

- **The FT-SE 100 index** consists of the 100 largest UK companies by market capitalisation. Its advantages, in comparison with the FT-SE-A All-Share, broadly can be summarised as follows:

  - good coverage of the market – it represents 70 per cent of UK stockmarket capitalisation;
  - lower trading costs to replicate the fund compared with the All-Share and Mid 250;
  - greater exposure to larger companies which tend to do better in a recession than smaller companies;
  - substantial overseas exposure to international economies through the larger multinational companies.

- **The FT-SE Mid 250 index** consists of the next 250 companies

13

below the FT-SE 100. These are companies capitalised at between approximately £150m and £1bn. Its characteristics in comparison with the above indices broadly can be summarised as follows:

- more concentrated coverage of the market – it represents approximately 22 per cent of UK stockmarket capitalisation;
- the index has outperformed the FT-SE 100 over the past five years;
- companies are less export-orientated than the FT-SE 100, and therefore represent a more concentrated investment in the UK;
- higher returns than the FT-SE 100 during an economic recovery, but less exposure to the more volatile smaller companies in the FT-SE-A All-Share.

Diversification clearly is a chief advantage of the FT-SE-A All-Share index trackers but unlike the FT-SE 100 funds, which tend to use full replication of the index, the All-Share is rarely replicated in full.

Importance of charges for trackers

As a private investor, it is worth keeping a lookout for surveys which quantify and analyse tracking errors and other technicalities. In addition, once you have selected your preferred index, charges are one of the most important criteria on which to base your selection.

■ UK EQUITY HIGHER-INCOME PEPS

Most Pep plan managers offer a UK equity higher-income fund but if your favourite manager does not have one available, look for the nearest equivalent. If yield is important to you, a broad guideline at the time of writing would be to consider funds with an income yield of 3 per cent or above.

Unlike the index trackers, where cost is one of the major, if not *the* major factor to consider when making your choice, with the actively managed funds what you are really paying for is performance – in this case a combination of a good yield with the prospect of good long-term capital growth.

Clearly then, the importance attached to charges must be kept in proportion. The difference between the investment performance of these funds is likely to far outweigh the difference in charges.

> **The difference between the investment performance of actively managed funds is likely to far outweigh the difference in charges.**

Percentage of funds in UK equities

You might think that a fund labelled 'UK equity' would be invested in, well, UK equities. This is not strictly true. A more detailed examination of the Peps in this category shows considerable variations in the asset allocation of what are apparently similar funds. In certain cases the entire portfolio is invested in UK equities, but in some cases the percentage of UK stocks can fall below 60 per cent.

If you are looking for a high-yielding Pep, you should ask what other assets the fund holds. There are two likely answers. Where part of the fund is invested in convertibles and bonds, the manager's intention is to use these assets to boost the yield and to provide a degree of diversification (see page 99).Whether you are comfortable with a substantial bond holding will depend on the views you and/or your adviser have on the prospects for bonds and equities.

Alternatively, the manager may choose to invest part of the fund in overseas equities. This maintains your high equity exposure, but also provides greater diversification. Most managers also hold a small percentage of the fund in cash.

Number of shares

If you are keen to spread risk, you might prefer to invest in a fund which has a large number of holdings, provided this is cost-effective for a fund of that size. Tracker funds should not be used as a benchmark for actively managed unit trust Peps, but nevertheless it is interesting to note that funds which track the FT-SE 100 fully replicate the number of stocks, while those that partially replicate the All-Share typically hold between 350 and 550 stocks. Very few UK equity funds have more than 130 stocks.

Income yield

To be classed as a higher-yielding trust, the fund must produce a yield of 110 per cent of the yield of the FT-SE-A All-Share Index.

However, ideally this income should not be achieved at the expense of long-term capital growth – which is the main attraction of equity income funds as opposed to bond funds. If a fund has a particularly high yield, it is worth looking at how that yield is achieved. In particular, check whether the annual management charge is deducted from the income generated by the fund or from capital. Since most managers deduct this charge from income, if instead the manager deducts from capital, the fund will show an artificially high yield compared with other funds in the category.

■ CORPORATE BOND PEPS

Corporate bond Peps represent an attractive alternative to the building society for income seekers – particularly those who in the past have been prepared to tie up their money for five years with a tax-exempt special savings account (Tessa), and who therefore are used to the discipline of longer-term investment.

In theory, there is no reason why confident and experienced investors should not choose their own individual bonds within a self-select Pep. However, given the investment limit of £6,000 a year, there is the same danger as with directly held equities that you could end up with a portfolio concentrated on too few stocks.

To date the corporate bond Peps which have proved most popular are the 'guaranteed' variety. For the bulk of bond funds which do not offer a guarantee, it is important to view with caution the assumption made by some promoters that these Peps offer investors absolute safety and security. If you are thinking of going this route, do take a close look in particular at the real risk of capital erosion. In any event it is important to regard these funds as medium- to long-term – that is, to be held for a minimum of five years.

Rather like tracker funds, charges are a more significant factor in the selection process than is the case with equity funds.

Asset mix

With fixed-interest securities, the investment return is determined more by the level of interest rate than the issuing company's profitability. Provided the company remains sufficiently secure to honour the future coupon payments (the regular interest) and redemption payment (the return of the original capital), you know exactly what your return will be if you hold the bond to maturity.

However, if you or a fund manager sell a bond before its maturity date, then the value of the future coupon and redemption payments will depend on the prevailing interest rates at the time of sale. If interest rates are high, then the value of the fixed-interest security will be lower because you could get a similar return for less money elsewhere. Conversely if interest rates are low, then the value of the fixed-interest security will be higher because it provides a greater stream of income than you could get from alternative sources.

This volatile pattern of behaviour is more apparent with fixed-interest securities which have a long period to run to maturity, since they are more likely to be traded before redemption date.

At any one time, a unit trust will hold securities with a variety of outstanding terms to maturity, and consequently its unit price will vary according to the interest rates at that time.

This makes the characteristics and behaviour of bond funds very different from equity funds. Changes in interest rates will make the unit price of bond funds all vary in a similar way, and there is less room for fluctuations in investment performance than there is for equity funds.

However, corporate bond funds can also invest in instruments known as 'convertibles' (see below) that share some of the characteristics and behaviour of equities. There is scope for greater variation in investment performance with these funds – and volatility.

Qualifying assets

The assets which can be held in a corporate bond Pep are as follows:

- **Debentures:** Corporate bonds secured on specific company assets. Most debentures offer a fixed rate of interest which must be paid before the company distributes dividends to shareholders.

■ **Preference shares:** There are two common classes of equity capital: ordinary shares, which have no guaranteed dividend payment but which carry voting rights; and preference shares. The latter usually carry a fixed dividend and must be repaid in full before ordinary shareholders if the company is wound up. However, bond holders are paid before preference shareholders. This gives you some idea of where they stand in the security pecking order. Other features worth noting are that preference shares generally offer a higher yield than corporate bonds due largely to their higher-risk profile. The market for preference shares is small and far less liquid than for bonds. Preference shares have no voting rights.

■ **Convertibles:** If a company does not want to dilute the ownership further by issuing more shares, it might instead issue convertibles (also known as a 'convertible loan stocks' or 'convertible bonds'). These are debt instruments that can be converted into ordinary or preference shares at a fixed date in the future, and at a fixed price. The main attraction of convertibles to the investor is that, as a hybrid between equities and bonds, they offer the potential for both income and capital growth.

These three categories form the main qualifying assets held in corporate bond Peps, but the funds can also invest in 'non-qualifying securities and investments'. The main options here include cash/term deposits and other short-dated instruments, plus British government securities (gilts).

As a general rule, volatility is reduced if a lot of cash is held and often increased if convertibles are held (because of the closer link to equity prices). The bonds themselves can prove volatile, and as a result, experts advise you to invest in corporate bond Peps only if you can afford to leave your money untouched for the medium- to long-term. If you are comfortable with this prospect then corporate bond Peps can be a suitable way of generating a stable tax-free income.

Volatility and mean term to maturity

Bonds are bought and sold on the open market and often do not remain in the same hands until the maturity date. Now there is a big difference in the risks associated with bonds held to maturity (pretty secure) and bonds that are traded before that date (much more risky).

Corporate bond Pep managers should be able to indicate the 'mean term to maturity' or average term to redemption of the bonds held within a fund (excluding preference shares which usually do not have a specific maturity or redemption date). This can be used as an indication of the potential volatility of the fund. As a rule of thumb, the longer the mean term to maturity, the more potentially volatile the capital value, and vice versa.

This is because, although an individual bond does give a 'guaranteed' return if it is held to maturity (the guarantee being as solid as the company which issued the debt), the return is not guaranteed if it is sold early. You can see how a fund which holds a lot of long-dated bonds could run into problems if it had to start selling up in order to pay back investors who wanted to pull out early. For this reason, where a lot of the bonds held within a fund are long-term, the potential volatility of your capital return is increased if you pull out early.

In fact, the government is partly responsible for this situation because it insists that qualifying bonds must have at least five years to run to maturity. This directs capital towards the long-term needs of industry (an underlying motive for introducing corporate bond Peps), but at the same time forces the fund to take on the risk of volatility of capital.

Having said that, bonds with a longer term to maturity also tend to offer better returns, so this may work to your advantage, provided you are comfortable with the potential additional risks.

■ SUMMARY

- **Unit trust tracker Peps offer a combination of broad diversification and modest charges. With charges as low as £30 a year to manage £6,000 spread over 100 stocks, with immediate access and no tax, this type of fund represents a very good deal indeed.**

- Many index trackers outperform actively managed funds.

- Once you have selected your preferred index, charges and tracking error are the most important criteria on which to base your selection.

- Unlike index trackers, where charges are probably the most important criteria for selection, with actively managed funds, performance is what really counts.

- Check what percentage of a UK equity fund is actually held in bonds, convertibles and overseas equities, and consider whether you are happy with this asset mix.

- Corporate bond Peps are suitable for income seekers who want a better deal than a building society, provided you can afford to tie up your money for a minimum of five years.

- They are lower risk than equity Peps, but bear in mind that historically, equities have outperformed bonds over the long-term.

- Find out how many stocks are held by a corporate bond Pep to check how well it is diversified.

- The income yield on a bond fund may be artificially inflated if the annual management charge is deducted from capital, instead of the usual practice of deducting from the fund's income.

■ GLOSSARY OF TERMS

Active management selects shares on the basis of analysis of companies, sectors, economic forecasts, and national and international trends.

Annual management charge This is deducted by your plan manager to cover investment and administration costs. It also includes 'renewal' commission which may be paid to your adviser from Year 2 onwards. This is the most important charge over the long-term.

Bid/offer spread The difference between the price at which you buy (offer price) and sell (bid price) your units. This includes additional items such as stamp duty, which are not included in the initial charge, so the 'spread' shows the full cost of your plan.

Convertibles: These pay a fixed rate of interest but can be converted into ordinary or preference shares at a specified future date, and at a fixed price. Convertibles are a hybrid between equities and bonds – they offer the potential for both income and capital growth.

Corporate bonds are IOUs issued by companies. In return for borrowing your money the company pays a fixed rate of interest and returns your original capital in full on a pre-determined future date.

Coupon The rate of interest paid by a bond or gilt.

Debentures: Corporate bonds secured on specific company assets.

The FT-SE-A All-Share index consists of around 900 companies and represents about 95 per cent of UK stockmarket capitalisation.

The FT-SE 100 index consists of the 100 largest UK companies by market capitalisation and represents about 70 per cent of UK stockmarket capitalisation.

The FT-SE Mid 250 index consists of the next 250 companies below the FT-SE 100 and represents approximately 22 per cent of UK stockmarket capitalisation.

13

Index tracking or 'passive' investment management replicates in part or in full the constituent shares of a specific index.

Initial charge The cost of buying your Pep, including sales commission to your adviser, if applicable.

Market capitalisation is the stockmarket valuation of a company, which is calculated by multiplying the number of shares by the market price.

Preference shares Shares which pay a fixed dividend or income but carry no voting rights.

DIY OR SELF-SELECT PEPS

The Inland Revenue rules on what investments you can hold in your Pep are very flexible – it is only the Pep managers who introduce restrictions in order to ease their administration and investment processes and to reduce costs.

Clearly, if you have comparatively small amounts to invest it does not make sense to run your own portfolio of individual shares, partly because trading in small volumes is disproportionately expensive and partly because you would end up with a high risk portfolio concentrated in too few stocks.

For most investors, therefore, the collective fund route is the most appropriate. However, even here you do not have to stick to just one manager. The rules allow only one manager per year (although you can transfer to another manager if you wish), but there is no reason why you should not build up a spread of managers over time. Within reason, of course. Advisers suggest that more than two or three managers will prove complicated from the adminis-

> The self-select plan simply acts as the Revenue-approved wrapper into which you place your choice of investments, selected from the Revenue's approved list of qualifying and non-qualifying assets.

tration point of view, while the set-up charges may mount if you spread your investments too thinly.

If you are planning to make maximum investments each year, and you already own a portfolio of pooled and directly held equities outside your Pep, a more flexible route is to use a 'self-select' plan offered by many firms of stockbrokers. The plan simply acts as the Revenue-approved wrapper within which you buy your choice of investments, selected from the Revenue's approved list of qualifying and non-qualifying assets.

■ INVESTMENT SNAPSHOT

If you invest with just one unit or investment trust manager, any dividends earned must be re-invested with that manager or taken as tax-free income. With a self-select Pep, dividends can be re-invested in the investment of your choice, while cash held within the plan can be re-invested later.

This means you can hold any combination of unit trusts, investment trusts, corporate bonds and equities, provided no more than one-quarter of the total fund is held in non-qualifying assets. You can also hold cash within the fund and earn interest on this while you are waiting to re-invest the money, provided you do not withdraw more than £180 per tax year from uninvested cash. If you exceed this limit, all the interest you withdraw will be taxable.

■ INTERNATIONAL EXPOSURE

Self-select is the easiest way to invest in the widest possible range of international stocks, because you have unrestricted access to unit and investment trusts which invest up to half of their assets outside the European Union. You also have unrestricted access to trusts that specialise in markets outside the EU. Up to 25 per cent of your fund can be held in these non-qualifying funds.

In addition you can invest directly in any EU share, although the cost of doing so combined with the risk of holding individual non-UK shares makes this unsuitable for most investors. You should also bear in mind that for non-UK shares it may not be possible to reclaim the withholding tax.

■ CASH OPTION

Again, where you invest with just one manager, if you are concerned about markets and want to withdraw, generally you have to cash in units or sell shares and come out of the Pep.

A self-select plan can revert to cash when markets are unstable or falling, and earn interest while you are waiting to re-invest in approved securities. In a general Pep you can hold cash for a 'reason-

14

able period' pending re-investment. In a single-company plan the limit for holding cash is 42 days.

■ HOW MUCH ADVICE?

Stockbroker services are discussed in more detail in Chapter 1. However, it is worth recapping on the different levels of advice available with a self-select Pep:

- **Discretionary:** This is where your stockbroker makes all the investment decisions for you and simply reports back to you after the event. The service is ideal for busy people who want the flexibility of a self-select Pep, but do not have the time and/or inclination to follow the markets and undertake the responsibility of stock picking and fund selection.

- **Advisory:** This is where there is a dialogue between the stockbroker and client before any investment decision is made. You might wish to run an idea past your stockbroker or he/she may suggest an investment to you. Either way you have the final veto. This is ideal for active investors who take a great interest in the markets and want a hands on portfolio underpinned by expertise of the stockbroker.

- **Execution-only:** This is for the total enthusiast. With an execution-only service you pick up the phone and place your order. There is no discussion or advice and you are wholly responsible for the outcome. Cheap but not necessarily cheerful, unless you are confident that you have the time to follow markets on a very regular basis.

■ HOW MUCH DOES IT COST?

There is no easy answer to this question. Just as unit and investment trust charges vary considerably, so too do stockbroker fees. If you are interested in a self-select service, read Chapter 1 on how to choose your adviser, and use the Association of Private Client Investment Managers and Stockbrokers' directory to draw up your shortlist (the address is given in Appendix II).

Typical costs for UK equities, convertibles and collective funds include a dealing charge of about 1.65 per cent on amounts up to £10,000, and 0.5 per cent on the next £90,000. Gilt-edged and other fixed-interest securities tend to be cheaper – for example 1.5 per cent on the first £5,000, 0.75 per cent on the next £15,000 and so on. Other charges include dividend handling – for example £7.50 per dividend and reporting services (valuations, newsletters etc), which could be anything between £15 and £150 depending on frequency.

A typical self-select plan includes the following charges: purchase of unit trusts 0.02 – 0.41 per cent plus £5, plus the usual underlying annual management charge; purchase of shares £5 plus 0.25 per cent or £1 plus 0.15 per cent for non-qualifying investment trusts.

Sharelink, one of the leading execution-only self-select services at the time of writing had dealing charges of 1.5 per cent of the transaction value with a minimum of £20 and a maximum of £37.50. Administration for a general Pep is 0.1875 per cent per quarter with a minimum of £5 on the first £16,000. For portfolios larger than this, the charge is a flat-rate £30. The charges for single-company plans are the same, although the minimum is £4 per quarter.

Within these prices, the company includes the following services at no extra charge: quarterly statements and valuations, an income facility, and administration of call payments (for example, the second instalment on payments for privatisation issues). Transfers in from other Pep managers are also free. Interest is paid on cash held within the fund.

As a general rule, if you see yourself as a regular saver, then you would probably be best served by seeking advice on the selection of the fund and signing up with one Pep manager each year. Stockbrokers are not really equipped to handle regular savings plans although some do offer this facility for those investing the full £6,000 annual Pep allowance in this way – that is £500 a month.

■ SELF-SELECT CORPORATE PEPS

Most corporate peps allow investment only in the shares of the sponsoring company. However some companies take a more enlightened view, and provided you invest and maintain a minimum holding (usually a specific number of shares), you can invest in other shares, either on an unlimited basis or choose from a range specified by the company.

BAA and Redland are among the few companies that offer this service through their Pep manager, Barclays Stockbrokers. If you think about it, it makes sense for companies to adopt a more flexible approach to their sponsored Peps. For example, where the Pep is used primarily for employee share schemes, it is important for employees not to put all their eggs in one basket. If the company has a bad year, employees with long service could have a sizeable holding and may feel disillusioned and angry with their employer – the exact opposite of what these schemes are intended to achieve which is a sense of loyalty and goodwill. In future, it is possible more companies will adopt this approach and effectively create an affinity group with shareholders, seeing shareholders as customers as well as investors.

> **Provided you invest and maintain a minimum holding with some corporate Peps, you can invest in other shares either on an unlimited basis or choose from a range specified by the company.**

The BAA and Redland plans allow shareholdings of any UK-listed company (including qualifying investment trusts and corporate bonds) to be held within the Pep, subject to a minimum of £1,000 shares being retained at all times. The plan also provides advantageous dealing rates for shares in privatisation companies.

For more details on single-company plans, see Chapter 15.

■ SUMMARY

■ A self-select Pep acts as a Revenue-approved wrapper for all your Pep investments, including direct shares and collective funds.

■ The main advantage is that you can trade freely between all the different investments provided you stick to the overall maximum of one-quarter in non-qualifying funds.

■ Dividends can be re-invested in any approved investment – not just within the fund that generated the income.

■ You can revert to cash if markets are volatile and keep this within the self-select plan for re-investment at a later date.

■ You have the option to use a stockbroker to run the plan entirely (discretionary), to help you with your investment choice, although you make the ultimate decisions (advisory) or simply to buy and sell on your instructions (execution-only).

■ Some corporate Peps can also be used as a quasi-self-select plan because, provided you keep a minimum holding in the sponsoring company, you are free to invest in other shares.

Further information

ShareLink's Pep helpline is 0121-233 9955.

For details of the self-select corporate Peps, contact Barclays Stockbrokers at 2nd Floor, 21 St. Thomas Street, London SE1 9RY. Tel: 0171-403 3833.

Active investors may be interested in ProShare, which provides independent advice to its members on share ownership issues. ProShare also runs a 24-hour telephone information service which gives share prices of all listed companies and details on new issues and publishes a useful guide to information sources for the private investor. You can also join ProShare investment clubs. Contact ProShare, Library Chambers, 13–14 Basinghall Street, London EC2V 5BQ. Tel: 0171-600 0984.

14

15

SINGLE-COMPANY PEPS AND COMPANY SHARE OPTION SCHEMES

For obvious reasons, single-company and corporate plans are far more specialist and risky than general Peps, yet for investors with large portfolios who can comfortably accommodate the risks associated with individual share holdings, they can be both cost-effective and tax-efficient. Moreover, whether they achieve these aims can be assessed with comparative ease.

■ HOW THEY WORK

There are two types of Pep aimed at investment in the shares of a single company, both of which can be based on an employer's company share option schemes.

- **Corporate Peps** use your general Pep allowance of £6,000 to invest in the shares of one company. A few company-sponsored corporate Peps also allow you to include shares other than the sponsoring company. These 'self-select' corporate plans are covered in Chapter 14 on page 131.

- **Single-company Peps** allow you to invest up to £3,000 a year in just one company's shares. This allowance is in addition to the £6,000 for a general Pep.

If you are interested in single shares, most advisers recommend that you use your annual general Pep allowance for collective funds or for your self-select portfolio, and that you use your single-company Plan for individual shares. (However, do note the greater flexibility offered by certain corporate Peps mentioned above.)

■ **INVESTMENT SNAPSHOT**

Although primarily used to hold the ordinary shares of UK companies, single-company and corporate Peps can also be used to hold qualifying EU shares.

In the case of single-company Peps, if your shares have come from Inland Revenue-approved all-employee savings-related share option or profit-sharing schemes you do not even have to sell them if you wish to retain the same holdings within your plan. This option also applies to general Peps, including corporate Peps, for shares acquired by a public offer – privatisations for example. Where the privatisation includes loyalty bonus shares – extra shares earned if you hold your original stake for a given period – these do not count towards the annual Pep subscription limit.

■ EMPLOYEE SHARE OWNERSHIP AND SAVINGS SCHEMES

Share option schemes allow you to buy shares in your employer's company at less than market value. You can also avoid income tax on what is effectively a benefit in kind – that is, the difference between your buying price and the market price.

The important point to remember about these schemes is that the 'option' is a *right* to buy, not an obligation. If direct investment is not for you, but the share price is attractive, you can exercise your option and sell immediately afterwards, pocketing any profits, in most cases with no tax to pay. Between one-third and one-half of employees do just that. In some cases, the company even provides subsidised dealing facilities.

There are two main types of scheme approved for special tax treatment by the Inland Revenue – Save As You Earn and company share option plans (also known by their previous name – 'executive schemes').

Save As You Earn

Under the SAYE contract, you agree to save between £5 and £250 each month for either three or five years, after which you receive a

15

The most attractive feature of the Save As You Earn scheme is that the option price of the shares can be fixed as low as 80 per cent of the market value at the date the option is granted.

tax-free bonus. With the five-year contract, if you leave your money in the account for a further two years, you qualify for an extra bonus. The option to buy is valid for a maximum of six months after the contract matures.

The most attractive feature of the SAYE scheme is that the option price of the shares can be fixed as low as 80 per cent of the market value at the date the option is granted – that is, when you start the contract.

There is no annual interest as such, but the scheme details should set out the equivalent rate by calculating what the value of the bonuses you receive at the end of your contract are worth when spread over the entire savings period. It is important to assess this rate carefully, because if you decide not to buy the shares, this will be the rate your savings will have earned over the period.

The tax-free bonus is worth the value of 18 months' contributions for the seven-year contract, nine months for the five-year contract and three months for the three-year contract. The equivalent tax-free annual interest rate is 5.87 per cent, 5.53 and 5.26 respectively.

From time to time, the government may change the bonus allocation, but once you take out a contract, it is set for the full period. This means the contract behaves like any other fixed-interest product, so your gamble is that the bonus will prove competitive in relation to prevailing interest rates over the savings term. Employees who pull out early are penalised.

If you do want to buy, what will your contract be worth? Assume you have saved £10,000 including the bonuses. The company will calculate the number of shares your fund would have bought at the discounted rate set at the time the option was granted. So, if the original share price was £1 and your option was to purchase at 0.80p, then you would have an option to buy 12,500 shares with your contract. If the current price of the shares is well above the option price, you will have bought cheaply and made a profit. If the share price has dropped to below the option price, clearly there is no point in buying.

Company share option plans (executive plans)

The main alternative to SAYE is a company share option plan, which in 1995 replaced the discretionary share option scheme. These were, and still are, commonly referred to as executive share option schemes because they are often only open to executives and directors. The plans are not linked to a savings contract – so you have to use spare capital to purchase.

Under the plan, you do not pay income tax on the grant of an option or on any increase in market value of the shares in the period before you exercise the option. You can purchase the shares between three and 10 years after the option was granted. Once you have made a purchase, you have to wait another three years before you can exercise a further option to buy. Given the long period in which you have to choose, you might wish to take advice on when the experts consider the price is right.

The new schemes are not so attractive as the old executive schemes where the shares could be offered at a discount of up to 15 per cent and the maximum value of options per employee was the greater of £100,000 or four times salary. With the new plan, the shares cannot be offered at a discount and there is a limit of £30,000 on the value of all the shares on option held by an employee.

15

Unapproved schemes

Some companies run 'unapproved' executive share option schemes. These do not offer the tax advantages of company share option plans, but in theory there is no limit to the size of the option. However, options granted from 27 November 1996 will, on exercise, be subject to income tax under the Pay As You Earn (PAYE) system. This leads to difficulties if the employee's income tax charge is so large that it exceeds his salary, and the company is unable to deduct it from monthly pay.

Profit-sharing schemes

You might also come across a profit-sharing scheme (not to be confused with profit-related pay, which is being phased out). This allows your employer to set up a trust to give you an immediate gift of tax-free shares equivalent to a proportion of profit. The shares remain in the name of the trustees.

The maximum limit in value per employee is the greater of £3,000 a year, or 10 per cent of annual salary, subject to a ceiling of £8,000. Provided you do not sell the shares before the end of the third year after allocation, there is no income tax to pay, although there may be a capital gains tax (CGT) liability.

To Pep or not to Pep?

Where the company share option scheme is open to all employees (so this does not include the schemes offered only to, say, executives and directors), you can transfer the shares to a Pep. As mentioned, provided you transfer within 90 days, you do not have to sell and re-purchase the shares, so you save on dealing costs and, possibly, capital gains tax.

> Unlike the unit and investment trust plans, where, with the exception of index trackers, you are paying for active management in pooled funds, with a single-company or corporate Pep, there is no investment management, so your only advantage is the tax shelter provided by the Pep wrapper.

One of the main attractions of the company-sponsored plans is the charges, which in theory at least should be lower than the non-sponsored variety, although it has to be said that the charges of some of the high street banks in particular are also very competitive.

Sponsored or not, these plans should be comparatively cheap. Unlike the unit and investment trust plans, where, with the exception of index trackers, you are paying for active management in pooled funds, with a single-company or corporate Pep there is no investment management, so your only advantage is the tax shelter provided by the Pep wrapper.

If, like most investors, you do not use up your annual CGT exemption (£6,500 for 1997/98), the main attraction of the Pep is the shelter from income tax. A simple comparison between the Pep annual management charge and the saving you would make by not paying tax on the company's gross dividend yield provides a good indication of whether it is more cost-effective to buy the shares through the sponsored Pep or direct.

As a general rule, the FT-SE 100 companies maintain a sustainable dividend policy. Provided the future prospects for the company do not alter substantially, the result generally is a fairly stable yield. There are exceptions where the yield is very high, which indicates changes afoot in corporate structure or perhaps a radical change in dividend policy.

Clearly, the higher the yield, the greater the tax saving. Where the yield is 5 per cent, a 40 per cent taxpayer would save 2 per cent of its value, less the annual management charge, which typically is 0.5 per cent for single-company Peps. But with dividends of around 2 per cent, the tax saving achieved by using the Pep wrapper is minimal or non-existent.

Finally, if you do not want to hang on to your company's shares, look out for the Pep managers who offer to sell shares at little or no cost in return for an equivalent investment in one of their unit or investment trusts.

15

■ ARE INDIVIDUAL COMPANY SHARES SUITABLE?

It is important to consider the place of a single share in your portfolio. Investment advisers generally recommend that the minimum number of shares in a portfolio is 10, and that no one share should account for more than 10 per cent of the portfolio. Hence the broad rule of thumb adopted by Pep specialists BESt Investments, for example, who recommend that any investor with an equity portfolio of £30,000 or more (in unit and investment trusts, shares and other Peps) should consider taking advantage of the £3,000 annual allowance for a single-company Pep.

However, there are two potential problems with single-company shares. The first is to avoid over-exposure to any one company. This can be achieved by choosing a different share each year, so that gradually you build up a small portfolio of direct holdings.

The second is selection. Some investors do not want the responsibility of choosing a single-company share but if you do not have a stockbroker you could get one of the big institutional fund managers do the job for you.

■ SUMMARY

■ In general, both corporate Peps and single-company Peps can only be used for the purchase of the shares of just one company within any tax year.

■ A few corporate plans offer access to other shares. These 'self-select' corporate Peps are discussed in Chapter 14.

■ Corporate Peps operate under the general Pep rules where the annual allowance is £6,000.

■ Single-company plans allow you to invest £3,000 in a single company's shares. This is in addition to the general Pep allowance.

■ You can transfer the proceeds of a Save As You Earn or share option scheme into a single-company Pep, provided the scheme is open to all employees and is not just for one section of the workforce (executives, for example). You must complete the transfer within 90 days of the scheme maturing.

■ A good way to check whether it is worth buying shares through a single-company plan is to compare the Pep annual management charge and the saving you would make by not paying tax on the company's gross dividend yield. As a general rule, you should use your single-company plan for high-yielding shares.

Further information

For further details of employee share schemes, contact your local Inland Revenue office for leaflets on the subject. These may also be available in bank and building society branches.

A useful guide to employee share ownership is published by ProShare. Contact ProShare, Library Chambers, 13–14 Basinghall Street, London EC2V 5BQ.

LIFE ASSURANCE INVESTMENT OPPORTUNITIES

Life assurance investment policies offer an alternative form of collective investment which in some ways is very different from unit trusts, investment trusts and open-ended investment companies (see Chapter 11). This chapter explains how these policies work, how they compare with alternative investments and for whom they are suitable.

■ YOUR CHOICE: THE THREE MAIN CATEGORIES

Despite the confusing array of investments offered by insurance companies to the public, most fall into one of three main categories:

- **Maximum investment plans (MIPs)** are regular monthly or annual premium investments and usually run for 10 years. Once this term is complete you can either take the proceeds or leave the fund to continue to benefit from investment growth. You can also make tax-efficient annual withdrawals.

- **Insurance company investment bonds** are similar to MIPs, but here you invest a single premium or lump sum.

- **Endowments** combined investment with a substantial element of life assurance.

With maximum investment plans and insurance company investment bonds, your premiums are invested in a choice of funds, most of which are unit-linked, similar in concept to unit trusts in that your premiums buy units in a collective fund and the value of those units rises and falls in line with the value of the underlying assets.

Although sold by life assurance companies, most of these regular and single premium plans offer minimal life cover as their main pur-

■ **INVESTMENT SNAPSHOT**

In 1996, the Inland Revenue issued a consultation document containing proposals to re-write the rules on the taxation of life assurance policies. If implemented, these may prevent higher-rate taxpayers from using these polices to defer for up to 20 years the higher-rate income tax liability. They would also stop investors from using policies held in trust – usually offshore – to reduce or avoid inheritance tax.

pose is investment. If you die, the company might pay out 101 per cent of your original investment or the value of the fund, whichever is greater.

> **Although sold by life assurance companies, most of these regular and single premium plans offer minimal life cover as their main purpose is investment.**

The third category – the traditional endowment – is most commonly used as a repayment vehicle for a mortgage. (Endowment mortgages are discussed in more detail in Chapter 20.) As mentioned above, the distinguishing feature of an endowment is that it combines a significant element of life assurance with your savings plan, so that if you die during the term of the policy, the combination of the value of your fund plus the life assurance is sufficient to repay the debt.

There are three investment options. With profits and unitised with profits, endowments invest in a mixture of equities, bonds and property and have a rather idiosyncratic method of distributing profits. This is discussed below. You can also invest in unit-linked endowments, which share the same investment characteristics as other unit-linked funds.

■ **TAXATION OF LIFE ASSURANCE POLICIES**

The whole area of the taxation of life assurance policyholders is under review, but at the time of writing the Inland Revenue was seeking consultation on its proposals and had not issued a date for any changes to come into effect. To avoid confusion, this chapter explains current practice.

At the end of the investment period, the proceeds of a life assurance policy will be treated as though the fund had already paid the equivalent of basic rate tax. For lower- and basic-rate payers, that is the end of the story. But what happens next for higher-rate payers depends on whether the policy is classed by the Inland Revenue as 'qualifying' or 'non-qualifying'.

With a qualifying policy, there is no further tax liability for higher-rate payers. However, to attract this special tax status, the policy must abide by various conditions. First, it must be a regular premium plan where you pay a pre-determined amount each month or each year. Second, it has to be a long-term plan – usually a minimum of 10 years. Third, it has to provide a substantial amount of life cover.

> The income tax cannot be reclaimed so, generally, life assurance policies are not suitable for non-taxpayers. Moreover, the capital gains tax paid by the fund cannot be offset against an individual's exemption – as is the case with unit and investment trusts.

This means that single premium investment policies are non-qualifying, but the regular premium MIPs may be classed as qualifying, depending on the term and level of life cover provided. Mortgage endowments, which tend to be long-term regular premium plans, usually are qualifying due to the substantial element of life cover.

16

The important point to note about life assurance policies is that the income tax cannot be reclaimed so, generally, these policies are not considered suitable for non-taxpayers. Moreover, the capital gains tax paid by the fund cannot be offset against an individual's exemption – as is the case with unit and investment trusts. Financial advisers tend to regard this feature as a serious drawback.

Unique tax feature of bonds

However, there are circumstances in which the unique features of investment bonds can be attractive to certain investors. With bonds there is no annual yield as such, since income and growth are rolled up within the fund. But up to 5 per cent of the original capital can be withdrawn each year for up to 20 years. The Inland Revenue treats these withdrawals as a return of capital, and therefore at the time of payment they are free of tax, so the higher-rate tax liability is deferred until you cash in your policy. (Withdrawals above 5 per cent are treated by the Inland Revenue as though they are net of basic rate tax – so the higher-rate liability must be paid, not deferred.)

'Top slicing relief'

Even if you invest in a non-qualifying life policy, you may be able to reduce or avoid the deferred higher-rate tax bill due to the effect of 'top slicing relief'. 'Top slicing relief' averages the profit over the number of years the bond has been held and adds this profit slice to an investor's income in the year the bond matures. If part or all of this falls into the higher-rate bracket, it would be taxed. However, with careful tax-planning, investors can avoid this liability by encashing the bond when they become lower-rate taxpayers – in retirement for example.

Higher-rate taxpayers who have used their full CGT allowance may also find bonds and MIPs attractive because the 5 per cent withdrawals do not have to be declared for income tax purposes in the year of withdrawal.

■ LIFE ASSURANCE VS UNIT AND INVESTMENT TRUSTS

Unit and investment trusts are discussed in detail in Chapter 11. Briefly, a unit trust is a collective fund and, in a similar way to insurance company investment bonds and MIPs, it can invest in a wide range of assets. Some unit trusts offer capital guarantees or guarantee to provide part of the rise in a stockmarket index and protect you from the falls. As with investment bonds, investors in unit trusts buy units in the collective fund and the value of these units fluctuates in line with the value of the underlying assets.

An investment trust is not a trust as such, but is a British company, listed on the UK Stock Exchange, which invests in the shares of other companies in the UK and overseas. As public companies, investment trusts are subject to company law and Stock Exchange regulation.

There are two factors that affect investment trust share prices – the performance of the underlying assets in which the company invests (this is the sole factor which determines the price of units in a unit trust or investment bond) and the supply and demand for the shares. The latter factor may make the shares worth more or less than the underlying value of the company's assets.

If the share price is lower than the value of the underlying assets, the difference is known as the discount. A large discount can make the shares very attractive. If it is higher, the difference is known as the premium. Investment trusts can also borrow money to invest – an activity known as gearing. These features make investment trusts potentially more volatile than unit trusts and investment bonds.

Tax treatment

Unit and investment trusts can be held inside a personal equity plan. In this case there is no income and capital gains liability either on the fund itself or on you, the investor. This makes Peps the most tax-efficient investment after pensions, and most advisers recommend that you first use up your annual Pep investment allowance (£6,000 per person for the 1996/97 tax year) before considering other types of collective funds.

Unit trusts and investment trusts held outside a Pep are also considered more tax-efficient than life assurance funds in most circumstances, because there is no capital gains tax on the fund. Instead this liability falls on the individual, so gains can be used to boost income, if desired, and the liability offset against your annual CGT exemption (£6,500 in 1997/98). Dividends are paid net of lower-rate tax. This can be reclaimed by non-taxpayers, so again this is more tax-efficient than life assurance investments where you cannot reclaim the income tax paid by the fund. With unit and investment trusts there would be a potential additional income tax liability for higher-rate payers.

■ INVESTMENT CHOICE

However, one advantage of bonds over most unit trusts is that insurance companies generally offer a low-cost switching facility between a large range of funds. Otherwise the charges for the two types of funds are broadly similar, although the tax status of life offices usually allows them to operate with slightly lower annual charges and this can have a significant effect on your fund's growth over the long-term. Charges are discussed later in this chapter.

The investment choice under life assurance policies is as follows:

Unit-linked plans

Unit-linked plans offer a very wide choice, ranging from UK and international equities to UK and international fixed-interest securities, index-linked gilts, property, and commodity and energy shares. Your money buys units in the fund's assets and the unit price rises and falls directly in line with the performance of these assets.

Clearly it is possible to select different types of fund depending on your preferred asset allocation, but for investors just starting out and for those with limited amounts to invest, a managed fund is ideal. Managed funds usually invest in a range of the company's core funds – for example a managed equity fund would invest in the company's main UK and international equity funds. Managed funds may also include different types of assets – for example equities and bonds – to provide a better balance of risk or to generate a higher income than could be achieved with a pure equity fund.

'With profits' funds

'With profits' funds are simply heavenly if you thrive on jargon and obscurity – which is a pity really because they can play an important role in a more cautious investor's portfolio. The 'with profits' fund is the fund of the life office itself and invests mainly in a range of international and UK equities, bonds and property. The way the fund's profits are distributed resembles a cross between a building society deposit account and a unit-linked fund. Under the original structure for 'with profits' – now known as 'conventional with profits' – you are guaranteed a 'basic sum assured', and each year to this sum is added an annual interest or 'bonus' (sometimes referred to as a 'reversionary' bonus). Once this has been added it cannot be taken away, although the rate for future years is not guaranteed. To avoid dramatic fluctuations, insurance companies 'smooth' their bonus rates, holding back some of their profits in the good years to maintain a reasonable return in the bad years.

In addition to the annual bonus, you also receive a final or 'terminal' bonus at the end of your investment period or when you die. The final bonus is discretionary (that is, voluntary on the part of the insurance company), and tends to reflect recent performance.

The more modern version – the unitised 'with profits' fund – invests in the same assets, but does not offer a basic sum assured. Also, unitised 'with profits' funds have a feature which allows the insurance company to reduce the value of your units if there is a run on funds – after a market crash, for example. Most companies rarely use this 'market value adjuster', but its very existence does mean that your fund value is never totally guaranteed.

However, in favour of unitised funds is the ease with which you can switch to and from unit-linked funds – an exercise which can be difficult with conventional 'with profits'.

In recent years, bonus rates have fallen, partly due to cuts in interest rates and partly to compensate for what many commentators regard as over-generous bonuses paid in the late 1980s. This does not mean that 'with profits' policies represent poor value – some companies continue to achieve very good results over the medium- to long-term. However, it does mean that you cannot rely on bonus levels of the past continuing in future.

Distribution bonds

Distribution bonds, pioneered by Sun Life in 1979, are becoming an increasingly popular alternative to 'with profits', due to their 'safety first' approach to investment. Unlike a typical managed unit-linked fund, which would be primarily invested in equities, distribution bonds tend to have a much higher proportion of bonds, gilts, deposits and property. In this way, they cope well with most market conditions. They also tend to offer a higher yield than managed funds, and so can be particularly attractive for investors seeking a regular income.

16

Guaranteed income and growth bonds

These are also very popular for investors seeking a fixed rate of income or growth over a specific period (usually one to five years). The taxation varies according to the structure. Generally the rate of income or growth quoted is net of lower-rate tax but subject to higher-rate tax at the time of payment or at maturity. If you surrender the policy early, then the rate of return is not guaranteed and there can be financial penalties.

Friendly society policies

Friendly societies are often snubbed as the small fry of the investment industry. However, in contrast to life assurance funds, which have to pay both income and capital gains tax, friendly society funds are tax-free.

Unfortunately, there are several drawbacks which detract from this attractive feature. First, the amount you can invest is small – £270 a year (£300 if you pay your premiums on a more regular basis than just once a year), and most plans run for 10 years. There are societies which accept a lump sum investment to cover payments for the full 10 years.

Second, the performance of some friendly society funds tends to be lacklustre, but several offer good investment management, and in some cases a link to one of the big institutional groups.

The third disadvantage is charges, which tend to be high in relation to the amount invested. However, again there are exceptions, and several societies offer charges which compare well with personal equity plans.

In conclusion, for small investments – perhaps for a child or grandchild, these plans can be worth considering. However, do look carefully at past performance and charges, and compare these with what is on offer from Pep managers and unit and investment trusts which offer low-contribution regular savings plans.

■ CHOOSING YOUR POLICIES

Once you have identified your life assurance and investment require-ments, it is time to select the product. There are several important issues to consider, preferably with the help of an independent finan-cial adviser:

- **Performance** should be above average consistently over the long-term.
- **Charges** should be average or low compared with competitive products.
- **Product features.** The investment should be flexible so there should be no penalties if you stop or reduce premiums.

You also need help judging the financial strength of the life office. This is virtually impossible for a private investor, but advisers have access to surveys and databases which compare the financial position of insurance companies, and identify the weaker providers most at risk from the current spate of take overs and mergers. If the ownership of your insurance company changes hands, it does not necessarily mean your fund will suffer, but it does lead to a period of uncertainty.

16

Performance

The size of fund at the end of the investment term will depend on three main factors – the amount you pay to the financial institution, the amount actually invested after charges and the cost of the life assurance are deducted, and the investment performance.

Past performance, as the experts constantly remind us, is an imper-fect guide to the future. But, provided it is examined in conjunction with an analysis of the investment process and the stability of the investment team, it is certainly better than nothing.

Where a good adviser will help is with the analysis of past results, focusing on good consistent returns over the long-term. Ideally, your adviser should look at discrete results which show returns on a year-by-year basis. This is important, because a good cumulative result over five years could mask one excellent year followed by several years of mediocre returns. Discrete results are only to be found on the large statistical databases used by professionals – for example *Micropal* and *HSW Hindsight*.

Unit-linked prices are shown in the *Financial Times* and other national newspapers, if not every day, then at weekends. 'With profits' performance is more difficult to keep track of, and the annual bonus statement, which you usually receive in January, often is incomprehensible. A good source of information is *Money Management*'s annual surveys. Also, large firms of advisers will subscribe to a comprehensive performance and a product feature database like *Aequos* from The Research Department and the annual life and pensions survey from Buck Consultants.

Charges

Until recently, it was virtually impossible to tell how much of your investment disappeared in the life office's charges and sales commission paid to your adviser. Since 1 January 1995, providers have had to give all prospective clients a pre-sale 'key features' document which sets out the total deductions over the course of the investment period.

There are two main charges to consider – the initial charge, which is likely to be about 5 per cent on a unit-linked fund – and the annual charge – usually between 0.75 per cent and 1 per cent. Among other points, this document shows you what the effect of the charges will be and what you are likely to get back if you pull out early. Clearly this information is only of use if the charges of different companies are compared – preferably through an independent financial adviser.

Early surrenders and poor returns

Long-term life assurance investments tend to deduct the commission costs for the entire investment period during the first year or two. This is why so many people have got back so little from their policies if they have pulled out during this 'initial' period.

Your best bet is to avoid the commission structure altogether if you can, by paying your adviser a fee and asking for the commission payments to be stripped out of the policy. Alternatively ask for a single-premium commission structure, where about 4–5 per cent is deducted from each premium throughout the entire term. This means that if you are forced to stop your policy during these early years, your fund should still have a reasonable value.

An endowment – or indeed any investment – is portable when it comes to mortgage repayment. If you buy another house and need a larger mortgage, keep the policy you have already got, and top up with a repayment or interest-only mortgage backed by the savings plan of your choice. You do not need to take out another endowment – a Pep may be a more tax-efficient alternative if you are not already using up your annual allowance.

Beware of sales people who try to persuade you to surrender an existing investment in order to start a new policy for the whole of the mortgage. This almost certainly would lead to penalties and is bad advice.

Alternatives to surrendering a policy

If you simply cannot continue a policy for some reason, don't just stop payments without first considering the alternatives. You could, for example, make the policy 'paid up': which means you no longer pay premiums, but you do not withdraw your fund until the maturity date. You should still benefit from investment growth but do check the ongoing charges and what penalties apply before taking this step.

If you need the capital, you might be able to take a loan from the insurance company, based on the surrender value of your policy. Alternatively, you might get up to 30 per cent more than the surrender value if you sell your policy on the second-hand endowments market. In this case, an investor buys it from you, and takes over the commitment to continue the premiums, in the hope that the final payout will be well in excess of the purchase price plus the cost of the outstanding premiums.

The two main options are to auction the policy, or to sell it to a market maker who naturally, will charge a fee or take a percentage of the profit. (The profit is the difference between what you would have got as a surrender value from your insurance company and the actual price achieved.) A list of companies operating in the second-hand endowment market is provided at the end of the chapter.

16

■ SUMMARY

- 'With profits' funds are less risky than unit-linked funds, but then higher risk should, arguably, lead to higher reward.

- Unitised 'with profits' funds offer a halfway house between the two products, but remember that there are fewer guarantees compared with the conventional 'with profits' fund.

- Distribution bonds offer a careful mix of assets designed to help the fund withstand most market conditions, and are therefore suitable for the more cautious investor, particularly income seekers.

- Guaranteed equity funds, backed by the use of derivatives, also provide protection against stockmarket falls but the guarantee can be expensive.

- Guaranteed income bonds tend to offer better rates than building society deposits but you have to be prepared to lock in – usually for five years – during which time interest rates generally may rise and you might have done better elsewhere.

- Peps in particular but also unit and investment trusts held outside a Pep are more tax-efficient than life assurance investments, although in certain circumstances the life assurance route can be attractive to higher-rate taxpayers.

- Unit trusts, with the exception of the low-cost index-tracking funds, are generally slightly more expensive than life assurance investments – a factor which can be important over the long-term.

- Until recently it could be argued that life offices offered a much broader range of cautious funds, but with the advent of guaranteed unit trust funds and index trackers the gap is closing.

- If you have an endowment and want to cancel, consider all your options – for example, you might do better if you sell it through the second-hand endowment market.

■ GLOSSARY OF TERMS

Endowments combine investment with a substantial element of life assurance.

Insurance company investment bonds are similar to MIPs, but here you invest a single premium or lump sum.

Maximum investment plans (MIPs) are regular monthly or annual premium investments and usually run for 10 years. Once this term is complete, you can either take the proceeds or leave the fund to continue to benefit from investment growth. You can also make tax-efficient annual withdrawals.

Qualifying policies must follow certain rules, but can pay the proceeds free of higher-rate taxation.

Top slicing relief averages the profits of a policy over the term, and adds the profit slice to your income in the year you take the proceeds. Investors who were higher-rate taxpayers while saving, but are lower-rate taxpayers when they take the proceeds can avoid some or all of the higher-rate liability.

Further information

H E Foster & Cranfield is an auctioneer. Tel: 0171-608 1941. Other companies dealing with second-hand policies include Absolute Assigned Policies (0181-951 1996); Beale Dobie (01621 851133); Policy Plus International (01225 466466); Policy Register (0161-763 1919); Securitised Endowment Contracts (0181-207 1666); Surrenda-Link (01244 317999).

16

17

TAX-EFFICIENT
BUT VERY RISKY

This chapter covers a handful of investments that fall into the *very* high-risk category. As such they may offer substantial tax breaks and potentially high returns, but they should only be considered by those with a substantial amount of genuinely spare capital and then only after seeking expert advice.

The category includes enterprise investment schemes (EISs), venture capital trusts (VCTs), enterprise zone trusts (EZTs), timber and Lloyd's of London. All four carry the ultimate wealth warning – if things do go wrong, they are likely to go very, very wrong and you could lose the lot. In the case of EZTs and Lloyd's, mentioned briefly at the end of the chapter, you may have to pay in more money if the scheme's losses pile up.

> With these investments, if things do go wrong, they are likely to go very, very wrong and you could lose the lot.

With regard to the first four investments, it is essential to make a full assessment of the products' commercial viability. To do this, you must judge each arrangement 'naked' – that is, without the tax breaks. The best way to do this is to use the benchmarks outlined in Chapter 8 which allow you to compare the aims, the alternative products that may meet some of these criteria, the investment period, the primary risks and any other noteworthy features.

Remember also to compare the potential net returns on these investments with after-tax returns on low-risk products, such as short-term conventional gilts and National Savings certificates. If the realistic potential net return on what you are offered does not outstrip these rates significantly, pause to consider whether the very real risks are worth it.

■ INVESTMENT SNAPSHOT

With some of the early enterprise zone trusts, almost all of the tax relief benefits went to the property developer and not the investors.

Understandably, given the speculative nature of the investments, the financial services regulators do not allow companies to advertise potential rates of return. When you do discuss this with a particular company, make sure you consider all the major factors that can affect the final outcome. Look at how the rates are calculated, and remember that the most important criterion for any investment is how easily you can get your money out at the end. With EISs, VCTs and EZTs there are no guaranteed exits.

Your adviser should have a clear approach to judging the merits of these schemes, and in particular have met the management team and analysed its track record.

Take EZTs, for example. If the building in which you invest remains unlet, you may have to put in more money to cover the cost of insurance, security and marketing to prospective tenants. VCTs are considered less risky because they are a type of collective investment, and pooling should dilute the risk somewhat. They are also quoted on the stockmarket but, when you come to sell, the share price may be a lot less than the underlying net asset value.

The best source of advice on these schemes is likely to be a large firm of accountants who have a financial services department. In addition, there are a few specialist firms of advisers, for example BESt Investments and Allenbridge. Contact details are provided at the end of this chapter. Your adviser should have a clear approach to judging the merits of these schemes, and in particular have met the management team and analysed its track record. You also need an adviser who can accurately assess the launch and running costs, which tend to be high with these types of investments compared with mainstream products. What you want to know is whether the costs are justified, and whether they undermine the total return and the tax breaks on offer.

■ ENTERPRISE INVESTMENT SCHEMES (EISs)

An EIS aims to make a large capital gain from speculative equity investment in a single, small unquoted company. This is very much a 'hands on' investment if you want to become involved in the running of the business, but is attractive only to wealthy investors who have income to shelter and capital gains to roll over. The investment period is a minimum of five years.

The maximum investment in an EIS is £100,000 a year. Income tax relief is generally equal to 20 per cent of the amount invested (but reliefs may be restricted where there is insufficient income tax capacity). In addition, your investment qualifies for capital gains tax re-investment relief and you benefit from CGT exemption on gains made (excluding the re-invested gain). A loss on the disposal of the EIS investment can be offset against tax.

Don't forget – if you take the plunge, you could lose the lot. You could also lose the tax reliefs if either you or the company in which you invest breach the rules. As an alternative, you might consider a VCT (see below), quoted securities and the Alternative Investment Market (AIM). AIM is the London Stock Exchange's market for small, young and growing companies. Companies admitted to AIM must comply with the stringent rules of the Stock Exchange, but investors should take into account that these securities are higher-risk and less liquid than companies on the main exchange.

■ VENTURE CAPITAL TRUSTS (VCTs)

VCTs aim to make capital gains from a portfolio of speculative equity investments in smaller unquoted companies. (In other words, VCTs allow you to participate in EIS-type investments on a collective basis and hence to spread risk.) Again this is attractive only to wealthy investors who have income to shelter and capital gains to roll over.

Your investment is committed for a minimum period of five years if you want the full tax advantages. The maximum investment is £100,000 a year, but reliefs may be restricted if there is insufficient income tax capacity. Sums invested also qualify for capital gains tax re-investment relief. Income tax relief is generally equal to 20 per cent of the amount invested. In addition, there is an income tax exemption for dividends and a CGT exemption for gains (excluding re-invested gains).

Advisers suggest that possible alternatives to a VCT is, for those looking for a higher risk/reward profile, the EIS mentioned above. Other alternatives include smaller company or emerging market investment trusts and unit trusts, or a portfolio of quoted securities.

As with the EIS, in the worst possible scenario, you could lose your total investment. You could also lose the tax reliefs if either you or the company in which you invest breach the rules. VCTs are quoted on the stock exchange, so in theory there is an exit route, but the market is very illiquid with only about a dozen schemes available. Unlike EIS, there is no hands on involvement, so you are totally reliant on the expertise of the trust manager. There could be a discount to net asset value where the value of the underlying asset could be worth more than the share price.

There is a new breed of 'secure' venture capital trusts. These invest 50 per cent in loans which are guaranteed by high street banks and 25 per cent in fixed-interest securities such as gilts. This leaves only 25 per cent 'at risk' through investment in the shares of small unquoted companies. Even if all this was lost, some advisers believe that the income tax relief and other tax breaks mean that you could end up no worse off than if you had never made the investment.

■ ENTERPRISE ZONE TRUSTS (EZTs)

The aim of this scheme is to make an equity investment in property, where the purchase cost is subsidised by tax relief. As such, this is attractive to high-income-tax earners only as an income tax shelter – there is no CGT exemption or roll-over provision. A more precise description of an EZT is an enterprise zone property unit trust – so this is a collective investment where you own a part share of a property.

With an EZT, you qualify for full tax relief on investment in buildings, but not land. You may also benefit from tax relief on interest on borrowings made to fund the investment. The relief is offset against rents.

So what are the risks? Once again these are substantial – for example, you could suffer a partial loss of your investment through property depreciation. Moreover, if the property remains unlet after five years, investors may have to put in more money. As you would expect, the market is very illiquid – at the time of writing, there were only about a dozen schemes available.

Advisers warn that investors must be prepared to stay with the scheme for 25 years, so clearly this is for the very long-term investor. In fact, you can sell after seven years, but the practical minimum is 10 to 15 years. Bear in mind, there is a loss of tax relief if you sell early.

Finally, for those interested in property-based investments, it is worth looking at other collective funds – the investment trusts, unit trusts and open-ended investment companies.

■ TIMBER

If you prefer a more tangible asset than shares and regard yourself as an ethical investor, you can't get much greener than forestry. According to timber consultants, you can pick up a nice little wood for £5,000, and you may qualify for government assistance. The government recently announced a new range of measures to encourage non-farmers to establish woodlands and gain access to the large planting grants and annual payments which last 15 years while you await timber harvesting revenues. Woodlands can also be useful in estate planning due to the inheritance and capital gains tax exemptions.

But for a serious direct investment in timber, experts reckon you need about £100,000, although smaller investors can start with much less if they are prepared to invest on a group basis. There are even forestry unit trusts. However, this is definitely not a short-term investment. With timber you are talking long-term or *very* long-term, that is, you should assume an initial wait of 10 to 15 years before you can begin to draw a tax-free income through felling. Some stockbrokers recommend timber on this basis to wealthy income-seeking investors as an alternative to investing in commercial and residential property to generate rental income.

By *very* long-term, you should assume up to 40 years for soft-woods and 120 years for hardwoods – clearly only suitable for those prepared to invest for the second or third generation.

So what are the risks? Well, Mother Nature for a start, although storm, fire and pest are all insurable. Less easy to insure against is poor husbandry and the chance that when you want to get out there is no buyer or no road access to the land! Timber is classed as an extremely illiquid asset and even where there are buyers, you are at risk from a fall in timber prices or in demand from growing plantations.

The good news is that profits on timber are free of capital gains tax, but there is no tax relief on the costs – for example, planting, upkeep and transport to the mills. Your return will depend on the quality and amount of timber you have to sell, plus, of course, supply and demand.

■ LLOYD'S OF LONDON

'Names' are members of Lloyd's of London who put up their capital to act as collateral for the underwriting business of this specialist insurance market. The chief problem with Lloyd's has been that your liability was unlimited, and in recent years, names' losses have been substantial. Limited liability is now possible, although this type of investment should be restricted to those with large amounts of spare capital. Experts agree that unlimited liability membership is only for the very rich or the very brave.

Further information

The large firms of accountants are likely to be able to advise on all aspects of tax-efficient investing. In addition, there are a few specialist firms including Allenbridge, 16 Bolton Street, London WIY 8LY. Tel: 0171-409 1111. BESt Investments, 20 Masons Yard, Duke Street St. James's, London SW1Y 6BU. Tel: 0171-321 0100.

SAVING FOR LONG-TERM PROJECTS
School Fees and Mortgage Repayments

SAVING FOR SCHOOL AND COLLEGE FEES

An increasing number of parents send their children to fee-charging independent schools. The reasons for so doing vary. In many cases, the parents are seeking academic excellence and the greater attention given to children through the benefit of smaller classes. Parents may have views on the 'traditional values' upheld by certain schools, or a child may have special needs or a particular talent which would flourish with the right type of guidance.

Whatever your reasons, sending your children to public school is a major financial commitment and should not be undertaken lightly. If you cannot afford to pay for private schooling out of your income and/or capital, and yet you are concerned about the standard of local State schools, one option is to move to an area with a better reputation. However, if you decide to move to an area with better State schools, first check the schools' admissions policy. By law you have the right to apply to any school, although there is no guarantee you will get a place. If a school is very popular and its priority for admissions is brothers and sisters of existing pupils, rather than local catchment area, you still might not qualify automatically for a place. The admission rules are explained in a prospectus which each school must provide free on request.

Even if you are happy with the local State junior and secondary schools, don't forget further education and university costs. An increasing number of families do not qualify for local authority maintenance grants, so you should still save to cover the cost of your children's living allowances at university. As a rough guide you should expect to pay about £3,800 per annum at today's prices.

■ INVESTMENT SNAPSHOT

There are almost 2,500 schools in Britain which are independent of local and central government control.

■ WHAT DOES IT COST?

For those who do want private schooling for their children, planning ahead for school fees is essential, and that means starting when the children are toddlers, preferably babies. School fees vary considerably but the following figures, provided by the Independent Schools Information Service (ISIS), will give you a rough idea of the costs *per term*:

■ Junior/preparatory (age 7 to 13): Day £850 to £2,300; Boarding £2,200 to £3,150

■ Senior girls (age 11 to 18): Day £1,250 to £2,600; Boarding £2,600 to £4,200

■ Senior boys (age 11 to 18): Day £1,250 to £3,100; Boarding £2,700 to £4,500

These figures are based on the 1996/97 school year. For 1997/98 year you can expect an increase of about 5 per cent, ISIS said. In addition, you should find out about the cost of the uniform (this can be substantial), extra-curricular activities, and any other payments – for example, for examinations, lunches, school trips and so on. ISIS reckons all of this could add up to 10 per cent to your bill.

In practice, few parents aim to pay the total cost from savings. Grandparents often contribute to their grandchildren's education, and an injection of capital in the early years could make viable what initially appears to be an unrealistic savings plan. Many senior schools, and a few junior schools offer scholarships to particularly bright children, although these rarely cover the full costs. Further financial help may be offered through a bursary, which is a grant from the school to help with the fees. These details are provided in the ISIS directory. The government currently offers help for children of parents on low incomes through the Assisted Places Scheme although this will be abolished in future. National ISIS (the information arm of ISIS) publishes a booklet which lists the schools within the scheme.

> **Senior boys' boarding schools can cost anything between £2,700 and £4,500 per term.**

■ WHAT IS A SCHOOL FEES PLAN?

Despite the dedicated packages put together by financial institutions and firms of advisers, all that a successful school fees plan does is provide good cashflow management backed by a range of suitable investments. To construct the right portfolio of investments for your circumstances,

> **All that a successful school fees plan does is provide good cashflow management backed by a range of suitable investments.**

you need to know what the fees will be and the initial investment period before payments start.

You also need to factor in school fees inflation, salary inflation (if you intend to fund partly from income), and a sensible annual investment return. If you have some capital to invest at the outset and/or are prepared to pay part of the fees from income, clearly this will reduce the level of your regular savings.

If you want help with this exercise, seek genuinely independent advice. If you go to just one insurance company, with the aid of fancy software, you will be shown how you can achieve your goal if you invest mainly or wholly in insurance company products. You should also be cautious about plans and trusts that are linked to particular schools, as these may prove inflexible if you change your mind about the school. As a last resort, you could even tap in to the equity in your house or arrange an unsecured loan, but experts warn parents to think very carefully before taking this drastic step.

■ WHICH INVESTMENTS?

As the previous chapters have explained, the first and most important

18

consideration is your attitude to risk, since this will define the type of portfolio and which funds you select. The tax status of both parents must also be taken into consideration as must the time frame.

The last point is important because whichever investments you choose, your plan must cater for phased disinvestment to provide the regular drawdown for fees. You should also take out insurance to cover a regular savings plan, so it can continue if you die or become disabled and can no longer save. A combination of life assurance and critical illness insurance, which pays a lump sum on diagnosis of a major illness, might be suitable (see Chapters 2 and 3).

For the medium- to long-term, most advisers recommend parents use their annual general personal equity plan allowance (up to £6,000 for each parent). You might also consider an additional annual investment to single-company Peps (up to £3,000 per partner), but do read Chapter 15 and assess whether holding direct equities is wise for your circumstances and risk tolerance. Once you have used up your Pep allowance, then a combination of unit trusts, investment trusts and, possibly, insurance company bonds, would provide a good exposure to equities through collective funds. Corporate bond Peps might also be considered. If you have a capital lump sum to invest, and more than five years before you need to pay fees, a risk-averse investor might consider zero-coupon preference shares or gilts. Tax-exempt special savings accounts and National Savings are also suitable where there are only a few years in which to save.

Finally, do make full use of your annual allowances and exemptions (see Section III). For example, where one of the partners does not work, investors might consider transferring sufficient low-risk savings to the non-working spouse in order to make use of the annual personal allowance for income tax.

■ WHAT NEXT?

Many independent schools require prospective pupils to pass the Common Entrance Examination which is usually taken at age 11, 12, or 13. You can find out more details about the exam from the Independent Schools Examination Board. Although the exam is set centrally, the papers are marked by the school to which you have applied and each school has its own pass mark to ensure your child will be able to cope with its specific academic standard.

The Common Entrance Exam is broadly in line with the national curriculum. However, ISIS points out that independent preparatory schools spend the last two years preparing pupils for the exam, so clearly this gives children from independent schools a head start. If your child attends a State junior school, you should find out if there are specific subjects covered where private coaching would help your child to pass.

ISIS publishes an annual directory of about 1,300 independent schools throughout the UK and Eire. Before you start to look around, the organisation suggests you consider the following point to narrow down the choice:

- Day or boarding?
- Senior, junior or both?
- Single sex or co-educational?
- Academic or special requirements?
- Religious requirements?

All schools publish a prospectus, and some even produce a video to give you a more detailed impression of the school. Nothing serves so well as a visit, though, when you can make up your own mind about the head, the staff, the facilities and the pupils. The ISIS directory provides a useful checklist of questions you might ask. One particularly good suggestion is to try to speak to the parents of existing pupils – probably the best reference you can get.

18

■ SUMMARY

- **If you cannot afford to pay for private education, one option is to move to an area with a better reputation for State schools.**

- **Even if you are happy with the local State junior and secondary schools, don't forget further education and university costs.**

- **Find out about all the extras – the cost of the uniform, lunches, school trips, etc, could add an extra 10 per cent to your bill.**

■ Some schools offer scholarships, although they rarely cover the full cost.

■ A school fees plan is simply a cash management exercise backed by suitable savings and investments.

■ Make sure your plan is flexible.

Further information

Independent Schools Information Service (ISIS): This is the central source for information about private schools. ISIS has useful leaflets on how to select a school and publishes an annual census of schools comparing fees, pupil/staff ratios and other data. (It also lists advisers and insurance companies which specialise in school fees: but do remember the importance of independent advice, and avoid plans based solely on insurance products.) ISIS, 56 Buckingham Gate, London SW1E 6AG. Tel: 0171-630 8793/4.

Common Entrance Examination: For details contact the Independent Schools Examination Board, Jordan House, Christchurch Road, New Milton, Hants BH25 6QJ. Tel: 012425 610016/621111.

Department for Education: The DFE publishes leaflets which set out your rights and offer advice on how to choose a secondary school. Department for Education, Freepost 414, London WC1A 1BR. For information on assisted places, write to Assisted Places Team, Department for Education, Mowden Hall, Staindrop Road, Darlington DL3 9BG.

Unit and investment trust guides to school fees: For unit trusts phone the Association of Unit Trusts and Investment Funds on 0181-207 1361; for investment trusts phone the Association of Investment Trust Companies on 0171-431 5222.

INTRODUCTION TO MORTGAGE PLANNING

Most people would like to own their homes but finding the best way to achieve this aspiration can be daunting, not just for the first-time buyer, but also for those who have taken a wrong turning and ended up in negative equity trap, or with a completely inappropriate mortgage package. Untangling these complex problems can be an expensive and painful process, so it is worth spending time at the outset to get it right first time around.

There are plenty of sources of advice on mortgages and home ownership but probably the best guide to the basics is published by the Council of Mortgage Lenders (CML). *How to buy a home* is free and was the main source of information for this chapter (see Further information at the end of this chapter). The CML is a central body for the various types of mortgage lender – the banks, building societies, finance houses, insurance companies and specialist mortgage companies. For information on mortgage protection insurance, see Chapter 3, page 28. The Association of British Insurers (ABI) also publishes free fact sheets on mortgage protection and building and contents insurance.

■ WHO CAN HELP?

When you decide you want to buy, your first step is to find out what you can afford, through a combination of any savings you already hold and by taking out a loan – a mortgage. How to find the right type of mortgage is the chief subject for this and the following chapter, but it may help to recap briefly the various stages in the process of home purchase. This process in Scotland is different in some important respects, so if you are buying or selling north of the border, ask the CML for its guide *How to buy a home in Scotland.*

■ INVESTMENT SNAPSHOT

A rise of 5 per cent in house prices would lift more than half the number of affected households out of negative equity. However, to completely eradicate the problem would require an increase in prices of over 30 per cent.

But first, a word on independent financial advice. Most people can see the sense in approaching an independent financial adviser for a personal pension or any other long-term investment, yet when it comes to the mortgage, the inclination is to think in terms of the lender first. In fact, the days when you had to have a building society deposit account for several years and prove your worth as a saver before being granted the privilege of a mortgage are long gone.

These days, provided you have a stable income, there is a huge range of mortgage facilities available and an independent adviser will have access to all the latest offers. He will also be able to warn you about the drawbacks of some of the special deals – for example, early repayment penalties or lack of flexibility if you want to top up the mortgage at a later date when you move to a larger house. Given the ease with which advisers can identify the best mortgages, your time will be better spent considering how you intend to repay the loan.

As with the mortgage itself, the range of repayment options has developed considerably in recent years, and some lenders require little more than a verbal assurance that you *will* save one way or another in order to repay the debt. If you opt for an interest-only mortgage backed by an investment plan – most commonly an endowment, a personal equity plan or a personal pension – you are on pure investment ground and certainly do need independent advice. Most building societies and banks offer a very limited range of options because they are 'tied' to one life office – increasingly their own. For a discussion on the merits of independent advice, read Chapter 1. For an examination of the main investment links, read Chapter 2.

Once you have established the amount and have found a house you can afford, you will make a formal offer and apply for the loan. The lender will insist on a valuation to check that the house is priced correctly. This is not the same as a structural survey, which is strongly recommended. It is far better to know where the woodworm and dry rot are before you hand over your money.

The mortgage lender will offer you an advance and if the conveyancer, who looks after the legal side of the process, is satisfied that all is in order, you will proceed to exchange of contract. This is when you make a formal commitment to buy, and the owner of the house makes a formal commitment to sell. At this stage, usually you are asked to pay a deposit of up to 10 per cent of the selling price to the conveyancer. A few weeks later on completion, when you take ownership of the house, you must pay the balance.

■ HOW MUCH CAN YOU BORROW?

Lenders differ in the amount they will offer, but broadly this will be up to three times your annual earnings, less any existing commitments such as hire purchase agreements and other outstanding liabilities. If you want a joint mortgage, the multiple is likely to be three times the higher income plus once the other income or up to two and a half times the joint income. The lender will want to see confirmation of your income – either a letter from your employer or, if you are self-employed, audited accounts for several previous years.

Clearly the amount of debt you can comfortably manage will depend on your circumstances. For example, even if you have two decent incomes now, it would make sense not to over-commit yourself if you plan to start a family in the near future and expect one of your incomes to substantially reduce or disappear altogether for a few years.

Your mortgage and any capital you set aside from savings towards the house purchase need to cover several items other than the price of the house itself – for example, surveys, conveyancing fees, stamp duty, land registry fees and the removal costs.

Stamp duty is a government tax on the purchase of properties and must be paid where the purchase price exceeds £60,000. The current rate is 1 per cent on the full price, where this exceeds £60,000, 1.5 per cent for purchases between £250,000 and £500,000, and 2 per cent for purchases above this level. Land registry fees must also be paid for either registering the title to the property or the transfer where the title has already been registered. The fee for a £100,000 – £150,000 house was £230 at the time of writing.

You will also need to consider buildings and contents insurance, life assurance and, depending on existing cover, a payment protection policy.

■ WHAT IS A MORTGAGE?

> If you breach the terms of your mortgage contract – for example by failing to keep up the monthly payments – the lender has the power to take possession of the property and to sell it in order to recoup the loss.

A mortgage is the legal charge on your property which you give to the lender in return for the loan – a sort of IOU if you like. Together with any special terms and conditions, the mortgage 'deed' is the legal contract between you and the lender. The CML guide explains that the most important features are:

- ■ The names of the parties to the contract – that is the borrower and the mortgage lender.

- ■ The amount of the loan and your acknowledgement of receipt of the loan.

- ■ A promise by you to repay the loan, with interest, on the stipulated terms. These include the amount of the initial repayments and any special terms, for example, a fixed rate or a discount off the lender's variable rate for the first two years.

- ■ The granting of the legal charge of the property to the mortgage lender until the loan is repaid.

- ■ Your commitment, if applicable, to any insurance policies and to carry out any repairs and alterations – for example, the lender may insist the house is re-roofed within the first three months of ownership to maintain the property's value.

If you breach the terms of your mortgage contract by failing to keep up the monthly payments, the lender has the power to take possession of the property and to sell it in order to recoup the loss. Repossessions are a last resort, but unfortunately they were an all too familiar feature of the late 1980s and early 1990s when many borrowers had over-stretched themselves and could not keep pace with rising interest rates.

■ THE DIFFERENT TYPES OF MORTGAGE

Repayment

Historically the most common method was a repayment mortgage where your monthly payments include interest and capital, so that at the end of the mortgage term you have paid off the entire debt.

The interest element in the repayments on the first £30,000 of a loan qualifies for income tax relief, currently at 15 per cent. The tax relief is taken into account by the lender. So, on the first £30,000, if the mortgage rate is 7 per cent, the tax relief will reduce it to the net rate of 5.95 per cent (85 per cent of 7 per cent). This process is known as Mortgage Interest Relief At Source or MIRAS. Under MIRAS, you pay the net rate and the borrower reclaims the tax relief from the Inland Revenue.

Most lenders calculate the repayments of a loan up to £30,000 on a constant equal yearly and monthly basis. Table 19.1 shows the constant net repayments on a £30,000 loan advance over 25 years at 7 per cent where the actual repayments are 5.95 per cent after MIRAS.

Some lenders may calculate the monthly payments on an 'increasing net' basis. Under this system, the lender calculates the tax relief due on the interest you pay in a given year and deducts this sum from your gross repayments. The mortgage repayments are made net of tax relief, and you will obtain the maximum tax relief in the first years of the mortgage. However, because the amount of interest you pay decreases as you repay the capital, the amount of tax relief you receive also decreases, so your monthly repayments will increase over time.

Clearly, if you have a mortgage on a standard variable rate – or a discount of this – your repayments will rise and fall in line with the corresponding fluctuations in the lender's variable rate, which in turn is affected by interest rates.

19

Table 19.1: Repayments on a £30,000 advance over 25 years at 7 per cent (5.95 per cent after MIRAS)

Year	Annual repayment (£)	Principal (£)	Interest (£)	Balance at year end (£)
1	2,335.66	550.66	1,785.00	29,449.34
2	2,335.66	583.43	1,752.23	28,865.91
3	2,335.66	618.14	1,717.52	28,247.77
4	2,335.66	654.92	1,680.74	27,592.85
5	2,335.66	693.89	1,641.78	26,898.96
6	2,335.66	735.18	1,600.49	26,163.78
7	2,335.66	778.92	1,556.74	25,384.86
8	2,335.66	825.26	1,510.40	24,559.60
9	2,335.66	874.37	1,461.29	23,685.23
10	2,335.66	926.39	1,409.28	22,758.84
11	2,335.66	981.51	1,354.15	21,777.33
12	2,335.66	1,039.91	1,295.75	20,737.41
13	2,335.66	1.101.79	1,233.88	19,635.63
14	2,335.66	1,167.34	1,168.32	18,468.28
15	2,335.66	1,236.80	1,098.86	17,231.48
16	2,335.66	1,310.39	1,025.27	15,921.09
17	2,335.66	1,388.36	947.31	14,532.73
18	2,335.66	1,470.97	864.70	13,061.77
19	2,335.66	1,558.49	777.17	11,503.28
20	2,335.66	1,651.22	684.45	9,852.06
21	2,335.66	1,749.47	586.19	8,102.60
22	2,335.66	1,853.56	482.10	6,249.04
23	2,335.66	1,963.85	371.82	4,285.19
24	2,335.66	2,080.69	254.97	2,204.50
25	2,335.66	2,204.50	131.16	0.00
Total	**58,391.57**	**30,000**	**28,931**	**0.00**

To simplify administration, lenders often calculate the interest payments at the start of its financial year for the whole of that year, so this will not take account of any extra capital repayments you make.

Interest only

The alternative to a repayment mortgage is an interest-only loan where you make interest payments each month, but the capital debt remains static. At the same time, you save through an investment vehicle, and at the end of the mortgage term, you aim to build up a large enough fund to repay the mortgage and, possibly, create a surplus lump sum for your own use. Unless you go for an endowment, you also need to take out sufficient life assurance to repay the loan if you or your partner dies before your fund has grown to the required level.

For details on how an endowment, Pep or pension mortgage work, read Chapter 20, and also refer to the relevant chapters on these investments in Section III.

Your choice of interest rates

These days, it is very rare for a new borrower not to be able to find some sort of special deal on the interest rate. Your financial adviser will be able to run through the complete range at the time you wish to take out the loan, but this section describes briefly your main options. Bear in mind, as always, that there is no such thing as a free lunch. Somewhere along the line you must pay for the special feature, which usually means committing yourself to a minimum number of years with that lender or facing a penalty if you want to switch to a different mortgage or repay a capital lump sum to reduce the outstanding debt.

19

Annual percentage rate

Before looking at the various options, it is helpful to understand how the interest rate is calculated and applied. There are many variations on this theme – for example, a lender might calculate and charge the interest on a daily, monthly, quarterly or even annual basis, all of which affect the annual rate charged.

To enable you to make meaningful comparisons between lenders' offers, the government introduced the concept of the 'annual percentage rate of change' or APR. This represents the total charge for credit and takes into account the added costs of the loan, such as the valuation fees and lender's conveyancing charges, which are not included in the nominal rate. The APR is based on the gross rate of interest, so it does not take account of MIRAS.

One word of warning. The APR quoted for fixed-rate or discount schemes only applies to the offer period – it does not take into account the full variable rate which will kick in after the cheap rate has finished.

Variable rate

Lenders frequently change the interest rate for borrowers and savers and these increases and decreases are passed on to your monthly repayments. Where the institution has borrowers and savers – the building societies and banks for example – they need to retain a margin between the two, as this represents their 'turn'. If they have to pay more to savers to keep a competitive edge, they will have to pass on this increase to mortgage customers. Other factors which influence mortgage rates include fluctuations in the Bank of England's base rate and, for the 'centralised' lenders, the cost of raising funds on the money markets.

Fixed rate

This type of mortgage is particularly attractive to borrowers who want the comfort of knowing what their liabilities are for several years in order to budget accurately. Typically lenders are prepared to fix for one or two years, sometimes up to five. When the fixed-rate period ends you would switch to the lender's variable rate or perhaps be offered the chance to fix again.

The factors that influence a decision to go for a fixed rate as a borrower are similar to the considerations facing a saver – but in reverse. If general interest rates rise you will be protected from an increase in your repayments for the period covered. However, if interest rates fall, you will be locked into an uncompetitively high rate.

As with savers who go for a fixed-rate bond, for example, fixed-rate borrowers must watch out for early redemption penalties. Quite often these are so high that you are forced to stay put because it is too expensive to get out, even when you take into account much better rates elsewhere.

Discounted rate

Most lenders offer a discount of 1 per cent or 2 per cent off their variable rate usually for a period of one or two years. On top of this, a lender may provide a 'cashback', where a lump sum is paid to the borrower once the mortgage has been settled. This type of package can be very attractive if you want to keep payments down during the first few years, but if you are interested, make sure you are happy with the penalties for early redemption or for repaying part of your debt with a lump sum. In the latter case, you would forfeit the cashback, and you would have to pay, typically, the difference between the discount and standard variable rate on the lump sum you use to reduce the mortgage. Under this system, the longer you stick with the lender, the worse the partial repayment penalty will be, until, that is, you are clear of the penalty period.

Cap and collar mortgages

Under a cap and collar mortgage, the lender sets an upper and lower limit on fluctuations in the interest rate. This means you know the worst in advance – the rate cannot exceed the upper limit. However, if interest rates fall below the 'collar', you will be stuck with an uncompetitive package, just as you would be with a fixed-rate mortgage. Penalties are likely to apply if you want to re-mortgage to take advantage of better rates elsewhere.

19

■ MORTGAGE-RELATED INSURANCE

Due to the substantial size of the loan and the value of the property, it is important to make sure you have the right type of insurance. In some cases this will be a compulsory requirement by the lender although usually you can choose your own insurer so, as ever, do shop around or use an independent financial adviser to do so for you. It may seem easier at the time to go with the lender's choice, but this may prove an expensive mistake.

Buildings and contents insurance are essential, and both the CML and ABI guides offer some good advice for buyers. In this chapter, however, we limit the examination to the mortgage-related insurance that protects the lender if you default, and the personal insurances which either pay off the debt in the event of your death or help you maintain repayments in the event of long-term illness.

Mortgage indemnity

Financial institutions like to protect themselves if they lend you more than 75 per cent of the value of the property. The risk they face is that if you default they would need to repossess the house and sell it, probably for less than the purchase price, given they wouldn't want to keep an empty property on their books in order to wait for prices to rise. So, if you want a 'high loan to value' advance, lenders reckon they are justified in making you pay towards the mortgage indemnity insurance, which would reimburse them for some or all of the difference between the outstanding mortgage and the actual selling price.

> **The important point to remember about the mortgage indemnity insurance is that it protects the lender, not you.**

The important point to remember about the mortgage indemnity fee (it might also be called an additional security fee or high-percentage loan fee) is that it protects the lender, not you.

Life assurance

Life assurance is examined in detail in Chapter 16, but briefly, your life assurance should pay off all your outstanding liabilities. The mortgage is likely to be your main debt, but you should also factor in any other liabilities whether they are debts (hire purchase agreements and other loans), or regular commitments such as school fees for your children.

With an endowment mortgage, the endowment plan combines both the savings and the life assurance element. If you prefer to save through a Pep or pension plan, you must buy the life assurance separately.

There are several types of life assurance, but the simplest and cheapest is likely to be level term assurance, which provides a lump sum if you die during the insured period, but nothing if you do not. In addition, your life assurance should provide a lump sum which, when invested, would generate a replacement income, taking into account any company benefits such as dependants' pensions and lump sum death benefits. You should also consider family income benefit or some other type of life assurance to cover the partner who looks after the children. Family income benefit could, for example, be used to pay for a live-in nanny, to enable the surviving spouse to continue to work.

Payment protection

This is a variation on critical illness and/or permanent health insurance (see Chapter 3). If you suffer a chronic illness or become disabled, this type of policy would cover the cost of the mortgage and any related costs – insurances for example. The critical illness element would provide a lump sum if you suffered a major illness.

You might also be offered a third type of policy, known as accident, sickness and unemployment (ASU) insurance. This covers your monthly mortgage payments if you become too ill to work or are unemployed. The accident and sickness element is like a short-term PHI policy. Unemployment insurance is available through a few specialist insurers, but generally is very expensive, so ASU may be the only way to get it.

Following social security changes, if you are a new borrower, you now have to wait nine months before you can claim unemployment benefit to cover your mortgage – longer if you have savings of £8,000 or more. You can use ASU to insure the nine-month gap, and in some cases can cover yourself for up to two years.

However, experts warn you should treat this type of insurance as a way of buying some breathing space if you need to re-assess your finances in the light of illness or unemployment. It does not provide a long-term replacement income.

The same caveat applies to the limited versions of PHI and critical illness offered through a mortgage protection scheme. The main

19

point to note here is that, while the lender is concerned to ensure you keep up your monthly repayments, in practice you will need a great deal more than this to cover all your monthly outgoings and your liabilities. This is particularly important if you are self-employed, and therefore not covered by an employer's group scheme at work.

In conclusion, our advice is to check what cover you have through an employer's scheme and any existing private insurance, and read Chapters 23 and 25 to find out how the different policies work and how to calculate the total level of income and capital you need to insure.

■ READ THE SMALL PRINT

■ **Simplified acceptance for life assurance:** This is a short cut to buying the life assurance you need to cover your mortgage debt if you die. Buying life assurance can be time-consuming, and often involves completing a detailed questionnaire and attending a private medical. However, some providers will insure you without these requirements if you are under age 50 and need less than £70,000 of cover. To qualify, usually you must also provide satisfactory responses to three questions about whether you have visited your GP in the last few months, whether you are taking medication and whether you have had an HIV test, counselling or advice. You might also be asked if you have any dangerous pastimes – motor racing or hang-gliding, for example.

■ **Free temporary life cover:** Once you exchange contracts you are legally bound to the mortgage, but your life cover may not take effect until completion. To avoid the potential complications that would arise if a borrower died in the period between exchange and completion, some companies provide free cover for up to three months from exchange.

■ **Transfers from joint to single life:** Given that one marriage in three ends in divorce, it is important to check your policy will not need to be cancelled if the ownership of the house and endowment have to change from joint to single ownership. This is particularly important where your life assurance and investment are combined through an endowment since policies stopped in the early years are usually very poor value. Rather than cancel the policy on divorce, some providers allow one of the partners to continue the premiums unchanged or they might alter the life assurance and premiums to reflect the new ownership.

■ **Guaranteed insurability options:** This gives you the flexibility to increase the level of life assurance if you move house, improve your home or if your family situation changes, for example, on marriage or on the birth of a child. Some insurers will increase cover without a medical examination or detailed application form.

■ SUMMARY

■ **Seek independent financial advice on both the choice of mortgage and on the investment plan you use to repay the debt.**

■ **Most mortgage institutions will lend up to three times your annual salary, twice your joint salary, or three times the main and once the second salary.**

■ **Do check the penalties which apply to any special offers such as a fixed rate or discount on the variable rate.**

■ **Use the annual percentage rate (APR) to make comparisons between different lenders, but remember this will relate to the offer period if there is a discount or fixed rate.**

■ **Make sure your life assurance and income protection plans cover all your liabilities and requirements, not just what you need to repay the mortgage.**

■ **Check if the life assurance covers you for the period between exchange and completion.**

■ GLOSSARY OF TERMS

Cap and collar refers to interest rates which can vary between an upper and lower limit.

Discounted rates offer a reduction of, say, 1–2 per cent off the variable rate.

19

Fixed rate refers to interest payments which are fixed for a period of one to five years.

Interest-only mortgages require you to pay just the interest each month, and to save in a suitable plan (e.g., an endowment or personal equity plan) to repay the capital debt at maturity.

Mortgage indemnity insurance is an extra payment charged by the lender if the advance is more than 75 per cent of the purchase price.

Repayment mortgages – here your monthly payments include interest and capital, so that at the end of the mortgage term you have paid the entire debt.

Variable rate refers to repayments where the interest fluctuates in line with the lender's main rate.

Further information

Council of Mortgage Lenders: For a free guide *How to buy a home* or *How to buy a home in Scotland*, send a large stamped addressed envelope to the Council of Mortgage Lenders, BSA/CML Bookshop, 3 Savile Row, London W1X 1AF. The CML also publishes a free leaflet on taxation and the home-buyer.

Association of British Insurers: For free fact sheets on mortgage protection insurance, buildings and contents insurance, write to the Association of British Insurers, 51 Gresham Street, London EC2V 7HQ.

INVESTING TO REPAY YOUR MORTGAGE

Next to your pension, the investment you choose to repay your mortgage is likely to be your most valuable asset. Historically, the big mortgage lenders favoured the endowment route, partly because the life offices paid handsome sales commissions, and partly because until the early 1980s endowments were favoured by the taxation system which granted tax relief on life assurance premiums. This tax advantage has all but vanished, yet endowments still account for a large proportion of mortgage repayment methods (about 60 per cent of current mortgages are arranged on this basis).

In recent years, the more expensive and inflexible endowments have been the subject of fierce criticism. Most notably, an Office of Fair Trading report on mortgage repayment methods, published at the end of April 1995,

> The tax advantages of endowments have all but vanished, yet they still account for a large proportion of the mortgage repayment market.

questioned the suitability of endowment mortgages as the most popular mortgage investment, and argued that many were sold because of the high commissions paid to advisers.

The OFT report coincided with the publication of a *Financial Times* survey on 25-year endowment mortgage charges, which showed that over half of the unit-linked endowments provided no return if you stopped payments after one year – and in some cases, three years. Where the endowment was stopped after 10 years, over one-third of companies failed to return the original premiums.

These findings, which came at a time of falling investment returns and rising mortgage rates, presented a powerful argument in favour

■ **INVESTMENT SNAPSHOT**

If you move house and already have an endowment, don't cancel it, but consider topping up your loan with a Pep or a repayment mortgage.

of the traditional repayment mortgage where monthly payments cover the interest and also pay off the capital debt (see Chapter 19). For the very risk-averse, this may well be true, but for many home-owners a good quality predominantly equity-based investment plan is likely to build up a fund which will repay the mortgage at maturity, and which will prove to be more flexible than the repayment version.

Of course you do have to bear in mind the caveat that an interest-only loan backed by an investment plan offers no guarantee that you will be free of debt at the end of the mortgage period.

The three most common investments recommended by advisers to repay mortgages are life assurance endowments and personal equity plans. In some cases, personal pensions are also used, but here you must be very careful not to reduce your retirement fund to an inade-quate level.

These three investments were examined in detail in Chapters 16, 12 and 25 respectively. To avoid duplication, in this chapter we limit the discussion to comments on how the mortgage link affects your investment planning with these products and to the pros and cons of each method.

You don't have to restrict your choice to these particular invest-ments. Lenders increasingly are taking a more flexible attitude as to how you repay your mortgage. Depending on your income and other savings, some are prepared to offer a mortgage without insisting that you establish an investment plan specifically earmarked to repay the debt. This is ideal for sophisticated investors who want to retain total freedom over their portfolio and may ultimately use a combination of investments to pay back the loan.

One word of warning on flexibility, however. If you move house and need a bigger mortgage, don't cancel the endowment policy – it may be better to top up using some other method such as a Pep or repayment. If the performance of your endowment is utterly dismal, then as a last resort it might be worth trying to sell it through the second-hand endowment market (SHEPs – see page 151).

Finally, borrowers keen to clear their debt early should always check for any penalties. As we discussed in the last chapter, most of the special offers – the fixed-rate and discount mortgages – impose stiff penalties if you want to reduce your debt through additional capital payments or you want to pay it off altogether.

■ ENDOWMENT MORTGAGES

The main difference between endowments and other investments is that endowments combine life assurance with the savings plan. Where you use other investments to back a mortgage – a personal equity plan for example – you have to buy life assurance separately.

One of the big selling features of endowments in the 1970s and early 1980s was life assurance premium relief (LAPR). This was abolished for new endowments taken out after March 1984. For endowments taken out prior to this date, the rate of tax relief is 12.5 per cent.

In recent years endowments have faced serious criticism. Evidence of widespread 'churning' for extra sales commission in the mid to late 1980s, when investors were persuaded to cancel an existing policy and take out a new product, tarnished the endowment's reputation. Many policyholders also assumed that the endowment guaranteed to pay off the mortgage at maturity. In fact this was never guaranteed but it has taken a period of falling returns to bring this point home.

As with any investment the size of the fund at maturity depends largely on three factors:

■ The amount you pay to the financial institution

■ The amount actually invested after charges and the cost of the life assurance are deducted

■ The investment performance.

In response to criticism, several leading endowment companies have altered their product structure to offer better value and greater flexibility – in particular by improving their terms for investors who stop a policy early. However, there are still some pretty awful endowments around which combine poor performance, high charges and are so inflexible that once you are in it is very hard to get out again without losing a lot of money.

If you think an endowment is the right sort of investment for you, do consider these points:

■ **Charges:** Past performance is an unreliable guide to the future, but when it comes to endowment premiums and charges we are dealing with known facts. Prior to 1 January 1995, providers did not have to tell you how much of your premiums disappeared in charges. Now the life offices must give all prospective clients a pre-sale 'key features' document that sets out the total deductions over the course of the investment period. Among other points this document shows you what the effect of the charges will be and what you are likely to get back if you pull out early. Clearly this information is only of use if the charges of different companies are compared. In some cases, the total bill for charges represents about one-third of the potential investment return. Ideally, you should only buy an endowment through an independent financial adviser who will check this is the most suitable investment to back your mortgage and who will select the best company in terms of performance, charges and flexibility.

■ **Cashing in early:** Unfortunately, the consequences of cashing in your endowment policy early remain dire with the majority of providers. Recent surveys indicated that over half of the unit linked endowments and one-third of the 'with profits' plans provide no return after one year. Several provide no return after two years. If you cash in after ten years, almost one-third of the endowments do not even return your original premiums.

■ **Beware low premiums:** When you shop around for a mortgage, bear in mind that a low premium does not necessarily represent good value, but may simply be a gamble on high investment returns which, if they fail to materialise, will force the life office to increase your premiums or leave you to face a significant shortfall in the fund needed at maturity to pay off your mortgage.

- **Early repayment can damage your wealth:** If you decide to pay off your mortgage early and terminate your endowment in the few years before maturity, you may be in for a shock. For a 25-year endowment, the difference between the return at Year 24 and Year 25 can be as much as 20 per cent of the total payout in some cases.

PEP MORTGAGES

In Chapter 16, we explained why in most cases unit trust and investment trust personal equity plans are more tax-efficient than endowments, since the funds grow free of income and capital gains tax and there is no further tax liability on withdrawals. You can also pay what you want, when you want provided you stick to the overall Revenue annual limits.

> **It's not a win-win situation with Peps. Where you gain on tax efficiency and flexibility, you can lose out on the higher charges.**

But it's not a win-win situation with Peps. Where you gain on tax efficiency and flexibility you can lose out on charges. Over the long-term, it is the annual management charges that really bite and in many cases these are substantially higher under a Pep than an endowment, with the exception of the index trackers.

Pep mortgages are similar to unit-linked endowment mortgages. However, instead of using an endowment plan to cover both the life assurance and savings required to pay off the debt, with a Pep mortgage, the Pep is used as the savings vehicle, and a separate life assurance policy is taken out to pay off the debt in the event of the death of one of the borrowers.

In the past, lenders were reluctant to accept Peps as an appropriate way of repaying a mortgage, but this is no longer the case. Indeed the Halifax, the UK's largest lender, has replaced most of its endowment mortgage range with Pep-based mortgage products.

Peps vs endowments: tax and charges

To summarise, there are two important differences between endowments and Peps that affect the return, namely tax and charges. The

Pep fund grows free of tax, while the endowment fund suffers a tax on income at a rate broadly equivalent to the basic rate of tax. Understandably, tax-efficiency is the main feature promoted by Pep companies.

The issue of charges is less clear-cut. Research indicates that Pep administration and investment management charges often are higher over a 25-year period when compared with an endowment, largely due to the higher annual management charge.

Where Peps should score is in the timing and distribution of charges, which usually are spread evenly throughout the investment period. With endowments, often a large proportion of the sales, marketing and administration charges that relate to the whole investment period are deducted during the first year or two, so if you stop the plan in the early years you may get next to nothing back.

Advisers warn that in most cases, it is unwise to stop endowment payments due to the impact of those high early charges. However, you could use a Pep to top up the mortgage if there is a need to increase the loan.

Pep appeal

Compared with endowments, Peps should offer investors the following benefits:

- Tax-free growth of fund.

- Flexibility to make partial withdrawals and to pay what you want when you want provided you stick to the overall Inland Revenue limit of £6,000 a year per person in a general Pep.

- Charges usually are evenly spread throughout the investment period, so you should avoid the poor returns often associated with those endowments which deduct high upfront charges.

- It is possible to change your Pep manager if performance is not satisfactory or charges are too high (but watch out for Pep exit charges). With self-select Peps, you are not limited to one investment manager, so over the course of the mortgage you can build up a portfolio of plans. This has obvious advantages from the point of view of diversification and spreading risk. However, if you opt for a Pep mortgage package, almost certainly you will be restricted to the same manager throughout the mortgage period. You may consider this a serious loss of flexibility.

■ If you want to pay off your mortgage early, you can stop the Pep investment at any time without penalty and use the proceeds to repay part or all of the mortgage. However, many mortgage lenders impose early redemption penalties, so do check this point carefully.

■ PENSION MORTGAGES

The tax-free cash available at retirement from pension arrangements, can also be used to repay a mortgage. As is explained in Chapter 25, with a pension plan, you get full tax relief on premiums and the fund itself grows free of tax. The pension itself is taxed as income.

In theory then, a personal pension plan should make a very tax-efficient repayment vehicle but there is an important caveat. If you fund your mortgage solely from this source you could leave yourself with a diminished fund at retirement with which to buy your annuity. Consequently, there is a real danger this would leave you with a low income in retirement.

■ SUMMARY

20

■ **The investment you choose to repay your mortgage is likely to be your most valuable asset after the house itself and your pension fund.**

■ **Lenders today are very flexible on which investment you use to back your mortgage, but the most popular choices are endowments and Peps.**

■ **Some endowments offer poor value, but some provide a good combination of consistent long-term performance and low charges.**

■ **Peps are more tax-efficient than endowments, but do check the charges, as these tend to be higher, particularly the annual man-**

agement charge. This can undermine your return over the long-term.

■ Pension mortgages are very tax-efficient, but be careful not to deplete your fund to the point where you end up with a low income in retirement.

■ Don't pay off your mortgage early without first checking any penalties under the investment plan and the mortgage itself.

Source material

OFT report *Mortgage Repayment Methods* and *Financial Times* survey, 'Endowment Mortgages', both 28 April 1995.

HOME INCOME PLANS

Home income plans offer elderly people who are 'house-rich, cash-poor' the opportunity to tap into the equity in their homes and use this to generate an extra income. These plans are particularly attractive because you don't have to sell up and move. You can take the money as a regular income or as a lump sum, depending on the scheme rules. All you have to do in return is pay interest on the loan, where applicable, and agree that the debt will be repaid out of the proceeds of your house sale when you die.

Perhaps this sounds too good to be true? Well, it was for thousands of pensioners in the late 1980s who were encouraged by high-pressure salesmen to re-mortgage part or all of their homes and use the proceeds to invest in insurance company bonds. These schemes relied on the flawed assumption that bond investment returns would always outstrip mortgage interest rates. They didn't. House prices tumbled, interest rates soared, the stock market crashed and thousands of elderly homeowners were left with a mortgage debt larger than the combined value of their house and the insurance bond. In 1990 these investment schemes were banned, and the Investor's Compensation Scheme has already paid out £45 million to 2,500 victims. There are still many claims outstanding.

> Some of the original 'equity release' schemes relied on the flawed assumption that bond investment returns would always outstrip mortgage interest rates. In the late 1980s they didn't. House prices tumbled, interest rates soared, the stock market crashed and thousands of elderly homeowners were left with a mortgage debt larger than the combined value of their house and the insurance bond.

■ INVESTMENT SNAPSHOT

In households where the owner is 65 or older, about 54 per cent are owner–occupiers without a mortgage.

But with increased longevity and cuts in State welfare provision, asset-rich, cash-poor pensioners are turning for financial assistance to a second generation of much more respectable equity-release plans. The government is also expected to promote these schemes as one way for the elderly to afford substantial insurance premiums to cover part of their long-term care needs in later retirement (see Chapter 4).

■ SAFE AS HOUSES?

Following the bad publicity of the earlier plans, four companies – Allchurches Life, Carlyle Life, Home & Capital Trust and Stalwart Assurance – joined together in 1991 to form SHIP, the Safe Home Income Plans company. SHIP secretariat is based at the independent advisers and home income plan specialists Hinton & Wild. The code of practice offered by members of the organisation is as follows:

■ You have complete security of tenure and are guaranteed the right to live in the property for life, no matter what happens to interest rates and the stock market.

■ You have freedom to move house without jeopardising your financial situation.

■ You will be guaranteed a cash sum or regular income; your money will not be sunk into uncertain investments.

■ HOW DO THEY WORK?

There are two basic types of safe home income plans – where a mortgage on the property is used to produce an income, and those which involve the sale of part or all of your property to produce an income or cash lump sum. In each case the loan is paid off when you die.

Mortgage annuities

This type of plan allows you to re-mortgage part of the value of your house – usually up to £30,000. The lump sum is used to buy a 'purchased life annuity' from the lender, which in return guarantees an income for life. This pays the fixed rate of interest on the mortgage, and what's left is yours to spend how you wish. Under some plans (NPIs, for example), you do not pay mortgage interest, but the annuity income is lower to compensate.

The income generated by the annuity will remain static or, at an extra cost, will rise at a fixed rate or in line with inflation (see Chapter 26). The only wild card that could alter this income would be a change in the taxation of annuities. Governments are unlikely to change the tax treatment for the worse, given the age and financial position of those who buy this type of annuity.

SHIP states that the minimum age for a mortgage annuity plan is 69 for a single person; in the case of couples, their combined ages must total at least 145, with the younger age 70 or over. Below these ages, the annuities are unlikely to offer attractive rates. The loan usually is repaid on the death of the individual, or on second death in the case of a couple.

The normal minimum loan is £15,000 and the maximum is £30,000, although the over-80s may be able to raise slightly more. Typically this could buy a gross flat-rate annual income guaranteed for life of £1,200 for a woman aged 75, rising as high as £4,000 for a man aged 85. This is the surplus income after the mortgage interest net of MIRAS (mortgage interest relief at source – see Chapter 20) is deducted. MIRAS is available at the concessionary rate of 24 per cent, rather than the usual 15 per cent. Women tend to outlive men and so receive a lower rate.

21

Purchased life annuities are regarded as tax-efficient because only part of the income is taxed. The rest is treated as a return of capital.

Reversion plans

This is where you sell, rather than mortgage, part or all of your house. Reversion plans fall into two categories. With a **reversion annuity**, the purchase price is used to buy an annuity which operates in the same way as the mortgage annuity described above, although obviously there is no mortgage interest to pay so your income is higher. However, because you have sold rather than mortgaged, you will not gain from any rise in house prices on that portion of your property. The exception is the Stalwart reversion plan which links its annuity to its property fund, and therefore passes on some of the gains in property price rises in the form of increased income. If you are concerned about the downside risk, Stalwart will guarantee 50 per cent of your annuity rate.

Under the **cash option** you sell part or all of your home in return for a lump sum which is tax-free provided the house is your main residence. You continue to live there, rent free, until you die. You can, if you wish, use the money to buy an annuity, but this is not obligatory.

According to SHIP, the minimum age for reversion plans is 65 to 70. The minimum sale is usually between 40 per cent and 50 per cent of the value of the property, and with most companies you can sell up to 100 per cent. SHIP says that for homes priced over £70,000, the benefits under a reversion plan often are appreciably higher than the mortgage plans.

How to decide

Your choice of plan will depend partly on your age, and your view on whether house prices are likely to rise over the period of the loan. But there are other factors involved. For example, you should consider how the additional income will affect your tax position and the possible loss of means-tested social security benefits. In particular, care is needed if you receive income support or council tax benefits, as these may be reduced or lost altogether. Clearly the home income plan benefits must more than compensate for this loss.

You should also check how an equity release scheme would affect your inheritance tax position, and you may wish to discuss your plans with your family, since it will reduce your estate. Moreover, before entering into an agreement, ask what would happen if you have to leave your house, perhaps to move into sheltered accommodation or a nursing home.

Finally, do consider all the costs involved – for example the survey, legal fees and administrative charges. Some plan providers make a contribution, but the amounts vary.

■ SUMMARY

- **Home income plans may be suitable if you need to boost your income and have no other assets to draw on except the equity tied up in your home.**

- **You can sell all or part of an interest in your home and use the money to buy an annuity. The debt is repaid when you die and the house is sold.**

- **Make sure you fully understand the terms of the plan and seek legal advice before proceeding.**

- **Find out how the plan will affect your income tax position and whether there are implications for inheritance tax.**

■ GLOSSARY OF TERMS

21

Mortgage annuities allow you to re-mortgage part of the value of your house – usually up to £30,000. The lump sum is used to buy a **purchased life annuity** which pays the interest on the mortgage and provides an income.

Reversion annuities allow you to sell part of the interest in your house and use the proceed to buy an annuity to provide the income.

Cash reversion plans allow you sell part or all of your home in return for a lump sum. You continue to live there, rent free, until you die. You can use the money to buy an annuity but this is not obligatory.

Further information

Safe Home Income Plans: 0181-390 8166 (this is run by Hinton & Wild).

Allchurches Life: 01452 526265.

Carlyle Life: 01222 371725.

Cavendish Property: 0113-237 0666.

Foster & Cranfield: 0171-608 1941.

Hinton & Wild: 0181-390 8166.

Home & Capital Trust: 01234 340511.

NPI: 0800 707580.

Stalwart Assurance: 01306 876581.

PENSIONS

STATE PENSIONS

Despite the low level of the State pension, for many people it still forms an important element of their overall retirement income. It is helpful, therefore, to understand how your State pension is earned and how it relates to your private schemes and plans.

■ PENSION FORECASTS

Unfortunately, the calculation of the pension is ridiculously complicated. If, like most people, you feel there must be more to life than wading through a morass of documents, ask your local Department of Social Security for a pension forecast (form BR19). This should provide a fairly intelligible explanation of your entitlement. You can get a pension forecast provided you have more than four months to go to pensionable age.

> If you want to find out what your pension is worth, and you feel there must be more to life than wading through obscure documents, ask your local Department of Social Security for a pension forecast (form BR19).

If you just want to find out what your additional pension will be, ask for leaflet NP 38. This type of forecast should help you decide whether or not to contract out of the additional pension scheme, for example if you want to take out a personal pension plan.

Each forecast takes between three and six weeks to process, longer if you are widowed or divorced, where the assessment will be more complicated.

■ INVESTMENT SNAPSHOT

People mistakenly believe the National Insurance Fund is storing up assets to pay their pension. Well, there isn't a fund. Social security is based on the 'pay-as-you-go' system, so no sooner have you paid in your NI contributions than the DSS uses them to pay someone else's benefits.

■ HOW THE STATE PENSION WORKS

The pension has two elements – a basic flat-rate pension, known as the old age pension, and a pension which is linked to the level of your earnings, known as the 'additional pension' or 'Serps' (State earnings-related pension scheme). Eligibility to both pensions is built up through the compulsory payment of National Insurance (NI) contributions on part of your earnings. The National Insurance system is explained on page 201.

> Don't fall into the trap of thinking that you will automatically receive the full rate of pension even if you have worked for 40 years before retiring.

The maximum single person's basic State pension for the 1997/98 tax year is £62.45 per week, while the maximum additional or Serps pension is just over £100 per week. State pensions rise each year in line with retail prices, are taxed as earned income and should be included in the end-of-year tax return.

The official pension age – 65 for men and 60 for women – is the minimum age at which men and women can claim a State pension in the UK. By the year 2020, the UK will have a common pension age of 65 for both men and women. This move to equal pension ages will result in a rather complex phasing period. Basically, women born after April 1955 will have to wait until age 65 to claim. Older women should check with the Department of Social Security to find out their proposed retirement date. The phasing period will last 10 years between 2010 and 2020.

Don't fall into the trap of thinking that you will automatically receive the full rate of pension, even if you have worked for 40 years before retiring. The State pension system works relatively smoothly if you are employed from age 16 up to State pension age. However, the career pattern of many people involves periods in self-employment, periods spent not working in order to raise a family, periods in and out of company pension schemes, and a whole host of other variables.

■ NATIONAL INSURANCE AND THE STATE PENSION

State pensions come under the general heading of 'social security benefits' which also include benefits paid to people who are sick, disabled, out of work, or on a low income. Most of these benefits are paid for out of the National Insurance Fund, which is built up from National Insurance contributions levied on earnings and paid by employers, employees and the self-employed. Purists might disagree, but essentially NI contributions can be regarded as another form of direct taxation.

National Insurance for employees is levied on what are known as 'band earnings', that is earnings between lower and upper limits (known as the lower earnings limit or LEL and the upper earnings limit or UEL). These are £62 and £465 per week for the 1997/98 tax year. The contributions are deducted automatically from an employee's pay packet while the self-employed pay a flat-rate contribution each month to the Department of Social Security and an earnings-related supplement which is assessed annually through the tax return.

The married woman's stamp

Women's State pensions are particularly complicated due to a two-tier National Insurance contribution system which still allows some older women (those who were married or widowed before 5 April 1977) to pay a reduced rate, known as the 'married woman's stamp'. The married woman's stamp originally was popular because it meant a much lower deduction from the weekly or monthly pay cheque. But if you pay this rate, you do not build up a right to a State pension in your own name. Instead you have to claim through your spouse's NI contribution record, and claim a Category B State pension which is worth about 60 per cent of the full rate.

22

The basic 'old age' pension

To get the full weekly rate of the basic pension, currently worth £62.45, you must have 'qualifying years' for about 90 per cent of your working life – broadly speaking, that is years in which you paid the full rate of National Insurance contribution for the complete period. In some cases you will be treated as though you had received qualifying earnings if you are eligible for certain benefits, for example Home Responsibilities Protection, invalid care allowance, unemployment benefit and sickness benefit, among others.

To get the minimum basic pension payable (25 per cent of the full rate), you normally need a minimum of 10 qualifying years.

It is not possible to claim the State pension before you reach official pension age, but it is possible to defer claiming for up to five years and earn increments.

Married couple's pension

The combination of the single person's pension and the spouse's pension form what is generally known as the married couple's State pension, which is worth £99.80 for the 1997/98 tax year.

If a woman qualifies for a single person's (Category A) State pension in her own right but it is worth less than the Category B pension, when her husband reaches age 65 or retires to claim his pension, she will receive a composite pension worth a maximum of the full Category B rate.

Under the current system the Category B pension, sometimes referred to as a 'dependency increase', is most frequently paid to the husband on behalf of his 'dependent' wife. Government proposals are likely to equalise the conditions for eligibility so that an older woman can claim a Category B pension for her husband, provided he does not have earnings or other pensions worth more than the value of the dependency pension.

The basic pension and your company scheme

'Integrated' company schemes are very common. Under this system, the level of pension promised by the company scheme takes into account the basic State pension. Effectively, this means that the employer does not provide any pension for earnings up to the lower earnings limit (£62 per week in 1997/98) or a multiple of this. Low earners and those who do not qualify for a State pension in their own right can suffer as a result.

■ ADDITIONAL PENSION ('SERPS')

The second tier of the State pension is the element which is linked to part of your earnings, known as 'additional pension' or 'Serps' (State earnings-related pension scheme). This pension, worth a maximum of £103 for the 1997/98 tax year, is paid at the same time as the basic pension, that is at age 65 for men and between age 60 to 65 for women, depending on when they retire.

If you are an employee and you are not contracted out of Serps, either through a company pension scheme or an appropriate personal pension plan, automatically you will be a member and pay for the pension through your National Insurance contributions.

Unlike the basic State pension, where the minimum qualifying contribution period is about ten years to get any benefit at all, a right to Serps builds up from day one. The value of the pension depends on the level of your earnings and the contribution period. It will also depend on when you reach pension age, because the Government has reduced Serps for those who retire after 5 April 1999. This, combined with the planned phased increase in women's pension age from 60 to 65, which kicks off in 2010, makes the calculation of the additional pension an extremely complicated exercise.

22

How Serps is calculated

Your Serps pension will be worth 25 per cent of your National Insurance band earnings averaged over the period 1978/79 and 6 April 1999. For benefits built up after this date, the formula is reduced over a ten-year period from 25 per cent to 20 per cent of band earnings averaged over your entire working life.

If you are a member of a company pension scheme which is contracted out of Serps, or if you have an 'appropriate' personal pension, your additional pension is replaced by the private scheme or plan.

■ APPEALS

Given the complexity of the State pension system it is not surprising that from time to time the DSS makes a mistake in the calculation of benefits. If you claim a social security benefit – whether it is your pension or some other form of payment – and you are unhappy about the decision made by the adjudication officer or adjudicating medical authority, you can request a review or make an appeal. However, first you should read leaflet NI 260 *A guide to reviews and appeals* to make sure you understand the rules.

■ SUMMARY

■ **To find out what your State pension is worth, ask your local DSS for a pension forecast.**

■ **Don't assume you will receive a full pension automatically. The qualifying rules are very complex and you usually have to have worked all your life to get the maximum benefit.**

■ **You can defer the date when you take your pension, but you cannot draw it early.**

■ **If you think the DSS has miscalculated your pension you have the right to appeal.**

■ GLOSSARY OF TERMS

Band earnings are the earnings between £62 and £465 per week for the 1997/98 tax year, on which National Insurance is levied.

Contracted out refers to employees who have replaced their Serps pension either through a company scheme or a personal pension.

The married woman's stamp is a reduced rate of National Insurance contribution which can be paid by women who were married or widowed before April 1977.

National Insurance is a form of taxation levied on band earnings (between £62 and £465 a week in 1997/98).

Qualifying year – your NI contributions count towards your State pension only if you pay for a complete year.

Serps – the State earnings-related pension scheme, which is based on National Insurance band earnings.

Further information

The Department of Social Security (DSS) publishes several guides to national insurance and social security benefits which are available, free of charge, from local DSS offices. Some leaflets are also available from post offices, libraries and Citizens Advice Bureaux.

Legal aid: You can find out more about Legal Aid in England and Wales from the *Legal Aid Guide*, available from: Legal Aid Head Office, Newspaper House, 8–16 Great New Street, London EC4 3BN. The equivalent service and guide for Scotland are available from: The Scottish Legal Aid Board, 44 Drumsheugh Gardens, Edinburgh EH3 7SW.

22

COMPANY PENSION SCHEMES

For most employees membership of the company pension scheme represents the most important benefit after the salary itself. But don't assume just because there *is* a company scheme, that it is automatically going to see you right in retirement. Scheme benefits vary considerably, and you may need to top up your pension if your employer is less than generous.

Company schemes are very tax-efficient. The employer's contributions are tax deductible, the employee's contributions are paid free of basic and higher rate tax, the pension fund builds up tax-free, and a significant chunk of the final benefits can be taken as tax-free cash at retirement. The pension, whether drawn from a company scheme or from a life office in the form of an annuity, is subject to your top rate of income tax.

> With a money purchase scheme the investment risk falls fairly and squarely on you, the scheme member. There are no guarantees.

There are two main types of occupational schemes: 'final salary', also known as 'defined benefit', and 'money purchase', also known as 'defined contribution'. With a final salary scheme, the employer bears the investment risk and backs the pension guarantees. With a money purchase scheme, the investment risk falls fairly and squarely on your shoulders as the scheme member and there are no guarantees.

■ FINAL SALARY SCHEMES

Final salary schemes, still the most prevalent among employers in the UK, base the pension calculation on the number of years of service and your salary at or near retirement. A typical scheme guarantees to provide a pension that builds up at the rate of 1/60 of your final salary for each year of service up to an Inland Revenue maximum of 40/60

■ INVESTMENT SNAPSHOT

Since 1988, employers have not been able to make membership of the scheme a condition of employment.

– that is, two-thirds final salary at retirement (restricted for some higher earners – see below).

How much do you contribute?

Employees can contribute up to 15 per cent of gross pay to an occupational scheme, although the most common rate is about 5 per cent. 'Pay' in this context is defined as basic salary plus, in some cases, benefits such as overtime, bonuses, and the taxable value of fringe benefits. If overtime or sales commission form a significant proportion of your gross earnings and this is not taken into account in your pensionable pay you could consider top up provision through additional voluntary contributions (see Chapter 24).

The pension itself may be based on your average salary during the last three years before retirement or possibly your average salary during the period of scheme membership. A minority of schemes base it on the period of maximum earnings, which is ideal if you are in a job where earnings peak mid-career rather than towards the end of your working life.

Contributions and benefits for higher earners

Over the past five years the Revenue has restricted the pensions of certain high earners. In particular, some employees are subject to a cap of £84,000, for the 1997/98 tax year, on which contributions and the final pension can be based. The cap applies to members of final salary schemes set up after the 1989 budget and members who joined any final salary scheme after 1 June 1989. For these employees the maximum contributions for the 1997/98 tax year are limited to £12,600 (15 per cent of £84,000), while the maximum pension will be about £56,300 (two-thirds of the cap).

23

Unapproved schemes

There are two main types of pension to cater for earnings above the cap. 'Funded unapproved retirement benefit schemes' (furbs) are company schemes that are recognised by the Revenue, but are 'unapproved' for tax purposes. Under a furbs, the employer sets aside contributions to build up a pension fund for the employee's earnings in excess of the cap. Furbs usually operate on a money purchase basis. The furbs member will still remain in the main company scheme, and receive benefits in the usual way up to the level of the cap.

The fact that the furbs has an identifiable fund, written under trust for the employee, makes it the most secure arrangement for individuals affected by the earnings cap.

Under a furbs, the employee is taxed on the employer's contributions which are classed as a benefit in kind – rather like membership of the company's private medical scheme. However, the employer can treat these contributions as a trading expense for corporation tax purposes. Also, there is no employer's National Insurance contribution on these payments. The furbs fund is subject to income and capital gains tax.

Where the fund is used to buy an annuity the income is subject to tax. However, the entire benefit can be taken as a tax-free lump sum on retirement – a far more attractive option and the most common choice. The death in service lump sum benefits can be paid under discretionary trust and therefore should be free of inheritance tax.

An alternative option under Inland Revenue rules is the unfunded unapproved retirement benefit scheme. In these arrangements your employer does not pay any contributions and there is no fund earmarked for the employee. Instead the pension benefits are paid out of company funds when the employee retires. When this happens the employer receives an allowance against corporation tax.

With this arrangement there is no tax liability until you receive the benefits but when that happens all lump sums and pensions are taxed as earned income. Where the employer decides to buy an annuity for the employee, the purchase price will be taxed as well as the resulting regular income. Death benefits, as with the furbs, should be free of inheritance tax if paid under a discretionary trust.

Topping up your company pension

By law every scheme, with a few minor exceptions, must provide an additional voluntary contribution (AVCs) scheme which allows members to top up their company scheme benefits. In practice very few people end up with the maximum permitted pension so most will benefit from AVCs. Since 1987, employees also have been able to contribute to individual top-up plans known as free standing AVCs (FSAVCs), which are sold by insurance companies and other financial institutions. These options are discussed in Chapter 24.

Transfers

This is one of the most complex pension issues. If you change jobs after two years' membership in a scheme you cannot claim a refund of contributions but instead have three main options.

- You can leave your pension where it is. This is known as a preserved or 'deferred' pension since your right to a pension from that company scheme is put off or deferred until you reach pension age. By law the value of a deferred pension must increase in line with the retail price index (RPI) up to a cap of 5 per cent. This is known as limited price indexation or LPI.

- You can transfer the benefits to the new company scheme. This has the advantage of keeping all your benefits under one roof, but for various reasons you may not receive the same number of 'years' in the new scheme as you had built up in the old scheme.

However, despite the vagaries of deferred pensions and inter-company pension transfers, usually these two are the best options.

23

- The other alternative is to transfer your benefits to an insurance product – either a personal pension or a 'buy-out' bond. This transaction will incur costs and the plans do not offer the guarantees associated with a final salary company scheme pension. Transfer options should always be considered with the help of an independent pensions adviser.

Integration

About 50 per cent of company schemes reduce the pension by 'integrating' with the basic state pension. The idea behind this is to provide a maximum two-thirds final salary pension including the State benefit. Of course it also cuts company pension costs. Where a scheme is integrated, no pension is paid for the first slice of salary up to the NI lower earnings (see page 201). No employee or employer pension contributions are levied on this amount either.

Contracting out of Serps

Most final salary schemes are contracted out of the State earnings-related pension scheme (Serps), and as a result the employer and employees pay a reduced rate of National Insurance contribution with the balance invested in the company pension fund. Where the scheme is not contracted out, the employee would receive the Serps pension and the company pension on top of this.

Tax-free cash

The maximum tax-free cash you can take from your company pension scheme is one and a half times your final salary after 40 years service. This is limited in the case of some higher earners (see page 207). If you take the tax-free cash – and almost everyone does – your pension will be reduced (the system is slightly different in public sector schemes).

Pension increases

Company schemes typically increase pensions by 3–5 per cent each year. However, you need to check which increases are guaranteed, and which are 'discretionary' (a voluntary payment on the part of the trustees when the fund has a surplus). Public sector pensions automatically increase in line with the full retail price index.

Family protection benefits

Most final salary schemes provide other important family protection benefits in addition to the pension itself, for example death in service benefits worth up to four times annual salary, widow's and dependent children's pensions and similar death in retirement benefits. Disability pensions and private medical insurance are also common features of the overall benefits package.

Most final salary schemes provide other important family protection benefits in addition to the pension itself, for example, death in service benefits worth up to four times annual salary, widow's and dependent children's pensions and similar death in retirement benefits.

■❶How does your scheme rate?

If you want to check how your company pension scheme rates, consult your scheme booklet and compare the benefits listed with our ideal scheme.

Retirement pension: Paid from age 65 (age 60 would be a real bonus), based on service and final earnings.

Accrual rate (that is, the rate at which the pension builds up): One-sixtieth of final pay for each year of service.

Pensionable earnings: All earnings (apart from overtime or similar bonuses paid only during earlier years of employment).

Final pay calculation: The higher of either total earnings in the year prior to retirement or average annual earnings over any three-year period ending within 10 years of retirement, uprated in line with the retail price index.

Pensionable service: Total service including maternity leave and certain temporary absences.

Lump sum on retirement: Revenue maximum (that is, the maximum amount of pension that can be converted to tax-free cash – normally one and a half times final remuneration after 40 years, possibly limited by the earnings cap).

Pension increases: Linked to the retail price index.

Ill-health pension: Equivalent to the amount the employee would have received had he remained in service until normal retirement age, at his or her current rate of pay.

23

Death in service benefits: This should include a dependent adult's pension of four-ninths the member's total earnings at death plus pensions for dependent children. Also a lump sum of four times annual earnings.

Death in retirement benefits: This should include a pension worth two-thirds of the member's pension to be paid to a nominated adult dependant plus a pension for any dependent children under age 18.

Scheme leaver benefits: The whole of the preserved pension should be increased in line with RPI up to retirement.

Source: Based on Union Pension Services *'Pension Scheme Profiles'*

However, if you are not married to your partner, check whether he or she is still entitled to the benefits.

■ MONEY PURCHASE COMPANY SCHEMES

Money purchase schemes can be attractive because you have an identifiable pot of money which you should be able to take from job to job. Contributions are invested to build up a fund which, at retirement, is used to buy an annuity from an insurance company. An annuity pays an income for life in return for a lump sum.

The most important point to bear in mind with money purchase is that the level of income your fund buys is not guaranteed, but will depend on four factors:

- ■ how much you and your employer contribute
- ■ the investment performance of the fund
- ■ the level of charges deducted from your fund by the pension company
- ■ annuity 'rates' – that is, the level of income your fund will buy at the time you retire.

How does your money purchase scheme rate?

Use the following checklist to find out if your employer's money purchase scheme is well-designed. Ideally it should:

■ Aim (but it cannot guarantee) to match the pension and risk benefits equivalent to your old final salary scheme.

■ Invest minimum employer and employee total contributions of between 6–15 per cent of annual salary, depending on age (the older you are the more you need to pay in – see Table 23.1 on page 214).

■ Delegate the investment management to a major institutional fund manager which has a proven track record in the pensions market.

■ Incur modest administration and investment charges which are shown to be among the most competitive for group schemes.

■ Impose no financial penalties if you leave the scheme when you change jobs, you reduce contributions, or you want to retire early.

If you don't want to make the investment decisions your scheme should also offer a 'working life strategy'. This is a managed fund which provides you with the long-term growth potential of equities in the early years but protects your capital as you approach retirement by automatically phasing a switch from equities into cash and bonds.

Some employers are introducing money purchase schemes, and asking members to switch from the old final salary scheme. If you are offered a choice between staying in your employer's old final salary scheme and joining the new money purchase scheme, you need practical advice from someone who fully understands how both schemes work. In particular, check that there are no material changes to the level of life assurance offered – typically three times your annual salary.

Contributions

Some money purchase schemes follow the same maximum contribution and benefit rules as final salary schemes. However, most new schemes are set up as group personal pensions (GPPs). Under a GPP, your individual personal pension plan can be used to contract out of Serps and to invest additional regular or single premiums to boost the pension provided by the NI rebate.

Personal pension contribution limits start at 17.5 per cent of 'net relevant earnings' (equivalent in this context to pensionable pay) for employees up to age 35, and rising in stages to 40 per cent for employees age 61 and over. Employer contributions must be included in these limits, but there is no obligation for employers to pay anything other than the redirected NI contributions.

The contribution level is the litmus test of a good GPP. Table 23.1 gives you an idea of what you would need to contribute to achieve a pension similar in value to those offered by final salary schemes. The Table (based on a real example provided by employee benefits consultants Godwins), shows the total contributions for a scheme designed to achieve broadly the same benefits as a final salary scheme where the pension builds up at a rate of 1/60 of final salary a year, allows for 3 per cent annual increases to the pension and provides a spouse's pension. Death in service benefits of four times salary are included, but in this case disability insurance is paid by the employer – otherwise the contributions necessary would be higher.

Table 23.1: Combined employee and employer contributions required to match a typical final salary scheme

Age	Total contribution (half paid by employer) % pa
16-24	6
25-29	7
30-34	8
35-39	9
40-44	10
45-49	11.5
50-54	13.5
55-59	15.5
60+	16.5

Source: Godwins

Family protection benefits

Death and disability benefits under money purchase schemes can be minimal so it is important to check what your employer provides here. If you are not happy with the level of cover offered, top up your family protection insurance through additional life assurance and disability or income replacement insurance. Private medical cover could also be considered.

Flexibility and portability

Flexibility is supposed to be one of the main attractions of money purchase pensions since the employee has an easily identifiable and apparently portable pot of money. The important point to check here is what happens to your pot if you leave the scheme when you change jobs.

■ SPECIAL SCHEMES FOR EXECUTIVES

Senior executives often belong to a fast-stream version of the main company pension scheme which builds up the pension more quickly and provides better benefits all round. But executives and directors can also be provided for through an entirely separate insurance arrangement known as an executive pension plan, or EPP. EPPs, although providing a pension linked to final salary, are occupational money purchase schemes designed for individuals or small groups of senior executives and directors.

In the past, EPPs have been popular, but today most advisers reckon that personal pensions, and particularly self-invested personal pensions (see Chapter 25) offer a package that is just as good and far simpler. Nevertheless, there are still some people for whom the EPP offers greater flexibility on contributions and possibly better and/or more flexible benefits, particularly as you can use an EPP in conjunction with the main company scheme (this is not possible with a personal pension).

So, for example, you could use an EPP to take contributions based on overtime and bonuses and then take the benefits from the plan as

23

part of your early retirement income. You could start to draw benefits from your main company scheme at a later date. However, unlike SIPPs and the small business schemes discussed in the next chapter, you cannot usually separate the administration and investment under an EPP and this inflexibility could cost you dear in terms of sales commission payments to advisers and the life office charges.

■ SMALL COMPANY SCHEMES

Small self-administered schemes come from the same stable as executive pension plans. These schemes are suitable for up to 12 members. Membership is usually restricted to the directors of the company because the fund can be used to invest in the business – for example to buy new premises. All investments must be at arm's length – so, in the case of a property purchase, the company would have to pay the scheme a commercial rate of rent.

SSASs are complicated and require expert advice.

■ DIVORCE

For most married couples, the husband's company pension is the most valuable asset after the family home. Over one-third of marriages in the UK end in divorce, but until 1996 there was no legal obligation to split the main breadwinner's (usually the husband's) pension fairly. Instead, in England and Wales, pension rights were dealt with at the discretion of the courts. In contrast, the law in Scotland is clear. Under the Family Law (Scotland) Act 1985 'matrimonial property' specifically includes the proportion of pension and insurance rights accumulated during marriage, and in most cases these must be divided equally between the partners.

The law in England and Wales is set to change but in two distinct phases. At present, the courts should 'earmark' the spouse's share of the pension and this will be paid out at retirement, although if the spouse re-marries, the earmarked pension, which is classed as deferred maintenance, reverts to the scheme member. After 2000 (the precise date is not yet known), the court will be able to demand an immediate split of the funds, so the lower-earning spouse can invest his or her share of the pension in a personal pension fund.

This whole area is very complex and you should seek professional advice on the calculation of your pension rights, particularly if you or your spouse have built up a substantial pension.

■ SUMMARY

- **In most cases it is in your interests to join the company scheme to take advantage of the employer's contributions.**

- **Higher earners may find the salary on which benefits and contributions are based is capped.**

- **If necessary, top up your scheme benefits with additional voluntary contributions (see Chapter 24).**

- **Transfer of pension rights is a notoriously complicated exercise. Seek expert independent advice.**

- **Make sure your money purchase pension does not impose penalties if you stop or reduce contributions.**

- **There are special schemes for executives and directors: executive pension plans (EPPs) and small self-administered schemes (SSASs). These can be very tax-efficient, but they are complex – again seek expert independent advice.**

- **The same goes for divorce. Make sure your solicitor assesses the value of your spouse's pension and takes this into account in the financial settlement.**

- **Seek legal advice or help from the union, if your company is changing hands and your pension scheme is affected.**

23

■ GLOSSARY OF TERMS

Accrual rate The rate at which your company pension builds up each year.

AVCs Additional voluntary contributions (AVCs) and free-standing AVCs allow you to top up your company pension in a tax-free fund.

Earnings cap This restricts to £84,000 (in 1997/98) the salary on which certain employees' pensions and contributions are based.

Final salary (defined benefit) schemes usually base the pension on your salary at or near retirement.

Funded unapproved retirement benefit scheme (Furbs) An unapproved pension scheme used to cover earnings above the cap. **Unfunded unapproved retirement benefit schemes** are also for capped employees, but the tax treatment is less favourable.

Money purchase (defined contribution) schemes build up a fund which is used at retirement to buy an annuity. This pays an income for life.

Further information

The National Association of Pension Funds publishes a series of leaflets on company schemes and related issues. Many of these will be available free of charge from your pensions manager, but if not write to the Association for a guide to its publications: The NAPF, 12–18 Grosvenor Gardens, London SW1W 0DH. Tel: 0171-730 0585. Fax: 0171-730 2595.

HOW TO BOOST YOUR COMPANY PENSION

To get a full company pension – limited to two-thirds of your final salary – normally it is necessary to work for 40 years for the same employer. This is because most company pensions build up at the rate of 1/60 of final salary for each year of service and the maximum is 40/60 or two-thirds (restricted in the case of some higher earners).

Today, very few employees follow this career pattern. Most change jobs a few times and spend at least some time out of employment to raise a family, in further education, due to unemployment, self-employment and so on. This can have a serious impact on your pension, but it is possible to fill in the gaps in a tax-efficient way. The investments designed for this job are called 'additional voluntary contribution' (AVC) schemes, where they are run by the employer, and 'free-standing' AVCs where they are set up on an individual basis by the employee. For the sake of brevity, in this chapter and elsewhere we use the accepted acronyms AVC and FSAVC.

■ WHAT DO AVCS AND FSAVCS OFFER?

The first point to note about AVCs and FSAVCs is that they are approved pension arrangements and almost as tax-efficient as company schemes. That means:

- Full tax relief on contributions;
- Tax-free growth of the fund;
- In certain cases a tax-free cash lump sum at retirement (depending on when you started payments).

> **■ INVESTMENT SNAPSHOT**
>
> Only one in ten employees in company pension schemes retires on the full two-thirds of final salary pension permitted by the Inland Revenue.

As with the main scheme, the pension itself is taxed as income. However, only employees can pay into an AVC scheme or an FSAVC plan. The employer cannot contribute.

Historically, under approved pension arrangements, these investment or savings vehicles generally locked your money away until you retired under your main company pension scheme. However, at the time of writing the government was considering ways to allow employees to draw the AVC/FSAVC benefit earlier.

■ YOUR EMPLOYER'S AVC SCHEME

This is a company top-up scheme set up by the employer or trustees to run in conjunction with the main scheme. However, in most cases the investment and administration of the AVC scheme is sub-contracted to a third party. The majority of AVC schemes are run by the life offices and, in the case of deposit-style accounts, by the building societies. There are also a few unit trust and investment trust companies in the market.

The choice of provider is usually left to the trustees of the main pension scheme and research from actuarial consultants indicates that they don't always take this particular role very seriously. This is unfortunate because the difference in results between the best and worst company can knock about 20 per cent off the value of your fund.

The contract or agreement to make AVC payments is between the employee and the employer, so if you want to check any details you must go to the trustees or pensions manager. Before joining, therefore, you should ask them on what criteria the selection of the AVC provider was based and how often the scheme is monitored. If the trustees are doing a good job, they will have access to the latest surveys on AVC performance. If your AVC company is not in the top ten for performance and charges, you should ask why.

It is also important to check how flexible your contributions can be. Ideally you should be able to pay what you like, when you like, within Revenue limits of course. But some life offices are likely to lock you in to regular monthly contributions, and if you stop or reduce payments you might be penalised (for details of how these charges work, see Chapter 1). This is another important point to check before signing up.

How does it work?

Most AVCs operate on a 'money purchase' basis. This means that although the main scheme may provide a pension linked to salary, the AVC scheme is likely to invest the contributions to build up a fund which, at retirement, is used to buy an annuity from a life office. This annuity provides a guaranteed income for life but the value of the annuity is dependent on the investment returns achieved by the AVC fund and has no link to the value of your final salary (see Chapter 23.)

Some AVC schemes – mainly those in the public sector – offer 'added years'. This means that contributions buy extra 'years' in the main scheme where the pension is salary-linked (see Chapter 23, page 206). The advantage of added years is that the pension you buy has a known value and is likely to be inflation-linked automatically while you are in the scheme. This is because it forms part of the main pension scheme benefit which increases in line with earnings inflation through the link with the employee's final salary. Having said that, the opportunity to buy added years is becoming less common and even where it is available, the cost can be high.

FSAVCs are individual contracts between the employee and the plan provider. The employer and scheme trustee are not involved, and do not even need to know about the arrangement unless you are paying very high contributions. As with AVCs, the FSAVC market is dominated by the life assurance companies – there are almost 100 of these – although again a few unit trust and investment trust groups also offer this product.

24

■ AVC vs FSAVC

Although similar in many respects, there are some important differences between company AVCs and FSAVCs. FSAVCs are as flexible as company AVCs in terms of contributions, although in both cases, if the scheme is run by a life office, it is important to find out exactly what charges you are paying and whether there are any penalties for stopping or reducing contributions.

At first glance, there seems little merit in looking outside the company scheme for a top-up arrangement, particularly since in many cases the employer helps to offset some or all of the AVC administration costs imposed by the life assurance company. Certainly if you are paying less than £50 a month, it is unlikely to be economic to take out an FSAVC.

> If you are paying less than £50 a month, it is unlikely to be economic to take out an FSAVC – stick to your employer's AVC.

The chief selling point of FSAVCs is their investment scope. While most larger company schemes offer an investment choice under their own AVC arrangements, there are many schemes which provide a single AVC option, often a deposit-style account run by a building society, or a 'with profits' fund run by a life office. For a full description of the different types of fund, see Chapter 25, page 233.

■ HOW MUCH CAN YOU PAY IN?

Despite the fact that AVCs and FSAVCs look very different from the main company scheme, it is misleading to regard them as a totally separate investment. In fact, the only time you can pay in to an AVC or FSAVC is when you are a member of a company scheme, while the amount you can pay in is dictated by the level of your contributions to the main scheme.

Under the Revenue rules, you can pay a total of 15 per cent of your earnings into the main scheme and AVC/FSAVC combined. Since most employees pay about 5 per cent, this leaves up to 10 per cent for the top-up scheme. If you are lucky enough to belong to a 'non-contributory' scheme, where the employer is the only one paying contributions, you can in theory invest the full 15 per cent of earnings into your AVC/FSAVC.

Some employees will be caught by the 'earnings cap', introduced by the 1989 Budget, which limits total pension contributions to 15 per cent of £84,000 (for the 1997/98 tax year). The earnings cap affects employees who joined a new occupational scheme set up after 14 March 1989 and for new members who joined an existing scheme after 1 June 1989.

Finally on this point, if you accidentally exceed the benefit limits, the AVC/FSAVC provider can refund excess contributions, but a tax deduction must be paid to the Revenue.

■ HOW YOU TAKE THE PROCEEDS

The rules here are unnecessarily complicated due to the introduction of various restrictions over the years. It all depends on when you started paying contributions.

■ Where AVC contributions began before 8 April 1987, the whole fund can be taken in cash, provided the total cash taken from AVC and main scheme combined is within Revenue limits.

■ From 17 March 1987, the Revenue restricted the level of salary on which the tax-free cash calculation was based. The ceiling was £100,000, so that the maximum cash taken from AVC and main scheme pension combined was £150,000 (one and a half times the £100,000 salary limit).

■ Where contributions to the AVC scheme started on or after 8 April 1987, the whole of the fund must be taken in the form of pension, although its value is taken into consideration when the tax-free cash from the main scheme is calculated.

■ Since FSAVCs were only introduced in 1987, there is no tax-free cash option.

So far the benefits all relate to pension. It is possible, however, to use part of your AVC allowance to buy additional life assurance. As with personal pension life assurance, effectively the premiums are tax-free.

24

■ FLEXIBILITY

Do check your FSAVC plan for flexibility and portability. As with a personal pension, you should be able to stop and start contributions, and increase or decrease payments without any financial penalty. If you change jobs you should be able to make the plan paid-up (i.e., terminate payments completely) or adapt it to your new needs.

If you are in doubt over your long-term employment plans, follow the golden rule of flexibility and pay for your advice by fees or pay single premium (one-off) contributions rather than commit yourself to a regular premium plan, which can give rise to hefty penalties if you are unable to keep up contributions for some reason.

■ PEPS AS PENSION TOP-UPS

In theory, you could use any savings plan as a pension top-up, but advisers reckon the most suitable and tax-efficient alternative to AVCs is a personal equity plan. Peps are discussed in Chapters 12 to 15, so this section is restricted to an examination of how they can be used for this specific purpose.

> The tax efficiency of Peps is different, but arguably comparable with AVCs and as such they do represent a sensible method of topping up a company pension.

The tax efficiency of Peps is different, but arguably comparable with AVCs, and as such, they do represent a sensible method of topping up a company pension and dealing with the 'earnings cap'. Indeed for some investors Peps will appear more attractive than the traditional top-up pensions.

In terms of tax-efficiency, with both AVCs and Peps the fund rolls up free of income and capital gains tax, but in other respects the tax treatment differs. For example AVCs qualify for full tax relief on contributions, but most of the benefits must be used to buy an annuity to provide a taxable income. With a Pep, there is no tax relief on contributions, but the fund can be withdrawn tax-free and does not have to be used to buy an annuity. Moreover, you have free access to the Pep fund whenever you like.

Higher earners in certain company schemes and those who have personal pensions are caught by the earnings cap. These investors can use Peps to build up a retirement fund to cover earnings in excess of the cap.

■ SUMMARY

- Some company AVC schemes offer 'added years' but in most cases AVCs simply build up a fund which is used to buy an annuity to provide an income in retirement.

- AVCs usually are better value than FSAVCs because the employer pays for some or all of the charges.

- Consider the investment options carefully. Younger employees should invest in a 'with profits' or managed unit-linked or unit trust fund rather than a deposit-style account.

- If you want an FSAVC, do seek independent financial advice to make sure you get the best value in terms of charges and performance.

- Check the trustees monitor the company AVC scheme regularly to assess the performance. Ask to see details of comparisons with other companies.

- Flexibility is very important. Check you can stop or reduce contributions whenever you want to without penalty.

- If you do not want a plan which locks away your investment until retirement, consider a personal equity plan (Pep) for medium- to long-term investment.

■ GLOSSARY OF TERMS

Additional voluntary contributions are tax-efficient schemes run by employers and are used to top up your main company pension.

Free-standing AVCs are individual plans used for the same purpose.

24

25

PERSONAL PENSIONS

If you are self-employed or you work for a company which does not run a pension scheme, you need to take action because by the time you retire, the State pension will have dwindled to a pittance and may even be means-tested. The investment designed to cater for this market is called a personal pension plan.

Personal pensions do two jobs. Both you and your employer can contribute up to a combined total of 17.5 per cent of your annual earnings (more for the over-35s) and build up a fund which, at retirement is used to buy an annuity. An annuity provides a regular guaranteed (taxed) income for life.

Second, personal pensions can be used to contract out of the State earnings-related pension scheme (Serps) on an individual basis, and in return receive a rebate of National Insurance (NI) contributions to invest in a plan of your choice. Employees who are not members of a contracted-out group scheme automatically are in Serps. (For more details on Serps, see Chapter 22.)

Your 'appropriate' personal pension (the rather daft technical name for plans used to contract out of Serps) can be bolted on to your main plan, or you could choose a different pension company. Spreading risk by investing with more than one company is a good idea in theory, but seek advice because the charges may outweigh the benefits if your contributions are small.

Like company pension schemes, personal plans are a very tax-efficient way of saving for retirement:

- contributions qualify for full tax relief
- the pension fund grows free of tax
- up to 25 per cent of the 'top-up' pension fund at retirement can be taken as tax-free cash. The rest of the fund must be used to purchase an annuity.

■ INVESTMENT SNAPSHOT

According to a leading firm of actuarial consultants there will only be about one dozen providers of personal pensions by the year 2000. At present, there are between 90 and 100.

Today over 5 million people have personal pensions, but the apparent success of the product has been marred by a major financial scandal over the mass mis-selling of plans in inappropriate cases, usually because the adviser or salesman stood to gain a high commission from the product

There is absolutely nothing wrong with the concept of personal pensions. All the problems have been a result of greedy salesmen, taking huge commissions, and greedy providers, imposing punitive, inflexible charges.

provider. This is discussed later in this chapter (see page 237). However, the important point to bear in mind is that there is absolutely nothing wrong with the concept of personal pensions. All the problems have been a result of greedy salesmen taking huge commissions, and greedy providers imposing punitive, inflexible charges. With care you can avoid both.

■ HOW TO GET THE BEST VALUE

With the help of a good independent financial adviser you should be able to narrow down your choice of pension companies by considering the following:

■ the financial strength of the provider: it is important to be confident your pension company can survive – this very competitive market is in the throes of merger mania

■ the performance track record, with the emphasis on consistency over the long-term and stability of staff

■ the level of charges deducted throughout the investment period

■ the flexibility of the contract, for example, there should be no penalties for reducing and stopping contributions, transferring the fund and early retirement.

25

■ CONTRACTING OUT OF SERPS

Employees who do not have access to an occupational scheme and employees whose company scheme is not itself contracted out of Serps need to decide whether they will get better value from staying in Serps or opting out and investing the rebate of National Insurance contributions the Department of Social Security pays. (The self-employed do not pay into Serps, and so cannot take out an appropriate personal pension.)

Unfortunately the future of Serps is not assured and the chances are it will be gradually phased out. However, political uncertainty is an unreliable factor on which to base decisions. All you can do is consider the facts as they are now and assume the government will pay the full value of the Serps pension you have earned if and when it closes the scheme.

Comparing the value of what your Serps benefits would be worth with the value of what you might get if you invest the rebate is a job for actuaries, not mere mortals. From April 1997, the government is re-calculating the rebates, so that they reflect what Serps would be worth at any age. This means that age is no longer a reason for opting out or going back (in theory anyway). Assuming you have no political bias on the issue, probably the main factor to consider is your level of earnings. If you earn less than £15,000 a year (some insurance companies suggest a much lower pivotal salary) you probably should stay in Serps, because your rebate will be worth about £600 or less and you will find that most providers' charges will render this level of single premium uneconomic, unless you are making substantial top-up payments yourself.

The other point to remember is that the regulators have issued guidance to pension companies recommending that employees should opt out only if it is sensible to do so for a minimum of three years. This is for the same reason mentioned above – it simply isn't worth opting out for one year and leaving £600 with a life office for the next 20 before you retire.

For the actuarially minded, the rebate is calculated as a percentage of an employee's 'band earnings' – that is, earnings between the lower and upper threshold for NI contributions. For the 1997/98 tax year the NI thresholds are £3,224 and £24,180 per annum, giving band earnings of just under £21,000. From April 1997, the fully age-related rebates start as low as 3.4 per cent of band earnings at age 16 and rising in stages to 9 per cent at age 46. So, if you are earning £24,180 or more the maximum rebate ranges from about £700 at age 16 to about £1,900 at age 46 or older.

The rebate is sent by the DSS direct to your personal pension provider after the end of the tax year to which it relates. It is always worth checking that your provider receives this promptly since a delay in investment will reduce the returns.

What can you buy with your fund?

The fund built up from the NI rebates is known as 'protected rights' – another daft name because the fund's value is not protected or guaranteed in any way: what you get depends on how well it is invested.

There are certain restrictions on what you can do with the fund at retirement. It cannot be used to provide tax-free cash, and the pension must be taken at the same age as the State pension, currently 65 for men and 60 for women (rising to 65 by the year 2020). The annuity purchased with the fund must provide for a spouse's pension worth 50 per cent of the personal pension planholder's and the annuity payments must increase by 3 per cent per annum. There are no restrictions on the annuity you purchase with your top-up plan.

■ TOP-UP PERSONAL PENSIONS

In addition to the rebate, you can and should contribute a significant proportion of your earnings into a personal pension since the rebate plan by itself will not provide an adequate pension. Employees base their contributions on what the Inland Revenue calls 'net relevant earnings', which are roughly equivalent to annual earnings from any self-employed activities (after deducting losses and certain business charges on income) or from employment where either there is no company pension scheme or you have chosen not to join the company pension scheme.

25

The annual contribution limits are shown in Table 25.1 (but see *High earners* below):

Table 25.1 Annual contribution limits for top-up personal pensions

Age	% net relevant earnings*
Up to 35	17.5
36–45	20
46–50	25
51–55	30
56–60	35
61-74	40

* All personal pension contributions (but not the emerging pension itself) are subject to the earnings cap which limits the amount of salary that can be used for pension purposes to £84,000 for the 1997/98 tax year.

You can run more than one top-up personal pension plan provided total contributions fall within these limits – but do consider the impact of start-up charges. However, you can only have one appropriate plan for each tax year.

Make sure that you are paying in a sensible amount each year – broadly between 6 and 16.5 per cent, depending on age. Your adviser should be able to help you assess the right contribution level. This will depend on how much pension you need and

> **Don't forget, employers can contribute to an individual employee's plan, although there is no legal requirement for them to do so.**

whether you have other sources of income. (See Table 23.1 on page 214 which shows how much you must pay in if you want to have a pension comparable to that available under a company final salary scheme.)

Don't forget – employers can contribute to an individual employee's plan, although there is no legal requirement for them to do so.

High earners

High earners with personal pensions are restricted by the 'earnings cap', introduced in the 1989 budget, which limits the amount of salary that can be taken into consideration for contributions.

For the 1997/98 tax year, the cap is £84,000 which means that the maximum contribution for an employee aged under 35 is 17.5 per cent of the cap – £12,330. In practice, it is hard to see how this would act as a restriction for younger people who tend to be financially stretched by family commitments and mortgage repayments. Older employees, however, often pay higher contributions if they have made little provision earlier in life.

Making extra large contributions

A special provision exists for employees and the self-employed who have unused tax relief in previous years. Under the Inland Revenue's 'carry-back' and 'carry-forward' rules it is possible to mop up unused relief for up to seven previous tax years. This is a complex exercise and should be discussed with your accountant or a pensions adviser with tax expertise.

■ LIFE ASSURANCE

It is also possible to use up to 5 per cent of the contribution limit to pay for life assurance, which effectively gives you tax relief on the premiums. Life assurance rates vary considerably, so do shop around. If your pension provider's terms are expensive, it might be cheaper to buy it elsewhere.

■ RETIREMENT ANNUITIES

25

Many people still have a retirement annuity plan – the predecessor to the personal pension. After July 1988 sales of these contracts stopped, but existing policyholders can continue to contribute to existing plans.

The contribution and benefit rules for retirement annuities differ slightly. Retirement annuity contribution limits are lower in terms of percentages than for personal pensions, but the total salary on which these contributions are based is not subject to the earnings cap. The limits are shown in Table 25.2.

Table 25.2 Limits for retirement annunity contributions

Age	% net relevant earnings
Up to age 50	17.5
51–55	20
56–60	22.5
61–74	27.5

Depending on your age at retirement and the prevailing annuity rates, it may be possible to take more than 25 per cent of the retirement annuity fund as tax-free cash, since the calculation is not a straight percentage of the fund. The other main difference between the two arrangements is that you cannot contract out of Serps with one of these older contracts – you must use an appropriate personal pension.

Finally on the older plans, it is possible to contribute to both types of plans at the same time, but you have to take care to keep within the Revenue's maximum contribution rules.

■ WHO SELLS PERSONAL PENSIONS?

It seems just about every financial institution (certainly over 90 companies at the last count) is in this market, which makes the choice all the more difficult. The market is dominated by the life offices, but an increasing number of unit trust and investment trust groups also offer plans and these are certainly worth considering. Most banks and building societies tend to sell the plans run by their own life office or have an arrangement with a separate life office to sell exclusively that company's plans. As in the Peps market, some of the big retail operations, like M&S and Virgin, also sell pensions.

There are several investment options to consider – unit-linked, unit trust, investment trust, conventional 'with profits', unitised 'with profits' and guaranteed funds. Before you get bogged down with the different options, remember that the main consideration is the underlying asset mix. Advisers tend to recommend that younger people should invest virtually 100 per cent in equities, because these offer the best long-term growth prospects. As you get older and closer to retirement, you need to switch gradually into safer assets such as bonds and gilts and by the time you are within a few years of retirement you should probably be entirely in cash (deposits) and gilts.

Having said that, if you intend to transfer to an 'income-drawdown' plan at retirement, which allows you to keep your fund fully invested, you may prefer to maintain a high exposure to equities. This new retirement investment option is discussed on page 248.

■ CHARGES

Charges are discussed in Chapter 1. Do remember, if your adviser is paid a commission, ask for your contributions to be classed as a series of single premiums or as 'recurring single premiums'. This means that each premium relates only to that particular payment so there are no heavy upfront deductions to cover commission costs for the full investment period. Over a 25-year plan, there would be little difference in total commission paid through regular and single premium plans. Where single premiums score is in flexibility. If you stop payments there are no early termination penalties.

■ WHICH FUND?

Unit-linked plans

Unit-linked plans are sold by life offices. Under this arrangement, your contributions buy units in a fund and the value of these units fluctuates in line with the market value of the underlying assets. Funds range from low-risk deposit, index-linked and gilt, to medium-risk UK and international equity funds, to higher-risk emerging markets funds. Companies make much of their often huge fund range, but in practice most people go for the managed fund which invests in a range of the provider's other main funds and in this way offers a bal-

25

anced spread of investments. Some companies offer investment links to top institutional managers. This is an excellent feature, but make sure the charges do not outweigh the potentially higher returns.

Charges vary depending on the type of fund, but on average you can expect to pay an initial charge of about 5 per cent and an annual management charge of about 0.75 per cent to 1 per cent per annum (more – often double – if you use the plan to gain access to an external manager). On top of this, you may pay monthly policy charges. Sales commission, where applicable, will be included in the initial and annual charges.

Unit trust plans

Unit trust plans offer a similar investment choice to unit-linked plans, and again the value of your units will fluctuate in line with the performance of the underlying assets (see Chapter 11). The choice of unit trust personal pensions was limited to about half a dozen at the time of writing, but more plans are expected to be launched over the next few years. Charges are similar to unit-linked funds, although the annual management charge may be higher. However, you can keep the bill down if you choose one of the index-tracking funds which generally offer access to a wide spread of equities at low cost.

Investment trust plans

Over the past few years, a handful of investment trust personal pensions have been launched (see Chapter 11). An investment trust is not a trust as such, but is a British company, listed on the UK Stock Exchange, which invests in the shares of other companies in the UK and overseas. It has a fixed number of shares, and most prices are published daily in the *Financial Times*.

The investment trust's share price is affected by the value of the company's underlying assets – as is the case with unit-linked and unit trust funds. However, it is also affected by the supply and demand for shares. This means that the share price does not necessarily reflect the actual value of the underlying assets. If the share price is lower than the value of the underlying assets, the difference is known as the discount. If it is higher, the difference is known as the premium. Buying at a discount is a good thing, buying at a premium is generally considered to be a bad thing. Investment trusts can also borrow money to invest – an activity known as gearing.

As a broad rule of thumb, investment trusts offer additional opportunities for active investors but they are also potentially more volatile. Charges tend to be lower than for unit trusts (with the exception of index trackers), particularly on some of the larger older investment trusts.

'With profits' plans

Until recently, these worthy but ridiculously complicated funds formed the backbone of the individual pensions market because they provided a reasonable degree of security together with good potential for long-term capital growth.

The mystical path to understanding the 'with profits' concept is littered with jargon. The 'with profits' fund (which in fact is the fund of the life office itself) invests mainly in UK and international equities, gilts and fixed-interest securities and property. Under the original 'with profits' contract (referred to by life offices as the 'traditional' or 'conventional' contract) the investor is guaranteed a substantial sum at the end of the investment period (known as the 'maturity' date) to which annual or 'reversionary' bonuses are added. The important point is that, rather like interest on a building society account, these bonuses are guaranteed and once allocated cannot be taken away.

The annual bonuses are 'smoothed' in order to provide a relatively consistent return. To do this, the life office holds back some of the profits in good years to boost returns in lean years. In this way, the plans tend to avoid the volatility associated with unit-linked and unit trust plans. On top of this there is a final or 'terminal' bonus which is discretionary, and tends to reflect actual performance over the past 12 months.

There are no explicit charges on a 'with profits' plan apart from a monthly policy fee. This does not mean that you don't pay charges, it simply means that you can't work out how they are calculated.

25

Generally the charges are deducted from the fund itself before the bonuses are declared – again rather like a building society account where charges are deducted before the interest rate is declared. Fortunately, now that companies must disclose in full the impact of their charges on your investment, it is possible to compare 'with profits' fund charges with other types of personal pensions.

Unitised 'with profits' plans

Unitised 'with profits' plans are supposed to occupy the middle ground between the conventional 'with profits' structure and unit-linked funds. One advantage of this is that investors with unit-linked plans can more easily switch into the lower-risk unitised 'with profits' fund – a common strategy in the run up to retirement when you want to consolidate gains and reduce risk.

Unfortunately unitised plans are, if anything, even more complicated than their conventional predecessors. Under unitised contracts, there is no guaranteed sum assured and so the provider does not have to set aside such large reserves to meet its obligations. Furthermore, the bonuses are declared in a very different format from the traditional contract. Most providers increase the value of the unit price, but a minority maintain a fixed unit price, and add bonuses through the allocation of extra units. Within these two systems, there is a host of variations on the way profit is distributed.

Quite a few providers do not offer a guaranteed minimum bonus at all. As with the traditional contract, unitised funds also apply a final bonus.

Unitisation also heralded the arrival of the controversial 'market value adjuster' (MVA). These adjusters are used as a safety net for life offices in the event of a mass exodus of clients following a drop in the markets. Effectively, the MVA allows a company to reduce the value of units whenever it likes and by however much it wants. In this respect, the guaranteed nature of the annual bonuses is not rock solid after all.

Charges are similar to unit-linked plans.

Guaranteed equity funds

If you want exposure to equities, but can't handle the white-knuckle ride of the stockmarkets, you might consider one of the relatively new 'guaranteed' funds which limit your exposure to falls in the stock market and provide a percentage of the gains.

Guaranteed equity funds are strange beasts, and in fact rarely invest in equities, but instead hold mainly cash and gilts. The fund manager buys derivatives to guarantee a certain rise in the index and to limit the percentage of any fall in prices. Of course the guarantee does not come free. In effect, what you lose is the equivalent of the stock market dividend yield. When you consider the fact that over a ten-year period, the yield on the FT-SE 100 index accounts for roughly half of the total return, its absence seems a high price to pay.

However, experts argue that you could be compensated for the loss of yield by the fact that the fund limits your exposure to any falls in the index, so you gain from potentially greater capital growth than unprotected investors. This is particularly relevant in volatile market conditions.

Charges are higher than for most of the other funds mentioned here – largely because of the cost of the derivatives which provide the guarantee.

Anything to do with derivatives is bound to be complicated, and the jury is still out on whether these funds really do what they are supposed to do. The old investment adage 'if you don't understand it, don't invest in it' probably applies here, although there may be a strong argument in favour of using these funds for income drawdown plans, where you keep your pension fund fully invested in retirement (see page 248).

25

■ THE MIS-SELLING SCANDAL

Personal pension plans can be used to accept a transfer value from a preserved company pension. This is a complex area and the subject of considerable controversy since the mass mis-selling of plans for this purpose in the late 1980s.

In December 1993, the Securities and Investments Board (SIB), the chief regulator for financial services, revealed that most personal pension sales since 1988 were based on poor advice and that employees would have been better off with their company pension scheme benefits, many of which are guaranteed.

Between one-quarter and one-half of the employees who transferred to personal plans came from local government and the public sector, which run some of the best pension schemes in the country. Estimates of the total bill for compensation run as high as £2.5bn, with average individual settlements of £8,000 to £10,000.

The motivation behind the mis-selling spree was simple greed. Insurance companies raked off huge profits to cover their administration and investment management costs. They also paid substantial commissions to sales representatives and independent advisers. All of which came out of the victims' pension funds.

In November 1996, the SIB decided to ditch the unworkable system it introduced in 1993 to identify and compensate victims. The new campaign, which was started in Spring 1997, will require almost all of the 570,000 investors identified to complete a detailed questionnaire about their company and personal pensions – information those selling the personal plans have largely failed to obtain. Investors who do not respond will be struck off the list and will not qualify for compensation.

Action plan

If you think you might qualify for compensation, contact the PIA Pensions Unit which has a dedicated investors' helpline (see Contact numbers at the end of this chapter) to deal with any queries involving the review process. The regulators identified three broad groups of potential victims:

■ Pension transfers – employees who transferred company pension benefits to a personal plan.

■ Opt-outs – employees who left a company scheme to take out a personal plan.

■ Non-joiners – employees who did not join a company scheme because they were sold a personal pension.

You might get help from your trade union. Several unions, particularly those in the public sector, are co-ordinating claims and court actions. You should also order a copy of the new SIB fact sheet.

It is important to re-join your company scheme, if you haven't already done so. However, if you do this, you cannot continue your personal plan, so check with your pension company if it will impose any early termination penalties. Under the circumstances you have a right to demand these should be waived. Seek independent advice if in doubt.

Don't forget, it is essential that you respond to the new questionnaire. If you bought your plan through an independent financial adviser, you have to be particularly careful to protect your rights. To comply with their professional indemnity insurance rules, advisers must write to clients to ask if they want their case to be analysed. If the client does not reply, the investigation simply will not take place.

How will the compensation be paid?

The regulators said that the aim of the review is 'to put investors back in the position in which they would have been if they had not taken out a personal pension'. The best outcome by far is to be fully re-instated in your pension scheme for the opt-out period. In this case the pension company will pay a lump sum, which will include the value of your personal pension, to your former pension scheme. Mind you, the SIB has no powers to force company schemes to accept re-instatement and where this is not possible – for example in the case of transfers of former benefits where you are no longer employed by that company – you are likely to be offered a guaranteed annuity which will replace lost benefits at retirement.

A third alternative is a top-up to your personal pension which, given the lack of guarantees, is not really satisfactory. Moreover, if you were sold a plan that combines high charges with poor performance, putting in more money only adds insult to injury. In this case you may wish to contest the offer or at least insist the money is

25

paid into a plan with a more reputable company. Always seek expert advice.

Table 25.3 The companies the SIB will be watching closely

Name of company	Number of priority cases	Assessments completed[1]
Prudential	41,439	10
Co-operative Insurance	36,931	1,324
Pearl Assurance	36,406	1,375
Legal & General	24,506	543
TSB Life	22,906	17
Britannic Assurance	19,222	3
Sun Life of Canada	16,693	419
Hogg Robinson Fin. Servs	13,716	1
Barclays Life	13,130	1,030
Abbey Life	12,981	8
Allied Dunbar	11,761	1,424
National Westminster	10,720	179
Sedgwick Noble Lowndes	9,787	10
Equitable Life	9,561	1,654
Lincoln Assurance	9,506	1
Royal London	8,285	362
Sun Alliance	8,249	135
Guardian Pensions Mgt[2]	7,968	237
GAN Life & Pensions	6,998	98
Windsor Life	6,885	72
United Friendly Life Assurance	6,289	54
Colonial Mutual	5,813	14
London & Manchester	5,635	22
Norwich Union	5,590	53
Refuge Assurance	5,114	62
Lloyds Bank[3]	5,028	48
Total	361,119	9,155

Note: This list was leaked from the PIA and first appeared in the *Independent* on 30 October 1996. Neither the PIA nor the SIB have denied that the information was correct.

[1] This is the number of cases actually completed. The figures do not reflect the fact that many of these organisations would also have a considerable number of cases under investigation.
[2] Guardian to review all non-priority cases.
[3] Not including Black Horse Financial Services.

If all else fails, you could ask the Personal Investments Authority Ombudsman for help (a free service) or even take the case to court. Do bear in mind that litigation is very expensive, and should be regarded as a last resort.

■ PERSONAL PENSION MORTGAGES

It is possible to arrange to pay off your interest-only mortgage through a personal pension plan (see Chapter 20), making use of the tax-free cash on retirement to repay the outstanding capital. This may be worth considering if you do not already pay maximum contributions, because you effectively get tax relief on your mortgage repayment investment vehicle.

However, do be careful not to undermine your pension at retirement, and make sure you are protected for periods of unemployment when you cannot continue pension payments. Finally, flexibility is essential. You need to be able to stop your personal pension without penalty if you change jobs and want to join your new employer's company scheme.

■ SELF-INVESTED PERSONAL PENSIONS

Self-invested personal pensions follow the same basic rules as standard personal pensions, but in addition allow you to exercise much greater control over your investments. Like self-select personal equity plans (Peps), the appeal of the SIPP lies in the product's ability to 'unbundle' the two key features of modern pension plans, namely, the administration and the investment. What generally happens is that the administration is carried out by a specialist life office, and you either tackle the investment yourself or appoint an investment manager (a stockbroker, for example) to construct and run the portfolio for you. If you are unhappy with the performance you can change the manager without having to upset the underlying administration arrangements.

SIPPs can also be used by partnerships. Schedule D taxpayers are excluded from the company-sponsored small self-administered schemes but they can use a SIPP with virtually the same effect and,

25

if they pool their contributions and funds, they can achieve beneficial economies of scale.

Investment choice

The choice of investments is very wide and includes the following:

- stocks and shares (e.g., equities, gilts, debentures) quoted on the UK Stock Exchange and including securities on the Alternative Investment Market
- stocks and shares traded on a recognised overseas exchange
- unit trusts and investment trusts
- insurance-company-managed funds and unit-linked funds
- deposit accounts
- commercial property.

A SIPP fund cannot purchase a firm's existing business premises from the partnership, but it can buy new offices into which the partnership can move, provided the property is leased back on a commercial basis. You can also use your SIPP fund to borrow on the strength of its assets to help with property purchase. However, the SIPP cannot lend part of the pension fund back to you, the investor.

You can also invest in a 'hybrid' SIPP. Under a hybrid, it is necessary to pay a minimum contribution each year to the life office, which also provides the administration, while any contributions above this minimum can be invested however you wish under the full SIPP rules. Hybrids might prove attractive and cost-effective where lower contributions are paid, but once total annual contributions exceed, say, £10,000, then a pure SIPP is likely to provide the best value for money as well as offering maximum investment control.

■ GROUP PERSONAL PENSIONS

Group personal pensions are becoming very popular, particularly among companies which do not want the expense and administrative hassles of a final salary pension scheme. The providers are the same as for individual schemes – mainly the life offices, but also a few unit trust and investment trust groups as well. More recently, some of the heavyweight institutional fund managers have moved into this market – a welcome development, particularly where they bring with them a first-rate performance track record.

If your employer offers a group personal pension, see the section on group money purchase schemes which starts on page 212. This will help you decide whether the terms are flexible and offer good value for money. In particular, you should check the amount your employer is prepared to pay on your behalf, and whether there are any penalties if you reduce or stop your own contributions when you change jobs.

At their most basic, group personal pensions are no more than a collection of individual plans. However the more sophisticated schemes, usually negotiated by a consultant, make full use of the potential for economies of scale to reduce administration and investment charges. More generous plans feature employer contributions, death benefits and disability benefits. Whether your group plan is generous or not will depend on how much your employer is prepared to pay.

Ideally, your employer will arrange the group personal pension on a 'nil commission' basis. This means that the commission costs are stripped out and your employer's adviser is paid a fee. The main advantage of this system is a clear, flexible charging structure – you can see exactly what you are paying, and if you change the amount of contribution or stop paying altogether there is no penalty. With any luck, your employer may cover the charges and not pass them on to scheme members.

■ SUMMARY

■ **Don't buy a top-up personal pension if you have access to a good company pension scheme. Company pensions generally represent better value for money, and usually provide good death and disability benefits as well.**

■ **If there is no company scheme invest in a personal pension and try to get your employer to contribute as well.**

■ **It may be worthwhile opting out of Serps with an 'appropriate' personal pension if you earn over £15,000 a year**

25

■ **Independent financial advice is essential (see Chapter 1). Check the performance, charges and flexibility of the plan as well as the company's financial strength.**

■ GLOSSARY OF TERMS

Appropriate personal pensions are used to accept the rebate of National Insurance contributions if you contract out of Serps.

Group personal pensions are a type of company scheme but in fact represent a series of individual plans.

Guaranteed funds use derivatives to limit your exposure to stock market volatility.

Income drawdown plans allow you to keep your personal pension fund fully invested in retirement up to age 75, while drawing a regular income.

Investment trust plans offer greater potential for the active investor but are potentially more volatile than unit-linked and unit trust plans.

Net relevant earnings are broadly equivalent to annual earnings from any self-employed activities (after deducting losses and certain business charges on income).

Market value adjuster (MVA). These adjusters are used as a safety net for life offices in the event of a mass exodus of clients following a drop in the markets. Effectively the MVA allows a company to reduce the value of units whenever it likes and by however much it wants.

Retirement annuity plans – the predecessor to the personal pension. After July 1988 sales of these contracts stopped but existing policyholders can continue to contribute to existing plans.

Self-invested personal pensions allow you to separate the administration and investment management so you can change the manager with the expense of switching the whole plan.

Unit-linked personal plans are sold by life offices. Your contributions buy units in a fund and the value of these units fluctuates in line with the market value of the underlying assets.

Unit trust personal plans are similar to unit-linked plans. Charges are clearer but tend to be slightly higher.

'**With profits**' plans invest in a mix of all asset classes and each year award a bonus or interest rate which, once added to your account, cannot be taken away. There are other bonuses – for example a discretionary final bonus at retirement. **Unitised** with profits invest in the 'with profits' fund but on a unitised basis – so your contributions buy units.

Contact numbers for pension transfer victims

■ The PIA Pensions Unit investors' helpline is 0171-417 7001.

■ For a copy of the fact sheet write to HMSO/SIB Distribution, Sovereign Press, PO Box 10971, London SE17 3ZG. Print your name and address and enclose a stamped addressed envelope.

■ The PIA Ombudsman: 0171-216 0016.

Further information

For full details on how to select a personal pension plan and the surveys which monitor performance and charges, see Chapter 1. For advice on how to check out a group personal pension, see page 242.

25

HOW TO BUY YOUR RETIREMENT INCOME

An annuity provides a guaranteed income for life in return for a lump sum investment. If you have a money purchase (defined contribution) pension arrangement, where the level of your pension is not linked to your salary, at retirement you can usually take a hefty chunk as tax-free cash, but the rest must be used to buy an annuity to provide your retirement income.

> The annuity 'rate' – or the level of regular income you secure in return for your lump sum – will depend on several important factors, including your life expectancy and interest rates.

Annuities are sold by insurance companies. The annuity 'rate' – or the level of regular income you secure in return for your lump sum – will depend on several important factors including your life expectancy and interest rates. If you are in ill health, you may be able to get a better rate if the insurance company thinks your life expectancy is less than the average for your age.

Most annuities offer a fixed income, but a handful offer an investment link to a 'with profits' or unit-linked fund, so here the level of income will also be determined by how well your fund performs.

■ INDEPENDENT ADVICE ESSENTIAL

You are under no obligation to buy your annuity from the company with which you have your pension arrangement. The 'open market option' allows you to take the proceeds of your pension fund away from the plan provider and to buy your annuity elsewhere. The top names in personal pensions are quite different from the top names in annuities, so it pays to shop around. However, do take into consider-

■ **INVESTMENT SNAPSHOT**

Women tend to live longer than men, so usually receive a lower income in return for the same level of investment.

ation any penalties or loyalty bonuses that affect your pension fund if you move it away from your original company.

■ ANNUITY OPTIONS

The DSS applies certain rules to the type of annuity you must buy with the fund you build up from your rebates of National Insurance contributions (see page 229). But with the rest of the fund, there are no specific rules. There are, however, several useful features which are sold as optional extras in addition to the basic annuity. Some of these may be essential,

The top names in personal pensions are quite different from the top names in annuities so it pays to shop around.

depending on your circumstances but they do reduce the annuity rate, so consider your priorities carefully.

- **Guaranteed annuities** guarantee to make payments for five years, and if you die during this period your beneficiaries will receive the outstanding amount.

- **Joint life basis** means that a full or reduced pension will be paid to your spouse if you die.

- **Escalating annuities** rise fully in line with retail price inflation or at a fixed rate each year – typically 3 per cent, or 5 per cent. Given you are likely to be retired for 20 years or more, some form of inflation-proofing is essential, but the cost is rather prohibitive. A 5 per cent annual increase, for example, would reduce the initial annuity rate by about one-third. If this sounds pricey, bear in mind that the purchasing power of £100 will be worth just £64 after 15 years of inflation at 3 per cent, and £48 if the inflation rate is 5 per cent. Several companies offer annuities linked to retail prices for about the same price as the 5 per cent fixed rate of inflation-proofing.

26

■ GUARANTEED BUT INFLEXIBLE

Annuities do have serious drawbacks which 'phased retirement' and 'income drawdown' plans aim to overcome. With a conventional annuity, once you hand over your money, you cannot change your mind about the choice of insurance company or the special features selected. In most cases your money is gone for good, even if you die shortly afterwards. As mentioned above, you can protect your fund – usually for five years – but this costs extra.

If you are ready to buy and are prepared to shop around through a specialist annuity adviser, you are already well on your way towards getting the best deal. The difference between the best and worst annuity rates at any given time can be as much as 20 per cent.

■ PHASED RETIREMENT

Until 1996, the main alternative to a conventional annuity was phased retirement where you generate your required annual income by withdrawing only part of your pension fund, leaving the remaining fund invested. The chunk withdrawn is used to provide an element of tax-free cash and the rest is used to buy an annuity. The pattern is repeated each year.

Phased retirement is not suitable for investors who want to use their tax-free cash for a capital project, because in the plan this is used instead to make up part of the income. However, if you don't need the lump sum, phased retirement may be suitable. It also offers full tax-free cash to your beneficiaries on death (avoiding inheritance tax), and can be easier to change your investment manager than under the newer income drawdown plans, where this is only possible through the self-invested version.

■ INCOME DRAWDOWN PLANS

The other important variable is timing – and this is where income drawdown plans can offer a welcome degree of flexibility compared with conventional annuities. Moreover, with income drawdown, you take control of both the timing and the amount of your income payments and at the same time keep your fund fully invested in a tax-free environment.

Of course, there is a catch. Income drawdown plans are marketed as the ultimate in flexible retirement planning, and as any seasoned financial adviser will tell you, 'flexible', in investment terms usually is synonymous with 'complicated' and 'risky'.

Taking a risk while you are young may be acceptable, but it poses serious problems in retirement when you have no earnings to fall back on if your savings are decimated by poor investment returns, high sales commissions and substantial running costs. So, before you take the plunge, make sure you understand the downside of income drawdown as well as the potential benefits.

Under income drawdown plans, you can still take your tax-free cash and then draw your taxable income direct from your fund. The income level is flexible, although it must fall between a minimum and maximum set by the Inland Revenue, based broadly on the annuity rate you would otherwise have secured with your fund at retirement. Within the pension fund, your investments continue to grow free of income and capital gains tax. If you die, your fund goes to your dependants, not the insurance company, so there are important tax and financial planning benefits as well. By age 75 at the latest, you must convert your fund to an annuity.

So far the odds in favour of income drawdown look good. However, the main risk with these plans is that, whereas with conventional annuities your pension income is guaranteed, with income withdrawal it is not.

You might think that you could make your position more secure by investing in something fairly safe – gilts and deposits for example. However, in most cases this would defeat the object of the exercise, which is to generate a return that will match or improve the income you would have received from an annuity. Annuity rates are based on medium- and long-dated gilts, which at the time of writing were yielding about 8.5 per cent per annum. So there is your absolute minimum target return, on top of which you must allow for investment and administration costs which will cost at least 1.5 per cent a year.

26

Mortality drag

There is also a rather important but obscure factor called 'mortality drag'. Basically, annuities work like an insurance pool – those who live get a cross-subsidy from those who die. Under income withdrawal, you get your money back if you die, but you lose this cross-subsidy, which experts reckon is worth about 1.5 to 2 per cent a year. In total therefore, you are looking for returns of about 12 per cent minimum, and the only sensible way to achieve this is to invest in an equity fund.

And therein lies the rub. If markets fall, your fund will plummet and take your retirement income with it. Clearly, if the fund was your only source of pension, you could end up in deep trouble. The only way out would be to invest in even higher-risk funds, and then the white-knuckle ride starts to get really scary.

Advisers recommend that you should not consider these plans unless you have substantial funds. This means a minimum of £100,000 in your pension pot, and plenty of other assets to support you in retirement if your pension fund falls in value. If you don't have other assets, then you probably shouldn't consider income drawdown, unless your pension fund is worth at least £200,000 to £250,000.

You also need good-quality advice. This is a very technical area, so your adviser must have expert back-up to cover all the pensions, investment and taxation aspects.

How to choose

There are several ways of setting up an income drawdown plan. You can buy an insurance company package that combines administration and investment management. A second option, widely favoured by advisers, is to separate these two features and run the fund yourself or appoint an investment manager to do the job for you (rather like a self-invested personal pension – see page 241). A third option is to go for a 'guaranteed' fund which limits the downside of stockmarket risk – but at a price (see below).

Buying from an insurance company

The first route – buying an insurance company package – is attractive from the point of view of simplicity. However, once you take your tax-free cash and start to withdraw an income, you cannot transfer your fund to another provider. If your plan restricts you to the internal funds of just one insurer you are stuck with that company – and its investment performance – until you buy your annuity. Hardly prudent, given the fact that you could be investing for 15 to 20 years. Packaged products are sold by about 20 life offices, although several also offer a choice of external fund management links.

Complete flexibility

Where you want complete flexibility over the investment management, and your fund size justifies the cost, you should consider the 'self-invested' route which separates the administration and investment management. This means you can run the fund yourself or appoint an investment manager to do the job for you. If you are unhappy with the performance, you can change your manager while leaving the administration intact. Under this type of plan, you can invest in a very wide range of funds and asset classes, including collective funds (investment trusts, unit trusts and insurance company funds), direct equities, bonds and commercial property.

The administration normally would be carried out by an insurance company although some financial institutions run their own plans and may also offer a discretionary investment management service, although this is not obligatory.

Guaranteed funds

Another option you might consider is a 'guaranteed' fund which limits your exposure to falls in the stockmarket and provides a percentage of the gains. This type of fund may be attractive to retired investors who need exposure to equity markets, but who can't afford to take the risks. (For further details on guaranteed funds, see page 237).

26

Finally, remember that the hallmark of good investment planning is knowing in advance when to get out. Under income withdrawal, by age 75 at the latest you must buy your annuity. To identify the best time to make your purchase, you need to keep an eye on equity prices, which affect your fund size, and on gilt prices, which determine the level of income your annuity will provide. Generally, when equity prices go up, gilt prices also rise. This means gilt yields fall taking annuity rates with them.

So, what you want is a rise in equity prices and a fall in gilt prices – but it rarely works out that way. Clearly, trying to spot the right conjunction of equity and gilt movements is rather like astrology and best left to the experts.

Income drawdown plan rules

If you have a personal pension or similar plan, at retirement you can take part of the fund (typically one-quarter) as tax-free cash and use the rest to buy an annuity. If you choose to defer the annuity purchase using a new income drawdown plan, the following rules apply:

■ You can buy the plan from age 50, but must convert the fund to an annuity by age 75.

■ You cannot make further pension contributions to the plan once it is in operation.

■ During the deferment period, investment income and capital gains continue to roll up tax-free.

■ The income you draw must fall between a minimum and maximum set by the Inland Revenue and be based on the annuity rate you would have purchased had you converted your fund at retirement.

■ Your plan must be reviewed every three years to ensure the income level you are drawing is still appropriate. If the fund has fallen too much, you must convert to an annuity immediately.

■ If you die before age 75, there are three options:
   i)   Your spouse can use the fund to buy an annuity.
   ii) Your spouse can continue to draw an income but must convert the fund to an annuity by the time you would have reached 75.
   iii) The fund can be taken as cash (less a 35 per cent tax charge).

Conclusion and warning

Conventional annuities offer a rock-solid guarantee and represent the best option for those who will depend solely or mainly on this income. Shopping around for the best conventional annuity rate certainly is essential. But think very carefully before you commit yourself to an income drawdown plan – or similar arrangement – which exposes your retirement fund to stock market risks.

■ PURCHASED LIFE ANNUITIES

Most people come across annuities when they retire and must buy a compulsory annuity with the proceeds of their pension fund. There is, however, a second type, known as a 'purchased life' or 'voluntary' annuity, which anyone can buy with their spare capital. These were discussed in Chapter 10 on page 96.

■ SUMMARY

- **Shop around – the best rates on the market at any given time can be 25 per cent more than the worst.**

- **Check if your pension company applies any penalties if you buy elsewhere or adds any loyalty bonuses if you stay put. Take these into consideration when shopping around.**

- **Do seek expert advice. Your adviser should specialise in annuities, and have the necessary software to check all the products available.**

- **Consider carefully which features you need – for example a spouse's pension and inflation-proofing.**

- **Think carefully before opting for an investment-linked annuity since your income is not guaranteed, and will fluctuate in line with investment returns.**

- **Do consider income drawdown, but only if you have a substantial fund and other sources of income. You must also feel comfortable with the equity market risks involved.**

26

■ GLOSSARY OF TERMS

Annuities provide an income for life in return for a lump sum investment.

Compulsory purchase annuities If you have a personal pension or similar plan, you must use most of the proceeds to buy this type of annuity.

Income drawdown allows you to keep your pension fund fully invested in retirement up to age 75 and to draw an income from your fund.

Phased retirement operates like income drawdown, but here you use your tax-free cash to generate part of your income.

Purchased life annuities can be bought voluntarily with spare capital.

WORKING AND RETIRING ABROAD

The whole area of expatriate pensions is in the throes of change and unless you are confident that your company provides the best possible arrangement in terms of value and security, it is wise to seek expert advice before signing up for that overseas assignment.

This chapter looks at the pension problems facing all UK expatriates, in particular arrangements within the European Union, then focuses on retiring abroad and taking your pensions with you.

One of the main problems for expatriates seconded within the European Union (and virtually anywhere else, for that matter) is the absence of a workable cross-border pensions regime. The tax structure of pension schemes is complicated enough on a national level, but when more than one regime are involved, the system breaks down and the tax officials engage in a free-for-all.

Most European pension systems work on the basis of tax deferment. This means that there is tax relief on contributions and the build-up of the pension fund, but all or most of the pension itself is taxed in full as income. Quite understandably, if a country grants tax relief on contributions, it will be keen to claim the tax on the pension itself. If it does not, a fiscal imbalance arises.

Clearly it is essential to know your rights, to understand the impact of a foreign assignment on your pension, and to be sufficiently well-informed to negotiate the best possible deal for yourself and your family.

The following details cover the main aspects to consider when negotiating your expatriate pensions package. Do bear in mind though that these points offer general guidance only. Your contract should relate specifically to the actual assignment and must be tailored to cater for any particular problem areas.

■ **INVESTMENT SNAPSHOT**

The European Union has tried hard to create a pan-EU pensions structure for so-called 'mobile' or expatriate workers, but so far has only really helped employees who are seconded abroad by an employer and stay with that company.

■ FOREIGN STATE PENSIONS

The UK pays a rather miserly pension, but elsewhere in Europe the benefits are much higher. In some countries – Spain and Greece for example – the pension is worth over 90 per cent of national average earnings, so it is important to keep track of any rights you build up to foreign State pensions since these may provide a valuable source of income in retirement.

Assessing the value of overseas State pensions is not easy. Different countries apply different qualifying periods which set out the minimum number of years you must pay into the local national insurance system before a pension can be claimed. In the UK it is normally necessary to work and pay full National Insurance contributions for at least 10 years before you qualify for a proportion of the basic State pension, although benefits under the earnings-related pension (Serps) build up from day one. In Belgium, however, an employee qualifies for a proportion of the State pension after just one year, whereas in Luxembourg, as in the UK, the minimum qualifying period is 10 years, and in Portugal and Spain the qualifying minimum is set even higher, at 15 years.

Fortunately, the EU has an excellent system in place which is designed to ensure that expatriate employees do not lose out on their State pension rights as a result of single or multiple assignments within the member states.

As a general rule, when you work abroad for more than one year (technically, from day one) you must pay National Insurance or social security contributions in the country of assignment. There are a few exceptions to this, particularly where the assignment is expected to last for less than a year, or where the work covers several different countries, in which case it may be possible to stay in the UK scheme

Assuming, however, that your assignments are for a longer period, then the Multilateral Agreement on Social Security allows you to combine the total number of years worked in the EU in order to meet minimum qualifying periods in each country.

To complicate matters further, State pension ages vary from country to country and payment of the pension is usually dealt with by each country's social security department and paid in local currency. Each element of the pension is subject to the annual increases that apply in the country of source.

For the expatriate whose career spans several countries, it can be something of an administrative nightmare keeping track of all these foreign State pensions, particularly where governments are in the process of changing the benefit structure to reduce costs. To avoid problems later, keep track of your social security number and the period you worked. Supply these details to the relevant authorities at retirement. Remember that payments in different currencies almost certainly will lead to fluctuations in terms of the pensions' purchasing power.

> For the expatriate whose career spans several countries, it can be something of an administrative nightmare keeping track of all these foreign State pensions, particularly where governments are in the process of changing the benefit structure to reduce costs.

State pensions outside EU

While the details above refer specifically to the EU, it is worth noting that the UK has social security agreements with many countries around the world, so claiming your State pension should not present any serious problems. For details on payment of a UK pension overseas contact the DSS.

■ COMPANY PENSIONS

For your main company pension, there are several options to consider, including remaining in the UK scheme, joining the local scheme in the country of assignment and setting up an offshore scheme or plan.

27

Retention in UK scheme

The important point to note about private pension schemes in the UK – whether set up by an employer or by an individual – is that under normal circumstances you can only contribute if you have UK earnings. These 'relevant earnings' are defined very clearly by the Inland Revenue, and as a rule do not include earnings paid by an employer while you are working abroad.

Fortunately, the UK tax authorities have one of the most flexible attitudes to employees who work abroad, and generally it is possible to remain in the UK company scheme for up to ten years, provided your employer meets certain qualifying rules. The advantages of this arrangement are obvious, particularly if you plan to retire in the UK. All your benefits come from one source in one currency and you do not have to track down pension benefits from foreign employers when you come to retire in 20 years' time.

Foreign company schemes

If you are going abroad to work for a foreign employer, you should also consider the local company pension scheme. Indeed, you may have no choice, if membership of the company scheme is a condition of employment – just as it often used to be in the UK until 1988. However, membership should entitle you to receive employer contributions and all the tax reliefs associated with locally approved pension arrangements. The downside is that you may have to work for several years to meet the minimum qualifying period for a pension and, even if you do, for legal reasons it may not be possible to transfer your benefits out of the country when you leave.

Tax problems

Taxation is the main stumbling block in any expatriate pension package, and even if you remain in the UK scheme you may hit problems. Clearly, employees who claim relief on contributions in one country, but pay tax on the pension in another country, upset the fiscal balance. As a result many foreign tax authorities will treat an expatriate's pension contributions paid by the UK employer to the UK scheme as extra income and will tax them accordingly.

One way round the problem is to try to get compensation in your pay package for the extra tax levied. In practice, however, many companies maintain the pension promise, but do not bother to fund it during the period the employee is abroad, particularly where this is for a short period. In other words, they guarantee the pension, but do not set aside specific contributions to cover that guarantee. No employer contributions, no tax penalty in the country of assignment.

When the employee returns to the UK and re-joins the UK company's scheme, the Revenue will allow pension provision for all the years in service, including the overseas secondment provided the maximum pension is in line with what would have been earned if the employee had stayed in the UK. The notional UK salary can take account of promotions and inflation. After 10 years the Revenue would normally insist that you leave the scheme, but even this may be negotiable by your employer.

■ OFFSHORE TRUSTS

Offshore pension trusts can be an effective and tax-efficient way of providing pension benefits for senior executives, particularly where the peripatetic nature of their career makes it impossible for them to remain within the UK company scheme.

The trust, often sited in the Channel Islands, can be designed to provide higher benefits and earlier retirement than the main UK company scheme. Where you plan to retire abroad the trust can even be set up to pay your pension in a different currency.

It sounds ideal but do be careful if you are offered something along these lines. Offshore trusts are complex and must be arranged by a reputable firm of employee benefits consultants and legal experts. Any arrangement should be backed by formal documentation and this should be checked by your own accountant or legal and tax adviser, provided they have expertise in this area. There can be all sorts of problems, for example, hidden tax charges, if you bring the fund back into the UK.

27

■ OFFSHORE PLANS

An increasing number of financial institutions sell long-term invest-ment plans to expatriates from the Channel Islands, the Isle of Man, Dublin and other offshore centres. Some of these are designed to mirror pension plans in the UK, but they should not be confused with the genuine article because they cannot mirror the tax advantages of an onshore, Revenue-approved plan. However, some do offer limited tax advantages, and it may be possible to transfer to a UK plan if you return home.

If you think this might be your only option, do watch out for high charges and sales commissions. Also, check that the contract does not lock you in to a fixed period of contribution. If your secondment is cut short and you return to the UK, you could face punitive early ter-mination penalties.

Be sure to consult an independent financial adviser who specialises in offshore products and in expatriate tax and pension planning. Make sure the adviser will also consider the wide range of offshore investment funds (similar to unit trust and unit-linked funds in the UK). These may provide better long-term growth prospects and prove more flexible than some of the insurance products.

■ RETIRING ABROAD

Your first financial consideration if you plan to retire abroad is to arrange for all your pensions and other sources of income to be paid abroad without double tax penalties. Expert advice on pension and inheritance tax planning is essential.

Claiming your State pension

The UK State pension is paid at age 65 for men, and between age 60 and 65 for women depending on when they retire. (The female State pension age is due to be raised in line with the male pension age, and there is a transition period between 2010 and 2020 to achieve this.)

According to the Department of Social Security (DSS), the State retirement pensions and widows' benefits can be claimed from anywhere in the world. However, annual cost of living increases are paid only if you live in a European Union country or a country with which Britain has a social security agreement which provides for uprating (see Table 27.1). This means that if you retire to Australia, Canada, New Zealand or any country not mentioned in the table, your State pension will be frozen either at the time you leave the UK or, for those already abroad when they reach State retirement age, at the time of the first payment.

Table 27.1 Countries where your State pension qualifies for the annual increase

Austria	Guernsey	Netherlands	Yugoslavia
Barbados	Iceland	Norway	(including
Belgium	Irish Republic	Norway	the newly
Bermuda	Israel	Philippines	independent
Cyprus	Italy	Portugal	former republics)
Denmark	Jamaica	Spain	
Finland	Jersey	Sweden	
France	Luxembourg	Switzerland	
Germany	Malta	Turkey	
Gibraltar	Mauritius	US	

Source: Department of Social Security

Clearly, the loss of the annual cost of living increases will rapidly erode the value of the pension over a 15 to 20 year retirement, and extra income from other sources will be required to compensate. The only good news is that if you return to live in the UK, your State pension will be paid at the full current rate. UK expats on a temporary visit home can also claim the full rate, but only for the period spent in this country.

If you go abroad for short periods, the DSS makes special arrangements to pay your pension. No action is necessary where the period is less than three months, and in this case your pension payments can be collected on your return.

For periods between three and six months, you can arrange for your bank or building society to transfer payments to a bank overseas. For periods over six months, the DSS will, on request, pay a

27

sterling cheque to an overseas bank. Alternatively you can collect the lump sum on your return. For over 12 months, a more permanent arrangement is made to pay your pension by automated credit transfer to your overseas bank. However, if you wish, you can leave the pension for up to a maximum of two years and collect the lump sum on your return.

Claiming your company or private pension

Company and private individual pensions can also be paid abroad. However, most statements that explain your future pension rights assume retirement is within the UK, so it is essential to check how retiring abroad will affect your tax position. For example, the tax-free cash lump sum that is an important feature of UK private pensions is not recognised in North America, and if you receive the benefit there it may be taxed along with the pension.

> **Also, remember that your pension will be subject to currency fluctuations. If the local currency in your retirement country rises against the pound, then the value of your UK pension will reduce in real terms.**

Also, remember that your pension will be subject to currency fluctuations. If the local currency in your retirement country rises against the pound, then the value of your UK pension will reduce in real terms. The only places where you are protected from this exchange risk are those which still use sterling, namely, the Isle of Man and Gibraltar.

Pensions from previous employment

Many people change jobs several times before reaching retirement, so it will be necessary to contact previous employers to check the value of any benefits you left in the former employers' schemes. These benefits are known as 'deferred' pensions. Where a company has been taken over or become insolvent and it is difficult to track down the trustees, the Pensions Register will trace your benefits free of charge (contact The Occupational Pensions Regulatory Authority – the address is in Appendix III).

If your career included overseas employment with foreign State and company pension entitlements, the tracing problems could be multiplied ten-fold. To add to the complications, foreign pensions schemes may have a different retirement age from the rest of your UK pensions.

Taxation

Once you have checked your sources of pension, it is time to examine how they will be taxed. Expert advice is essential here, and clearly the adviser must be conversant with the tax and pensions rules in the country of retirement. The object of the exercise is to pay tax on pensions and investment income just once – usually in your country of retirement.

Where the country you choose has a double taxation agreement with the UK (there are over 80 of these agreements in operation), the Inland Revenue will allow pensions to be paid gross. But first you will need a declaration from the foreign tax authorities stating that they are taxing you on your worldwide income.

This declaration should be sent immediately to your UK tax office. If there is a delay your pensions will be taxed twice – once in the UK, at the basic rate of income tax, and once again in your country of retirement. However, if there is a delay in sending the form, the Inland Revenue confirms that the withholding tax can be reclaimed when it receives the declaration from the foreign tax authority.

■ SUMMARY

Working abroad
- Can you stay in your present company's scheme?

- Will the company guarantee that you will be no worse off than if you had remained in the UK?

- If there is no company scheme, then consider a local pension arrangement, provided your expected period of employment will allow you to meet the minimum qualifying periods.

- If you look for an offshore pension, do beware the high charges

27

associated with some of these plans and do not lock in to a long-term regular commitment.

Retiring abroad

■ Find out if your State pension will receive cost of living increases.

■ Check the value of your UK company pensions using the Pensions Register to trace any benefits from former employment if necessary.

■ Check the expected value of any individual pension plans.

■ Trace any overseas pension benefits (State and private).

■ Find out how your pensions will be taxed in the retirement country.

Further information

Ask at your local DSS for leaflet NI 106, *Pensioners or widows going abroad* and NI 38, *Social Security Abroad.*

For further information write to: Department of Social Security, Overseas Benefits Directorate, Payments Group, Longbenton, Newcastle upon Tyne NE98 1YX.

APPENDIX I
Bluffers' Guide to Jargon

Accrual rate: The rate at which a pension scheme member's pension rights build up. In a 'sixtieths' scheme your pension would build up at a rate of 1/60 of your final salary for each year of service. In this case it would take 40 years to build up the maximum pension allowed by the Inland Revenue of 40/60 or two-thirds of final salary (subject to restrictions in the case of some higher earners – see *earnings cap*).

Accumulation unit: Units in a unit trust where the income generated is re-invested automatically, increasing the unit price. The alternative is *income units* where the income is distributed to the unitholders.

Active investment management: Active managers use in-house and external research, together with their own detailed knowledge of companies and their management teams, in order to actively select the stocks. See *passive investment management*.

Added years: Where the pension is expressed as a proportion of final salary, typically it will build up at the rate of 1/60 of final salary for each year of service. Some *additional voluntary contributions (AVC)* schemes allow members to top up their main pension scheme benefits by investing to build up extra 'years'.

Additional voluntary contributions (AVCs): Extra contributions to a separate fund paid by the member in addition to the main scheme contributions. Total employee contributions to the main scheme and AVC combined must not exceed 15 per cent of annual earnings. AVCs are normally run by insurance companies, building societies and, occasionally, unit trust groups. See also *free-standing additional voluntary contributions*.

Advisory management: An advisory investment management service means that you may discuss investment opportunities with your manager but no action can be taken without your prior approval.

Annual charge: The annual management charge made by your investment manager.

Annuity: An annuity provides a guaranteed income, usually for life, in return for a lump sum investment.

Appointed representative: Companies that have a contract with a life office to sell one or more of its products on an exclusive basis in return for a commission payment.

Appropriate personal pension: Introduced in 1988, the appropriate personal pension allows employees who are not members of a 'contracted out' company pension scheme to contract out of *Serps* on an individual basis in return for a rebate of National Insurance contributions which are invested in your chosen plan.

Arithmetic average: This is a simple arithmetic calculation – the sum of the total returns for a given category of shares, divided by the number of companies within the category.

Assets: A catch-all phrase which refers to the sectors in which funds invest, for example, UK equities, European Union equities and fixed-interest securities (bonds).

Association of Investment Trust Companies (AITC): The main trade body for investment trusts.

Association of Unit Trust and Investment Companies (AUTIF): The main trade body for unit trusts and open-ended investment companies.

Authorised unit trust: Unit trusts sold to the public must be authorised by the Securities and Investments Board, the chief regulator for financial services in the UK.

Band earnings: National Insurance for employees is levied on what are known as 'band earnings', that is earnings between lower and upper limits (known as the lower earnings limit or LEL and the upper earnings limit or UEL). These are £62 and £465 per week for the 1997/98 tax year.

Basic State pension: The basic or 'old age' pension is a flat-rate benefit paid to individuals who reach State pension age and have paid or been credited with sufficient National Insurance contributions during their working life.

Bed and breakfast: At the end of the tax year it is common practice to sell shares and re-purchase them the following day in order to crystallise a capital gain or loss to use in conjunction with the annual capital gains tax exemption (£6,500).

Bed and Pep: As for *bed and breakfast*, but this time the shares are re-purchased within the Pep. Pep rules require most Pep investments to be bought with cash, so this transaction is usually necessary if you want to transfer existing shares or units in a unit trust into your plan. The only exception is where you transfer shares to a single company plan, for example, from an employee share option scheme.

Beneficiaries: Literally, those who benefit from a trust. With a unit trust, the trustees run the fund on behalf of the beneficiaries – in this case the unitholders. With a pension fund, the beneficiaries are the scheme members and their dependants.

Bid/offer spread: The full initial cost of your investment in a fund. This includes administration, sales commission if applicable, dealing costs and stamp duty among other items. Typically, the spread is about 5–6 per cent but where the initial charge is reduced or abolished, it could be as low as 0.5 per cent.

Bid price: The price at which you sell units in a unit trust back to the investment manager. You purchase at the *offer price*.

Bond: UK bonds are issued by borrowers – for example the government and companies – which undertake to repay the principal sum on a speci-fied date, rather like an IOU. During the time the bond is outstanding a fixed rate of interest is paid to the lender. Not to be confused with insurance bonds which are collective investments sold by insurance companies.

Capital gains tax: The tax on the increase in the value of an asset when it is sold, compared with its value at the time of purchase, adjusted by inflation since the date of purchase.

Capital growth: An increase in the value of shares or assets in a fund.

Carry-forward/carry-back: A special provision exists for employees and the self-employed who have unused tax relief in previous years and want to make a substantial personal pension payment. Through the Inland Revenue's carry-back and carry-forward rules it is possible to 'mop up' unused tax relief for up to seven previous tax years by treating a payment this year as though it had been made in a previous tax year.

Commission: 1. On the sale of an investment or insurance product man-agement company may pay a financial adviser a commission. 2. The fee that a stockbroker may charge clients for dealing on their behalf.

Commutation: See *tax-free cash*.

Company representative: Also known as direct salesmen and tied agents. Company representatives are employed directly by the life office and work solely for that company.

Contracted out/contracted in: Most company pension schemes in the UK are 'contracted out' of the State earnings-related pension scheme (Serps) and pay a reduced rate of employee and employer National Insurance contributions. The difference between the full and reduced rate contribution is invested to provide a level of pension which broadly matches what members would have got under Serps.

Contract note: Confirmation of your share purchase.

Contribution limits: The Inland Revenue sets out maximum contributions that an individual can pay each year. In a company scheme employees can pay up to 15 per cent of 'pensionable pay', while in a personal pension, the limit is between 17.5 – 40 per cent of 'net relevant earnings', depending on age. The employer's contributions are not restricted under a company scheme but are included under the personal pension limits.

Convertibles: Fixed-interest securities which may be converted to equities at some future date.

Corporate bond: An IOU issued by a public company. See *bond*.

Corporate bond Pep: A general Pep which can invest in corporate bonds, convertibles, preference shares and Eurosterling bonds.

Corporate Pep: A general Pep which invests in the shares of just one company.

Coupon: The rate of interest paid by a bond or gilt.

Custodian: Usually a bank, whose primary function is to look after a fund's assets.

Death in retirement benefits: The pension and lump sum paid to the deceased member's spouse and/or other dependants where death occurs in retirement.

Death in service benefits: The pension and lump sum paid to the deceased member's spouse and/or other dependants where death occurs while still employed.

Debentures: Bonds issued by UK companies which are secured on the company's underlying assets – for example, property. Unsecured bonds are known as 'loan stocks'.

Deferred pensioner: A scheme member who changes employment and leaves behind his or her pension benefits. The benefits are known as a deferred pension because the pension is held by the scheme until retirement age.

Deficit: In pension fund terms, a deficit is identified when the fund cannot meet its liabilities in terms of the guaranteed benefits it must pay. See *surplus*.

Defined benefit: A US term for *final salary scheme*. This is a pension scheme which links your pension to your salary – usually at or just before retirement. Usually there is no direct link between what you pay in and the emerging pension.

Defined contribution: This refers to money purchase pensions, where there is no direct link between the pension and your salary at retirement.

Dependants: In the context of a pension scheme, the members' or beneficiaries' dependants are usually limited to the spouse and children under 18.

Derivative: Financial instruments are referred to as 'derivative securities' when their value is dependent upon the value of some other underlying asset. The value of the derivative security is *derived* from the value of the underlying security. See *future*, *option* and *warrant*.

Designated account: An account held in one name (often a child's) with a second name as additional identification.

Discount: If the share price of an investment trust is lower than the value per share of the underlying assets, the difference is known as the 'discount'. If it is higher, the difference is known as the 'premium'. As a general rule, a share trading at a discount represents good value.

Discretionary benefits: Non-guaranteed benefits, although in some cases they can become an expectation – typically, where pension increases above the guaranteed minimum are paid on a regular basis. Discretionary payments are paid at the 'discretion' of the trustees. The trust deed and rules, for example, may include a 'discretion' to allow trustees to pay death benefits and spouse's pensions to common law partners.

Discretionary management: An investment service where you give your manager total control over the day-to-day running of your portfolio or units. The manager makes all the investment decisions.

Distributions: Income paid out from an equity or bond fund.

Dividend: The owner of shares is entitled to dividends – the annual or six-monthly distribution to shareholders of part of the company's profits.

Dividend yield: See *gross yield*.

Earnings cap: Introduced in the 1989 Budget, the cap restricts the amount of salary on which pension contributions and benefits are based. For the 1997/98 tax year, the earnings cap is £84,000.

Enterprise investment scheme (EIS): Available by direct subscription. EISs offer a range of tax reliefs if you invest in the shares of mainly unquoted trading companies.

Enterprise zone trust (EZT): Available by direct subscription. EZTs are designated areas where tax reliefs and reduced administrative controls are used to attract new business, providing investment in property with income tax relief on most of the cost.

Equities: The ordinary share capital of a company.

Eurosterling bond: A corporate bond issued in pounds sterling by a company which wants to borrow money on the international markets rather than just in the UK.

Ex-dividend: The period of about six weeks before a fund or equity pays out its dividend/income. If you buy during this period, you are not entitled to that dividend.

Execution-only: With this type of service, the investment manager/stockbroker simply buys and sells at your request without offering any advice.

Exit charges: A charge deducted from certain funds if you pull out early – usually within the first five years. Some Pep managers have abolished their initial charges, but replaced them with an exit charge.

Fee-based adviser: Many firms of financial advisers do not accept sales commission. Instead they charge a fee calculated on an hourly basis, or occasionally on a per case basis. This means that the adviser's remuneration is not dependent on the sale of financial products.

Final salary scheme: Final salary schemes (in the US known as 'defined benefit' schemes) link the value of the pension to earnings – usually in the few years leading to retirement. Typically the pension builds up at a rate of 1/60 of final salary for each year of service up to a maximum of 40/60 or two-thirds final salary (subject to restrictions in the case of certain higher earners – see *earnings cap*). See *money purchase*.

Financial Services Act 1986: The Act which set up the system of self-regulation for financial services and a series of self-regulatory organisations (SROs) which regulate different types of financial institutions and the advisers and representatives who sell their products.

Fixed-interest security: Another term for bonds. See *bond*, *corporate bond*.

FT-SE 100 Index: The index which covers the top 100 companies on the UK Stock Exchange measured by market capitalisation (the number of shares times the share value).

FT-SE-A All-Share Index: The index which measures the bulk of the companies listed on the UK Stock Exchange – about 915 in total.

FT-SE Mid 250 Index: The index which measures the 250 companies below (by market capitalisation) the FTSE 100.

Free-standing additional voluntary contributions (FSAVCs): If your company pension is likely to fall short of the maximum two-thirds final salary set by the Revenue, it is possible to pay voluntary top-up contributions either to the company *additional voluntary contribution* (AVC) scheme or to an individual plan called a free-standing AVC (FSAVC).

Funded and unfunded unapproved schemes: These are pension schemes recognised by the Revenue but not approved for tax purposes. They are used to provide pensions for employees caught by the *earnings cap*.

Fund of funds: A unit trust which can only invest in other authorised unit trusts.

Future: A type of *derivative*. A futures contract is a legally binding agreement to buy or sell an amount of shares (or other instruments) at a fixed date in the future at a fixed price.

Gearing: The relationship between debt and assets. High gearing means that there is a large proportion of debt in relation to the assets held.

Investment trusts can borrow to invest in assets, unit trusts can do so only to a limited extent.

General Pep: Up to £6,000 a year can be invested in a general Pep which can hold a variety of 'qualifying' and 'non-qualifying' assets including equities, fixed-interest securities, unit and investment trusts.

Gilt: The most secure type of *bond* because they are issued by the UK government.

Gross yield: This is a method of assessing the income from an investment. It is the annual gross dividend expressed as a percentage of the current market price. This shows the rate of gross income return a shareholder would receive on an investment at the share price on the date specified – much as one might describe the interest received on a deposit account. The important point to note is that for equities, investment trusts and equity-based unit trusts held within a Pep, the yield is quoted gross but paid net. The Pep manager reclaims the tax.

Group personal pension: This is little more than a series of individual *personal pension plans*, although if the employer sets up the group plan he is more likely to make a contribution and, perhaps, provide life assurance and other benefits on top. The GPP is not defined as an occupational scheme and so the same contribution and benefit limits as individual personal pensions apply.

Guaranteed equity funds: Funds which limit your exposure to falls in the stockmarket and provide a percentage of the gains. They do this by investing mainly in gilts and cash and then buying derivatives to provide the guarantees. Guaranteed funds may be worth considering for *income drawdown* plans but otherwise it is not clear whether long-term equity investors get value for money given the cost of the guarantee. Some commentators regard guaranteed funds as the natural replacement for 'with profits' funds. But then nobody really understands how these work either.

Higher-yield unit trusts: A category of unit trusts which yields a minimum of 110 per cent of the *FT-SE-A All-Share Index*.

Income drawdown: Rather than immediately purchase an annuity at retirement, with a drawdown plan you can draw an income while keeping the rest of your pension fund fully invested up to age 75 at the latest.

Income unit: If you buy income units in a unit trust, you receive automatically your share of the income generated by the fund. However, you can opt to have the income re-invested within the fund. Compare with *accumulation units*, where the dividends are re-invested to increase the unit price.

Independent financial adviser: IFAs, as they are known in the trade, are not tied to any one life office, but instead search the market to find the best product for your needs.

Independent financial planner: These firms sell financial advice rather than products, and usually charge a fee for their time rather than take sales commission.

Index tracking: With a tracker fund, the investment manager uses a computer model to select stocks to simulate the performance of a specific stockmarket index. Index tracking is also known as 'passive management'. The alternative is 'active management' where the manager selects individual stocks on the basis of research into a company's prospects in the light of expected economic conditions.

Inheritance tax: A tax on wealth passed on at death. The nil rate band is £215,000. Anything over this is taxed at 40 per cent, although gifts between husband and wife are exempt.

Initial charge: A charge, typically 5 per cent, levied by the investment manager to cover administration and sales commission when you invest in a fund. However, the full upfront cost of your investment is shown in the *bid/offer spread*, which includes additional charges such as stamp duty.

Integration: Company pension schemes that are integrated with the basic State pension scheme do not provide a pension for the first slice of earnings up to the Lower Earnings Limit (LEL) for *National Insurance*.

Investment trust: A UK company, listed on the stock exchange, which invests in the shares of other companies in the UK and overseas. Investment trust companies have a fixed number of shares which are subject to the usual market forces, so the share price does not necessarily reflect the underlying net asset value. See *discount* and *premium*.

Key features document: The (supposedly) simple summary of the product you will receive before you sign up. The most important feature is the details on charges, but it should also include details on the risk level of the investment and the pattern of contributions to which you are committed.

Life office: A life assurance company authorised to sell life and pensions products. The term is also used to describe the life assurance arm of a composite insurer. Composites sells life and pensions products, and also general insurance such as household and motor cover.

Lower earnings limit: The threshold above which you pay National Insurance contributions – up to the upper earnings limit. The lower limit is £62 per week and the upper limit is £465 per week.

Loan stocks: Unsecured bonds issued by UK companies. Bonds secured on a company's underlying assets (property, for example) are known as debentures. See *bonds*.

Market maker: A dealer who can buy and sell shares.

Managed Pep: A plan where the investment decisions are made for you by the Pep manager.

Managed/mixed fund: This is a broadly diversified fund which invests in a range of the manager's other main funds, usually including UK and overseas equities, gilts, bonds and, in some cases, property.

Married woman's stamp: More correctly, the 'reduced' rate of National Insurance contribution women can still pay provided they were married or widowed before 5 April 1977. The reduced rate does not build up an entitlement to the basic State pension, among other benefits.

Misappropriation: The term used where pension fund money (or any money for that matter) is put to wrong use by someone who does not own it. Theft to you and me.

Money purchase: Money purchase or *defined contribution* schemes do not guarantee a pension linked to the member's final salary. Instead contributions are invested to build up a fund which is used at retirement to buy an annuity from a life office. The annuity provides the guaranteed regular income until death. See *annuity*.

Monthly income scheme: This type of Pep has the facility to pay out a fixed income each month. However, if the fund has not generated sufficient income itself, part of the payment may be met by cashing in units, and hence reducing the capital value of your investment.

Mutual life office: A mutual life office is effectively owned by its policyholders and, unlike a 'proprietary' company, it does not have shareholders.

National Insurance: A form of taxation levied on 'band' earnings – that is earnings between the lower and upper earnings limits (see *Lower earnings limit*). These are £61 and £455 per week (£3,172 and £23,660 per annum) for the 1996/97 tax year.

National Insurance rebate: A partial return of National Insurance contributions is rebated to individuals who contract out of the State earnings-related pension scheme (Serps) with an appropriate personal pension. See *Serps*.

National Savings certificates: Available direct from National Savings or via the Post Office. NS certificates offer a tax-free return.

Net asset value (NAV): The market value of an *investment trust*'s underlying assets. This may be different from the share price since the latter is subject to market forces and supply and demand. See *discount* and *premium*.

Net yield: The return on an investment after tax has been deducted. See *gross yield*.

Non-qualifying funds: Unit or investment trusts with more than 50 per cent of their assets invested outside of the European Union. The annual allowance for non-qualifying investments is one-quarter of the total Pep allowance, that is £1,500.

Net relevant earnings: Earnings on which personal pension contributions are based.

The Occupational Pension Regulatory Authority (OPRA): is a new regulator for company pensions, established under the Pensions Act 1995. It took over from the Occupational Pensions Board in April 1997.

Occupational pension scheme: A scheme sponsored by an employer to provide relevant benefits to employees.

Offer price: The price at which you buy units from the unit trust or Pep manager. You sell back to the manager at the *bid price*.

Open market option: Your right at retirement to take the proceeds of your personal pension (or similar) and buy your annuity elsewhere. Annuity rates (the income you buy with your pension fund) vary considerably so it is vital to shop around.

Occupational Pensions Advisory Service (OPAS): Provides a free service to pension scheme members, pensioners, deferred pensioners and their dependants who have a complaint about their scheme.

Option: A type of *derivative*. A call option gives the buyer the right (but not the obligation – hence 'option') to buy a commodity, stock, bond or currency in the future at a mutually agreed price struck on the date of the contract. Put options give you the right, but not the obligation, to sell.

OEICS: Open-ended investment companies are a new type of investment fund. They are similar to unit trusts, but will have a corporate structure, rather than be based on a trust, and they will have a single price rather than a bid/offer spread.

Passive investment management: Another term for *index tracking*.

Pensions: Available from a range of financial institutions, and also provided by many employers in the form of an occupational pension scheme. Pension schemes and plans approved by the Inland Revenue offer tax relief on contributions, tax-free growth of the fund and, in some cases, a tax-free lump sum at retirement. The pension income is taxed.

Pension age: The age at which you can draw your pension from the State scheme, your company scheme or your individual plan.

Pension forecast: A useful service provided by the Department of Social Security which tells you what your State pension is worth.

Pensions Ombudsman: An independent arbitrator for pension disputes – usually referred by *OPAS* (see entry). The ombudsman has statutory power to enforce his decisions.

Performance measurement: Used to check how well or badly the investment manager has done. There are usually two measurements; first, against an industry average, and second against a specific benchmark or target set by the trustees of the fund.

Personal equity plan (Pep): A Pep is a wrapper or basket which shelters Inland Revenue-approved stockmarket investments from the taxman. Both income and capital gains are tax-free for the lifetime of the investor. The current maximum allowable tax-free investment into a general Pep is £6,000 in any one tax year from 6 April to 5 April of the following year. A further £3,000 may be invested in a single-company Pep.

Personal Investment Authority (PIA): Under the Financial Services Act 1986, the PIA is the regulator for companies which market and sell retail investments such as Peps, pensions and life assurance savings plans.

Pooled funds: Another term for collective or mutual funds which invest in a range of different shares and other instruments to achieve diversification and economies of scale for the smaller investor who buys units in these funds.

Preference share (pref): This is similar to a *bond* in that it pays a fixed rate of interest, although its payment depends on company profits. Preference shares are first in the pecking order of payouts when an investment trust is wound up. See *stepped preference share* and *zero dividend preference share.*

Premium: If the share price of an investment trust is higher than the value of the underlying assets, the difference is known as the premium. Normally, investors are advised not to buy under these circumstances. If the price is lower than the *net asset value* (NAV) the difference is known as the *discount.*

Price earnings ratio: The market price of a share divided by the company's earnings (profits) per share in its latest 12-month trading period.

Property: In the context of pension fund investment, property means the ownership of land and buildings that are used by businesses or other organisations which pay rent to the owner. Ownership is often on a collective basis.

Proprietary life office: Proprietary life offices are quoted companies and have shareholders, unlike 'mutual' life offices which are effectively owned by their policyholders.

Protected rights: The fund which is built up from the rebates of National Insurance contributions under a personal pension and other types of money purchase pensions. See *money purchase.*

Purchased life annuity (PLA): See *annuity.*

Qualifying funds: Unit and investment trusts which qualify for the full £6,000 annual Pep allowance must have at least 50 per cent of their assets invested in the European Union.

Qualifying year A complete tax year in which the full rate of National

Insurance contribution was paid or credited. Qualifying years count towards your basic State pension.

Recognised stockmarket: A stockmarket approved by the Inland Revenue for certain investments such as Peps.

Redemption: The date at which a *bond* becomes repayable.

Redemption yield: The current dividend or interest rate increased or decreased to take into account the capital value if the bond is held to maturity.

Renewal commission: Often overlooked by the consumer, the renewal commission is paid by the life office to the adviser at certain intervals throughout the contract.

Retirement annuity: Retirement annuity contracts were the predecessor of personal pensions, and were similar in most respects except that they did not allow individual employees to contract out of Serps.

Return: The amount by which your investment increases as a result of interest or dividend income and capital growth.

Risk: A measure of the probability that the value of your savings and the income they generate will fall as well as rise.

Running yield: The current dividend or interest payments on a fund.

SICAV: This is the French equivalent of the UK's open-ended investment companies (OEICs), and stands for 'Securité d'investissement à capital variable'. SICAVs are the most popular retail investment on the Continent.

SSAS: Small self-administered schemes (SSASs) are approved occupational pension schemes for small businesses which allow far more flexibility than standard schemes. For example, they include the facility to self-invest to a high degree, and to take a loan from the fund. The maximum number of members is 12.

Scrip issue/dividends: A scrip issue is where a company turns part of its accumulated reserves into new shares. Scrip dividends cannot be put in a Pep because they do not carry a tax credit, so you cannot reclaim the tax.

Securities: The general name for all stocks and shares. Broadly speaking, stocks are fixed-interest securities and shares are the rest. The four main types of securities listed and traded on the UK Stock Exchange are UK equities, overseas equities (i.e., issued by non-UK companies), UK gilts (bonds issued by the UK government) and bonds/fixed interest stocks (issued by companies and local authorities).

Securities and Investments Board (SIB): The chief regulator for financial services in the UK. See *Financial Services Act 1986.*

Self-invested personal pensions (SIPPs): These are similar to personal pensions, but allow the individual to separate the administration and investment, and therefore allow the individual to exercise much greater freedom in the investment choice. Only viable for larger investments.

Self-select Pep: A plan which does not restrict you to the funds of one Pep manager but instead allows you to hold the entire range of 'peppable assets', including individual shares and bonds as well as unit and investment trusts.

Serps: The State earnings-related pension scheme was set up in 1978 to provide employees with a pension linked to average earnings between the lower and upper threshold for *National Insurance.*

Share exchange: A facility offered by plan managers whereby they take your shares, sell them and invest the cash in a Pep. In some cases, they may be able to absorb the shares into their funds and reduce dealing costs.

Single premiums/recurring single premium (SP/RSP): A one-off contribution that does not lock you in to any future payments. If commission is paid to the adviser, this also is on a one-off basis, so there are no financial penalties if you decide not to pay further contributions. Recurring single premiums should be treated as one-off payments for commission purposes, but do check this point.

Size-weighted average: The average return after weighting each company in the category by size of market capitalisation at the start of the period. This means that the performance of really small shares or trusts does not have a disproportionate impact on an index. Size-weighted average is the preferred method used by the independent measurers of the big institutional pension funds. See *arithmetic average.*

Split-capital trust: An *investment trust* which has different types of shares – for example, some offer a high income, but no capital growth, and some offer pure capital growth, but no income.

Stamp duty: A tax on the purchase (but not the sale) of shares, currently 0.5 per cent.

Stepped preference share: Stepped preference shares are shares in a *split-capital trust* which pay dividends that rise at a predetermined rate and have a fixed redemption value, paid when the trust is wound up.

Stockmarket indices: An index is a specified basket or portfolio of shares and shows how these share prices are moving in order to give an indication of market trends. Every major world stockmarket is represented by at least one index. The *FT-SE 100 Index*, for example, reflects the movements of the share prices of the UK's largest 100 quoted companies by market capitalisation.

Tax-exempt special savings accounts (Tessas): Available from building societies and banks. Tessas are deposit accounts which offer secure five-year tax-free growth for capital that might otherwise sit in an ordinary deposit account.

Tax-free cash: Under Inland Revenue rules, it is possible to take part of your pension benefits at retirement in the form of tax-free cash. This process is known as 'commutation'.

Tax year: Tax and investment allowances apply to the 12 months from 6 April to the following 5 April.

Timber: Available by direct subscription. Timber offers an eight- to ten-year investment for tax-free income through felling or a very long-term investment for the next generation.

Tracker funds: See *index tracking*.

Transfer value: The amount you take out of a pension scheme if you leave employment and want to transfer your pension benefits into the new employer's scheme or into an individual pension plan.

Trust deed: The legal document on which a unit trust is based. The use of a trust separates the fund from the management company's assets. The trustees manage run the fund on behalf of the beneficiaries – in this case, the unitholders.

Trustee: You can't have a trust without a trustee who, as legal owner of the fund, looks after the assets on behalf of the unitholders.

UCITS (Undertaking for Collective Investments in Transferable

Securities): A European Union term for a collective fund, such as a unit trust or OEIC which can be marketed in all the Union's markets.

Unapproved pension schemes: Schemes that are recognised by the Revenue, but are not approved for tax purposes. Used mainly to top up benefits for employees caught by the *earnings cap*. See *funded and unfunded unapproved schemes*.

Upper earnings limit: See *National Insurance*.

Venture capital trusts (VCTs): Available from a range of financial institutions and by direct subscription. VCTs allow you to participate in EIS-type investments on a collective basis.

Waiver of premium: With a regular premium pension plan, if you have this feature the pension company credits your fund with contributions under certain circumstances – for example, if you are too ill to work.

Warrant: Risky and volatile investments which give the holder the right, but not the obligation to buy investment trust shares at a pre-determined price within a specified period. This type of share has no voting rights and holders do not normally receive dividends.

Winding up: The term used to explain the legal termination of a pension scheme. Details on how the scheme should be wound up are set out in the trust deed and rules.

'With profits'/unitised 'with profits' pension funds: 'With profits' funds are invested in UK and overseas equities, gilts, bonds and property. Under a 'with profits' contract, the life office provides a guaranteed minimum sum at maturity, to which it adds annual or 'reversionary' bonuses which, once allocated, cannot be taken away. The annual bonuses are 'smoothed' to avoid volatility. On top of this, there is a discretionary (not guaranteed) final 'terminal' bonus which reflects recent performance of the 'with profits' fund.

Yield: The annual dividend or income on an investment expressed as a percentage of the purchase price. See *gross yield*.

Zero dividend preference share ('zero'): A lower-risk and pre-determined investment. They offer a fixed-capital return in the form of a redemption value which is paid when the trust is wound up. These shares are not entitled to income, and therefore there is no income tax liability.

Source: Some of the definitions were drawn from other publications, by kind permission of the publisher, including *Investors Chronicle Good Peps Guide*, by Debbie Harrison, published by Pitman; *Pensions Power*, by Debbie Harrison, published by John Wiley & Sons; *Unit Trust User's Handbook*, published by Pearson Professional; London International Financial Futures and Options Exchange *LIFFE Futures and Options: A Guide for UK Fund Managers*.

APPENDIX II
Sources of Information

■ INDEPENDENT FINANCIAL ADVISERS

Where we do not provide a telephone number, the organisations below prefer you to contact them by post. Before you contact a firm, you can check with the Securities and Investments Board that it is authorised and registered with the appropriate regulator. To contact the **SIB central register**, phone 0171-929 3652. Fees vary considerably from firm to firm, so if you have a tight budget, ask about the hourly rate and get a rough idea of the total bill in advance.

Stockbrokers

The Association of Private Client Investment Managers and Stockbrokers publishes a free directory of member firms, many of which provide a full financial planning service. Contact APCIMS, 112 Middlesex Street, London E1 7HY.

Financial planners and advisers

The Institute of Financial Planning, Whitefriars Centre, Lewins Mead, Bristol BS1 2NT. For the register of fellows, phone 0117-930 4434.

The Society of Financial Advisers, 20 Aldermanbury, London EC2V 7HY. Tel: 0171-417 4419.

For a list of three local independent advisers, contact **IFA Promotion** on 0117-971 1177. For fee-based independent advisers, contact the **Money Management Register** on 0117-976 9444.

Chartered Accountants

Seven hundred members of the Institute of Chartered Accountants qualify for Category C status and can offer a full advisory service. *Contact:*

The Institute of Chartered Accountants in England & Wales, Moorgate Place, London EC2P 2BJ. Tel: 0171-920 8100/8711.

The Institute of Chartered Accountants in Scotland, 27 Queen Street, Edinburgh EH2 1LA. Tel: 0131-225 5673.

You could also try the **Chartered Association of Certified Accountants** (ACCA), 29 Lincoln's Inn Fields, London WC2A 3EE. Tel: 0171-242 6855.

Solicitors

Solicitors are also strongly represented in the financial services market. *Contact:*

The Law Society of England & Wales, 113 Chancery Lane, London WC2A 1PL. Tel: 0171-242 1222.

The Law Society of Scotland, 26 Drumsheugh Gardens, Edinburgh EH3 7YR. Tel: 0131-226 7411.

The Law Society of Northern Ireland, Law Society House, 98 Victoria Street, Belfast BT1 3JZ. Tel: 01232-231 614.

You could also contact the **Solicitors for Independent Financial Advice** helpline on 01372 721172 and the **Association of Solicitor Investment Managers**, Chiddingstone Causeway, Tonbridge, Kent TN11 8JX. Tel: 01892 870065.

Actuaries

Contact:

The Association of Consulting Actuaries: Membership of the ACA includes most firms of consulting actuaries and individuals engaged in private practice. Only qualified actuaries with a minimum of three years' experience are entitled to become full members of the ACA.
Number 1 Wardrobe Place, London EC4V 5AH. Tel: 0171-248 3163.

Association of Pension Lawyers (APL)
The APL membership includes solicitors and other firms with a special interest in legal aspects associated with pension schemes.
c/o Paul Stannard, Travers Smith Braithwaite, 10 Snow Hill, London EC1A 2AL. Tel: 0171-248 9133.   Fax: 0171-236 3728.

Faculty of Actuaries
The Faculty will provide a list of members who can help with mis-sold personal pensions.
17 Thistle Street, Edinburgh EH2 1DF. Tel: 0131-220 45555.   Fax: 0131-220 2280.

Society of Pension Consultants (SPC)
The SPC is a representative body for firms and individuals working as pensions and employee benefits consultants.
Ludgate House, Ludgate Circus, London EC4A 2AB. Tel: 0171-353 1688.   Fax: 0171-353 9296.

■ OTHER USEFUL INVESTMENT ORGANISATIONS

Association of Investment Trust Companies (AITC)
The AITC is the trade body for investment trusts. It publishes a range of free information sheets on investment trusts which explain how they can be used for general and specific investment purposes. It also publishes performance details in its Monthly Information Service (MIS – a free sample copy is available to investors) and the Investment Trust Directory, which provides profiles of the AITC member companies together with a list of plan managers (price £15 or £12.50 if you buy it together with a subscription to the MIS).
AITC, Durrant House, 8-13 Chiswell Street, London EC1Y 4YY. Tel: 0171-431 5222.

The Association of Unit Trusts and Investment Companies (AUTIF)
AUTIF is the trade body for unit trusts and the new open-ended investment companies. It publishes a range of free fact sheets which explain how unit trusts can be used for general and specific investment purposes.
AUTIF, 65 Kingsway, London WC2B 6TD. Tel: 0171-831 9975.

The Stock Exchange publishes useful leaflets on buying and selling shares and on rolling settlement and nominee accounts. For copies, telephone 0171-797 1000 or write to the Stock Exchange, London EC2N 1HP.

Contacts for experienced investors and DIY investment enthusiasts

ProShare was set up to promote private share ownership for individual investors and publishes a range of useful guides as well as running a nationwide network of investment clubs. For details of membership contact ProShare, Library Chambers, 13–14 Basinghall Street, London EC2V 5BQ. Tel: 0171-600 0984.

Those looking for an execution-only service might consider **ShareLink**, one of the pioneers of this type of service in the UK. ShareLink also publishes a range of useful booklets.
ShareLink, Cannon House, 24 The Priory Queensway, Birmingham B4 6BS. Tel: 0121-200 2474.

Chase de Vere is a firm of independent financial advisers based in London and Bath. The firm's asset management department researches and analyses collective investments such as unit and investment trusts. Chase de Vere is the author of *Pep Guide*, the annual comprehensive guide to personal equity plans and plan managers.
Chase de Vere, 63 Lincoln's Inn Fields, London WC2A 3BR. Tel: 0800 526 091.

Stockbroker services

APCIMS represents well over 90 per cent of private client stockbrokers as well as an increasing number of other investment managers. Members have direct access to the stockmarket for buying and selling shares.

The directory of stockbrokers published by APCIMS (Association of Private Client Investment Managers and Stockbrokers, 112 Middlesex Street, London E1 7HY) provides a brief guide to the services offered by each firm and an indication of the minimum size of portfolio considered acceptable by the firm. The symbols used in the directory relate to the following services.

Dealing or 'execution-only'

This service is designed for investors who do not require advice, but who do need a stockbroker to buy and sell shares for them. There is no advice or management in this service so the costs of transactions generally are lower than with other services. Some stockbrokers specialise in this low-cost no-frills service so if this is what you are after, look them up in the APCIMS directory under 'E'.

Those who want help from a stockbroker have several options. In each case, you should be offered an initial interview without obligation.

Advisory

As the name implies, with an advisory service, you take the decisions based on your own ideas and the advice of your manager. Almost all firms of stockbrokers offer an advisory service. In practice, there are different types of advisory service. For example, you may want a more limited service where the manager advises on the purchase, sale or retention of individual stocks but you do not necessarily have to reveal full details of your investments. Alternatively, you may want a more comprehensive service and be prepared to give your manager full details of all your investments. This enables the stockbroker to give advice on individual stocks, capital gains tax and provide regular valuations on your entire portfolio.

Unlike the discretionary service described below, the advisory manager will not take any investment action without your authority.

Advisory services are indicated by an 'A' in the APCIMS directory.

Discretionary

If you want your investment manager to make all the decisions for you and to simply get on with it without checking with you before each transaction, then you are looking for a discretionary investment management service.

You do not lose control entirely however, since you and your manager will spend some time at the outset discussing your financial circumstances, your requirements and your investment views. This gives your manager a clear framework within which he or she must work. You might, for example, state that certain stocks within your portfolio should not be sold, or that for ethical reasons you do not wish to invest in certain types of companies.

You will also keep up-to-date with changes in your portfolio as the manager will send you a contract note every time a transaction takes place, and will also send you regular valuations.

Discretionary or portfolio management services are indicated by a 'P' in the APCIMS directory.

Comprehensive financial planning

In addition to the core investment management services, many stockbrokers offer a broader financial planning service. This can cover Peps, pensions, mortgages, life assurance, school fees, inheritance tax, cash and deposits, and tax-exempt special savings schemes, among others. Many stockbrokers run their own Peps, although you should consider whether you will receive as good a service from a stockbroker as a large institutional manager, given the huge research resources available to the latter.

Comprehensive financial planning is indicated by a 'C' in the APCIMS directory.

Useful organisations

Association of British Insurers (ABI)
51 Gresham Street, London EC2V 7HQ
Tel: 0171-600 3333   Fax: 0171-696 8999

The ABI is a trade association for insurance companies and provides useful statistics and other information on individual and company pensions.

Pre-Retirement Association (PRA)
Nodus Centre, University Campus, Guildford, Surrey GU2 5RX
Tel: 01483 39350

National association for pre-retirement education in the UK, providing training for counsellors and co-ordinating courses around the country.

■ PUBLIC/GOVERNMENT AGENCIES

Department of Social Security (DSS)
The Adelphi, 1-11 John Adam Street, London WC2N 6HT
Tel: 0171-962 8000

Government Actuary's Department (GAD)
22 Kingsway, London WC2B 6LE
Tel: 0171-242 6828   Fax: 0171-831 6653

Inland Revenue (Savings and Investment Division)
South West Wing, Bush House, London WC2B 4RD
Tel: 0171-438 6622

Occupational Pensions Regulatory Authority (OPRA):
OPRA took over from the (OPB) in April Occupational Pensions Board 1997
OPRA, Invicta House, Trafalgar Place, Brighton, East Sussex BN1 4BY
Tel: 01273 627600

Pension Schemes Office (PSO)
Lynwood Road, Thames Ditton, Surrey KT7 0DP
Tel: 0181-398 4242   Fax: 0181-398 7333
also at:
St Nicholas Court, Castle Gate, Nottingham NG1 7AR
Tel: 01602 243855   Fax: 01602 504355

APPENDIX III
How to Make a Complaint

If you think you have a complaint concerning your investments, you first need to find out to whom you should complain. This might not be immediately obvious because different types of financial institutions and advisers are authorised by different regulatory bodies. However, details of the regulator should be shown in the letter head of the company which sold you the investment. If you are in any doubt, contact the Securities and Investments Board, which keeps on a central register the details of all the companies authorised under the Financial Services Act.

The main regulator for sales of retail investment products is the Personal Investment Authority (PIA), which has its own ombudsman. However, you may also come across the Securities and Futures Authority (SFA), the Investment Management Regulatory Organisation (IMRO) and the chief regulator, the Securities and Investments Board (SIB), which still authorises some companies directly.

Most independent financial advisers are authorised by the PIA, but if you were advised by a professional firm, then you will deal with the appropriate 'recognised professional body' (RPB), for example the Institute of Chartered Accountants or the Law Society. Due to their complexity, pension complaints, particularly those which relate to company schemes, have their own system for complaints.

Not everything is regulated under the FSA. For example, most protection insurances, examined in Section II of this book, are classed as general insurance business and do not come under the aegis of the investment regulators, even if there is a significant element of investment within the policy, as is the case with some whole of life plans (a type of life assurance – see page 21) and long-term care policies (which cover nursing home fees for the very elderly – see page 35).

In these cases, if you had a problem, you would probably contact the Insurance Ombudsman or even the Department of Trade (DTI) – but again, the company which sold you the policy is obliged to tell you which is the correct complaints channel.

Most of the regulators and ombudsmen publish consumer guides to complaints which will help you prepare your case.

What to say

Different regulators have different rules, but in most cases they will expect you first to tackle the company which sold you the plan before taking your complaint further.

Clearly, your complaint stands a much greater chance of being taken seriously if you prepare your case well. The regulators and ombudsmen recommend the following procedure:

- Write first to the compliance officer at the company which sold you the plan.
- State clearly the nature of the complaint.
- Give contact details, including your daytime telephone number.
- Provide the name of the plan, the date you invested, and the name of your contact – the salesman or adviser who dealt with your case.
- Quote all relevant plan details and reference numbers.
- Photocopy letters and supporting material.
- Set a sensible deadline for the reply. You should receive an acknowledgement of your letter within seven days, but allow two months for the actual investigation before taking the case to the ombudsman or regulator.

Occupational pension schemes

The new Pensions Act (1995), which came into force in April 1997, requires trustees to establish a two-stage internal dispute resolution process for members who have a complaint. This system will be the first port of call for any scheme member who has a problem, or feels the scheme has in some way failed to provide the promised benefits.

If this fails to resolve your dispute, you can go to the Occupational Pensions Advisory Service. OPAS is a grant-aided, non-profit-making company limited by guarantee. It is an independent and voluntary organisation providing free help and advice to members of the public. As with other financial products discussed above, the first step is to contact the scheme authorities.

Only after you have attempted to resolve your problem this way will OPAS step in. The best way to approach OPAS is through your local Citizens Advice Bureau which will put you in touch with your nearest OPAS adviser. If there is no CAB locally, then send a brief letter direct to OPAS, enclosing any relevant material.

While OPAS has an outstanding track record on settling disputes, nevertheless there will always be the stubborn cases where the scheme authorities refuse to budge even if it is clear that they are in the wrong. If OPAS fails to rectify the problem, you can turn to the Pensions Ombudsman.

The Pensions Ombudsman was appointed under the Social Security Act 1990 to deal with complaints against and disputes with occupational schemes and personal pensions. He is completely independent and acts as an impartial adjudicator. His services are free, and he has statutory power to enforce his decisions.

Personal pension transfers

A new system to deal with complaints about the sale of personal pensions to employees in company schemes gets under way in Spring 1997. This will require almost all of the 520,000 investors identified to date to complete a new questionnaire about their company scheme and personal pension. This is vitally important. Investors who do not respond will be struck off the list and will not qualify for compensation. If you are concerned about the progress of your case, see page 000.

Personal pensions complaints cover a wide area and fall under the remit of both the PIA and the Pensions Ombudsman. If in doubt write to OPAS or the PIA, both of which act as an unofficial sorting office for pensions complaints and will make sure your details go to the right place.

The regulators and ombudsmen

The following guide explains briefly the role of the main regulators. Most of these publish a consumer guide to complaints. Labour plans to overhaul the regulators and bring them together under one roof – the SIB's.

The Securities and Investments Board (SIB) is the chief regulator under the Financial Services Act. Among other functions it registers every unit trust and lays down the regulations for unit trust pricing and charging. The SIB will give you information about your plan manager, including its regulator.
The Securities and Investments Board, Gavrelle House, 2–4 Bunhill Row, London EC1Y 8RA. Tel: 0171-929 3652.

The Investment Management Regulatory Organisation (Imro) is responsible for authorising and monitoring the activities of most unit trust management companies. However, all complaints about Imro firms must be directed to **The Investment Ombudsman**.
The Investment Ombudsman, 6 Frederick's Place, London EC2R 8BT. Tel: 0171-796 3065.

The Securities and Futures Authority (SFA) regulates stockbrokers, many of which run their own Peps. The SFA asks investors to write to their usual contact at the firm before writing to the compliance officer. If the complaint is not properly remedied, the firm is obliged to inform you of your rights and to send you a copy of a complaints guide.

The SFA pointed out that it cannot deal with complaints that either are already the subject of litigation or arose before 29 April 1988 (that is before the date the Financial Services Act came into force). The SFA said it will acknowledge your letter of complaint within one day of receipt, require answers from the member firm within ten working days, and aim to resolve all complaints within three months. If you are unhappy with the outcome you can take the case to arbitration.
The Complaints Bureau, The Securities and Futures Authority, Cottons Centre, Cottons Lane, London SE1 2QB. Tel: 0171-378 9000.

If you want to take the case to arbitration:
The Complaints Commissioner, c/o SFA Tribunal Secretariat, Cottons Centre, Cottons Lane, London SE1 2QB. Tel: 0171-378 9000.

The Personal Investments Authority (PIA) is responsible for regulating the sales and marketing operations of companies in the unit and investment trust market. Complaints regarding PIA members are dealt with by the PIA Ombudsman.
The PIA Ombudsman, Hertsmere House, Hertsmere Road, London E14 4AB. Tel: 0171-216 0016.

Some advisers are authorised by the **Insurance Brokers' Registration Council (IBRC).**
15 St Helens Place, London EC3A 6DS. Tel: 0171-588 4387.
63 St Mary Axe, London EC3A 8NB. Tel: 0171-621 1061.

The Occupational Pensions Advisory Service (OPAS), 11 Belgrave Road, London SW1V 1RB. Tel: 0171-233 8080. Fax: 0171 233 8016. (But remember, OPAS prefers you to contact one of its advisers via your local Citizens Advice Bureau if possible.)

The Pensions Ombudsman can be contacted at the OPAS address. Tel: 0171-834 9144. Fax: 0171-821 0065. (However, normally you would not approach him directly, but ask OPAS to mediate in your case first. Only if this fails and OPAS believes you have a strong case, would the matter be referred to the Ombudsman.)

The Banking Ombudsman
70 Gray's Inn Road, London WC1X 8NB. Tel: 0171-404 9944.

The Building Societies Ombudsman
Millbank Tower, Millbank London SW1P 4XF. Tel: 0171-931 0044.

The Insurance Ombudsman Bureau
135 Park Street, London SE1 9EA. Tel: 0171-928 4488.

Inland Revenue, Customs and Excise and Contributions Agency Adjudicator's Office
3rd Floor, Haymarket House, 28 Haymarket, London SW1Y 4SP. Tel: 0171-930 2292.

Registry of Friendly Societies
15–17 Great Marlborough Street, London W1V 2LL. Tel: 0171-437 9992.

Pensions Registry
The Pensions Registry and Tracing Service was launched in 1990 to help individuals trace their pension benefits if they have lost touch with a former employer. This often happens when a company changes its name and address, is taken over or becomes insolvent. The service is free.

Most requests for information on lost pensions are sorted out within two days, and the scheme reports a success rate of almost 90 per cent. Where delays occur this is usually because the applicant has insufficient information.

Complete form PR4 which can be obtained from a pensions consultant or from the office of the Occupational Pensions Regulatory Authority (OPRA), Occupational Pensions Board, Pension Schemes Registry, PO Box 1NN, Newcastle upon Tyne NE99 1NN. Tel: 0191-225 6393/94.

The Association of Pension Lawyers (APL) will provide a list of specialist pensions lawyers in your area. Tel: 0171-248 9133. Fax: 0171-236 3728.

INDEX